Tunes of the Twenties

and all that Jazz
The Stories Behind the Songs

by Robert Rawlins

Copyright © 2015 by Robert Rawlins
All rights reserved. This book or any portion thereof may
not be reproduced or used in any manner whatsoever without the
express written permission of the publisher except for the use of
brief quotations in a book review.

Printed in the United States of America

Library of Congress Control Number: 2015956197

First Printing, 2015

ISBN: 978-0-9965949-0-5

Rookwood House Publishing

www.tunesofthetwenties.com
www.rookwoodhouse.com

Dedication

To the songwriters who wrote the music,

the musicians who brought it to life,

and the listeners who embraced it.

Acknowledgments

Since I've been writing this book in my head for most of my life, it would be impossible to acknowledge everyone who helped make it a reality. Countless musicians and enthusiasts of the music have told me stories and given me ideas that have made their way into this book. I apologize for the many names unintentionally omitted.

Tunes of the Twenties took shape over the past four years, and the following people were crucial to its preparation:

- Nancy Rawlins, who oftentimes knows what I mean to say when I don't say what I mean.
- Emily Rawlins, who oftentimes knows what I shouldn't say even when I meant it.
- Carl Hausman, with his vast writing and publishing experience, who helped me establish a house editorial style most suited to this book.
- Jim Miller, whose keen eye for detail was very helpful.
- John McClernan, Franny Smith, Pat Mercuri, and Dan Tobias, all of whom were most generous with their vast knowledge of the genre.
- My many friends from the Tri-State Jazz Society and the Cape May Traditional Jazz Society who frequently asked, "When will the book be finished?"
- My good friend Paul Jost, a wonderful interpreter of these songs himself, who frequently said "Finish the book!"
- Sharla Feldscher and Seth Hanes, who provided publicity and website design.
- Sonja Jackson-Newton, who was very patient with me in designing and formatting the layout.
- John Rawlins, who oversaw planning, production, and printing.

— Robert Rawlins

Table of Contents

Preface . . . . *xiii*
Introduction . . . . *xvii*
Forward . . . . *xiii*
The Songs *1*
Ace in the Hole *1*
After I Say I'm Sorry *2*
After You've Gone *3*
Ain't Misbehavin' *4*
Ain't She Sweet *5*
Alabama Jubilee *7*
Alabamy Bound *7*
The Alcoholic Blues *8*
Alexander's Ragtime Band *10*
Alice Blue Gown *11*
All By Myself *13*
Angry *13*
As Long as I Live *14*
At a Georgia Camp Meeting *16*
At Sundown *17*
Aunt Hagar's Blues *18*
Avalon *19*
Baby Face *19*
Baby Won't You Please Come Home *20*
Back in Your Own Backyard *21*
Ballin' the Jack *23*
Basin Street Blues *24*
Beale Street Blues *26*
Bei Mir Bist Du Schon *26*
Between the Devil and the Deep Blue Sea *27*
Bill Bailey *27*
Birth of the Blues *28*
Black and Blue *29*

Black Bottom	29
Blue and Broken Hearted	30
The Blue Room	31
Blue Skies	31
Blue Turning Grey Over You	32
Blues My Naughty Sweetie Gives to Me	33
Bluin' the Blues	34
Borneo	34
Breezin' Along with the Breeze	35
Bugle Call Rag	35
By and By	36
Bye Bye Blues	38
Cakewalking Babies from Home	38
California Here I Come	39
Canal Street Blues	40
Careless Love	40
Chicago Breakdown (Stratford Hunch)	41
Chicago, That Toddlin' Town	42
Chimes Blues	43
China Boy	44
Chinatown, My Chinatown	46
Clarinet Marmalade	47
Come Back Sweet Papa	47
Copenhagen	48
Cornet Chop Suey	48
Cottage for Sale	49
Crazy Rhythm	49
The Curse of an Aching Heart	51
Dangerous Blues	52
Dardanella	54
The Darktown Strutters' Ball	55
Dear Old Southland	57
Deed I Do	58

Diga Diga Doo	58
Dill Pickles	60
Dinah	60
Dippermouth Blues	62
Do You Know What It Means to Miss New Orleans	62
Doctor Jazz	63
Don't Get Around Much Anymore	64
Down by the Riverside	64
Down Home Rag	65
Down in Jungle Town	67
East St. Louis Toodle-oo	68
Everybody Loves My Baby	69
Exactly like You	70
Farewell Blues	70
Five Foot Two, Eyes of Blue	71
The Fish Man (Le Marchand de Poissons)	72
Floatin' down to Cotton Town	73
Gee Baby Ain't I Good to You	74
Georgia on My Mind	74
A Good Man is Hard to Find	76
Goodbye	76
Grandpa's Spells	77
Grizzly Bear	78
Hard Hearted Hannah	79
Heebie Jeebies	79
High Society	80
Hindustan	83
Home, When Shadows Fall	83
Honeysuckle Rose	84
Hotter than That	85
A Hundred Years from Today	86
I Ain't Gonna Give Nobody None of This Jelly Roll	87
I Can't Believe That You're in Love with Me	88

I Can't Give You Anything but Love........................89
I Gotta Right to Sing the Blues............................90
I Never Knew (That Roses Grew)..........................90
I Never Knew (I Could Love Anybody like I'm Loving You)..............92
I Want a Big Butter and Egg Man..........................92
I Wish I Could Shimmy like My Sister Kate 94
I'm Confessin' 95
I'm Crazy 'bout My Baby..................................96
I'm Gonna Sit Right down and Write Myself a Letter 97
I'm Gonna Stomp Mr. Henry Lee 98
I've Found a New Baby...................................98
I've Got a Feeling I'm Falling..............................99
Ida, Sweet As Apple Cider 100
In a Shanty in Old Shanty Town..........................101
Indiana 103
Irish Black Bottom 104
Is It True What They Say about Dixie 104
It All Depends on You...................................105
It Don't Mean a Thing If It Ain't Got That Swing 106
Ja-Da 106
The Japanese Sandman 108
Jazz Me Blues..109
Jelly Roll Blues...111
Jitterbug Waltz...112
Johnson Rag...113
Jubilee...114
June Night 115
Just a Closer Walk with Thee............................116
Kansas City Stomps 117
Keepin' Out of Mischief Now.............................118
King Porter Stomp 118
Lazy River..119
Lazybones 119

Title	Page
Life Is Just a Bowl of Cherries	120
Limehouse Blues	121
Linger Awhile	122
Livery Stable Blues (aka Barnyard Blues)	124
The Lonesome Road	125
Louisiana	125
Love Is Just Around the Corner	126
Love Nest	127
Mahogany Hall Stomp	129
Makin' Whoopee	131
Mandy	132
Mandy Make Up Your Mind	133
Maple Leaf Rag	135
Margie	137
Mean to Me	138
Memories of You	139
Memphis Blues	141
Midnight in Moscow	141
Minor Drag	142
Mississippi Mud	143
Muskrat Ramble	144
My Baby Just Cares for Me	144
My Blue Heaven	145
My Buddy	146
My Gal Sal	148
My Honey's Lovin' Arms	149
My Melancholy Baby	151
My Monday Date	152
Nagasaki	153
New Orleans	154
Nobody Knows You When You're Down and Out	155
Nobody's Sweetheart	156
Oh by Jingo, Oh by Gee, You're the Only Girl for Me	157

Oh Didn't He Ramble	159
On the Alamo	161
Oriental Strut	161
Original Dixieland One-Step	162
Ory's Creole Trombone	163
Paddlin' Madelin' Home	163
Palesteena	165
Panama	166
The Pearls	167
Peg o' My Heart	168
Petite Fleur	169
Please	170
Poor Butterfly	171
Potato Head Blues	172
Pretty Baby	174
P.S. I Love You	174
Puttin' on the Ritz	175
Red Sails in the Sunset	176
Riverboat Shuffle	177
Rockin' Chair	177
Rose of Washington Square	179
Rose Room	181
Roses of Picardy	183
Rosetta	183
Royal Garden Blues	184
Runnin' Wild	186
Sailing down the Chesapeake Bay	187
San	189
St. James Infirmary	190
St. Louis Blues	191
Shake That Thing	192
She's Funny That Way	193
The Sheik of Araby	195

Shine	*196*
Shreveport Stomp	*197*
Sidewalk Blues	*198*
Singin' the Blues	*199*
Smile	*200*
Smiles	*201*
Some of These Days	*202*
Somebody Loves Me	*203*
Somebody Stole My Gal	*205*
Someday You'll Be Sorry	*207*
South	*207*
S'posin'	*208*
Squeeze Me	*209*
Stealin' Apples	*210*
Stompin' at the Savoy	*211*
Strut Miss Lizzie	*212*
Struttin' with Some Barbeque	*213*
Sweet Sue	*214*
Swing That Music	*215*
Tain't Nobody's Biz-ness if I Do	*217*
That Da-Da Strain	*218*
That's a Plenty	*220*
There'll Be Some Changes Made	*221*
There'll Come a Time When You'll Need Me	*221*
Thou Swell	*222*
Three Little Words	*223*
Tiger Rag	*223*
Tin Roof Blues	*224*
Tishomingo Blues	*226*
Tuck Me to Sleep in My Old 'Tucky Home	*228*
Twelfth Street Rag	*229*
Undecided	*229*
Wabash Blues	*231*

Walkin' My Baby Back Home 232
The Wang Wang Blues 233
Washington and Lee Swing 237
Way down Yonder in New Orleans 238
Weary Blues 239
West End Blues 241
When It's Sleepy Time down South 242
When My Baby Smiles at Me 243
When My Sugar Walks down the Street 244
When The Saints Go Marching In 245
When You're Smiling 246
Where Did Robinson Crusoe Go with Friday on Saturday Night? 247
Whispering 249
Wild Cherries 251
Wolverine Blues 251
The World Is Waiting for the Sunrise 252
Wrap Your Troubles in Dreams 253
Yellow Dog Blues 254
You Always Hurt the One You Love 255
You Can Depend on Me 256
You Took Advantage of Me 256
You're the Cream in My Coffee 257
Afterword 259
Chronology 261
Bibliography 265

FOREWORD

I've been passionate about jazz and popular music from the 1920s and 30s since I was a child, after discovering it on a Victrola at my grandparents' house. The sound hit me, and this music became my calling. I sought out all of the information I could find and began amassing a collection of Jazz Age artifacts and memorabilia (including more than 60,000 band arrangements).

As I collected old records, sheet music, and orchestrations, I used to wonder, who were these folks, what was their story, and how did all of the music come about? Asking older musicians or songwriters that I was able to meet from the old days usually got the response: "he was a great guy" (and maybe a dark story here and there) and that was about all.

Robert Rawlins has delved into the history, sought out the facts and stories, and brought the era back to life. I for one am very grateful! What's more, he cites not only vintage recordings, but also more recent ones, showing how the music continues to thrive and suggesting modern recordings so folks can hear what these songs actually sounded like.

I do wish I had this book when I was working the five seasons of Boardwalk Empire—it would have been a great help to me!

For anyone interested in popular music from the early 20th century, as Paul Harvey used to say, "Now, here's the rest of the story."

—***Vince Giordano***, *Leader of Vince Giordano and the Nighthawks*

PREFACE

"Tell a story." That was the advice of Lester Young, the celebrated tenor saxophonist of the Count Basie Orchestra. *Tunes of the Twenties* follows that advice. The songs in this book have stories to tell. They come from the streets of New Orleans, rural Mississippi, Tin Pan Alley, Broadway, Hollywood, churches that were home to haunting spirituals, and concert halls that presented classical masterpieces. Each one is unique, with a circumstance and a history that reflect the diversity of American culture and the dynamic of American business.

The titles offer clues to their past. Sometimes they narrow the origin to a legendary street: "Basin Street Blues," "Canal Street Blues," "Beale Street Blues," and "The 12th Street Rag." Or they hint at a story about places still standing or long gone: "Royal Garden Blues," "The Rose Room," "St. James Infirmary," and "On the Alamo." Then there are titles with names, often of real people: "Margie," Rosetta," and "Dinah." Some titles don't seem to make any sense at all: "Irish Black Bottom," "San," and "That Da-Da Strain." And some titles are just baffling: "Limehouse Blues, "Ballin' the Jack," "Thou Swell," and "Jitterbug Waltz."

These and over 200 other stories are collected for you in *Tunes of the Twenties*, a work that is sure to provide hours of browsing pleasure and leave you with a totally new vision of what music was like during the Jazz Age.

The title *Tunes of the Twenties* is true, but not to be taken literally. It refers to a style, an attitude, and a mindset, not necessarily a decade. While the majority of the songs in this book bear copyright dates from the 20s, many were written earlier, some later. A few traditional jazz staples, including "The Darktown Strutters' Ball," "Indiana," and "Ballin' the Jack" belong to the decade before. Other favorites, among them "Just a Closer Walk with Thee," "St. James Infirmary," and "When the Saints Go Marching In," came way before the twenties. Surprisingly, some of the Dixieland warhorses, such as "Is It True What They Say about Dixie?" "Swing

That Music," "Someday You'll Be Sorry," and "Do You Know What It Means to Miss New Orleans?" actually belong to the 1930s and 40s. And the great soprano saxophonist Sidney Bechet, living the final years of his life in Paris, continued to turn out great traditional jazz numbers into the 1950s, including "Le Marchand De Poissons" ("The Fish Vendor") and "Petite Fleur."

Tunes of the Twenties is meant to be a companion guide to my previous book *The Real Dixieland Book* (published by Hal Leonard Corporation, 2010). That book provides the sheet music to 250 traditional jazz classics. This book talks about the songs. And "talk" is the operative word. Each entry starts with the basic facts, but then veers off into its own direction. I strive not for completeness and consistency, but to reveal what I found interesting about each particular tune. And, in the spirit of the music I discuss, I try to make each story unique, funny, witty if possible, and sometimes irreverent. Obscure facts pertaining to a song's early history are included only when they reveal something important about the song.

In other words, if it wasn't interesting, I left it out.

Most of the songs in this book are still frequently performed today, and represent the cream rising to the top. Many songs from the 20s are no longer remembered, and a list of the top hits of the decade would look far different from the contents of the present volume. The test of time is often a good filter, and some songs really needed many years to catch on or be rediscovered. For instance, to the best of my knowledge, no jazz band ever played "When the Saints Go Marching In" prior to Louis Armstrong's 1938 recording, yet today it is the most frequently requested song for traditional jazz bands.

I threw in a couple of oddballs as well. I wanted there to be a mixture of different types of songs, which explains the inclusion of some rags, hymns, blues, and novelty songs that aren't frequently played anymore. When was the last time you heard "Borneo," "Dill Pickles Rag," or "Alcoholic Blues"? Knowing these obscure songs will enable musicians to broaden their repertoire, listeners to stump the band, and friends to share a fun fact or two over a cocktail. Regretfully, many good songs had to be left out because of space and copyright restrictions. (*The Real Dixieland Book*, which provided my song list, is a collection of both music and lyrics, and nearly all songs written after 1922 are still under copyright protection.) But as a cross section, the tunes included provide an excellent representation of the period.

Although not a primary focus of this book, I have provided recommended recordings for most songs. Since early recordings were released individually, and then reissued in various collections after LPs and CDs came out, it seemed a better idea to simply provide the recording date. An internet search with song, artist, and year will most like bring up the version referred to, either available for streaming, download, or purchase on a CD. For more recent recordings, it seemed more helpful to provide the year of the album release.

Obviously, I could only mention a few recordings for each tune, and these choices, to some extent, reflect my preferences. Like many who perform and study this music, I admire a handful of musicians I feel are absolutely essential to the style: Bessie Smith, Louis Armstrong, Bix Beiderbecke, Jack Teagarden, and Eddie Condon are all near the top of that list. Recordings by these musicians are reliably and consistently good, and you're not likely to be disappointed listening to any of their records. Notable recordings by non-jazz artists are occasionally referred to if there is something significant about them. As for recent recordings, I focused on the very recent and tried to mix it up. There has been an explosion of interest in early jazz over the past 10 years, with no shortage of talented musicians keeping the momentum going. New bands and singers are appearing so quickly that undoubtedly some have not crossed my radar screen.

Jazz developed into its first maturity during the 20s. Not surprisingly, the music had some strange bedfellows around this time, and any attempt to include only the "real stuff" is doomed to failure. Some would dispute that Paul Whiteman and Ted Lewis were real jazz musicians or that they even led jazz bands, but they nevertheless hired and often featured some of the finest jazz musicians of the day. Sophie Tucker, Eddie Cantor, and Gene Austin are even further removed from the jazz purist's mainstream, but you simply can't talk about the early years of jazz without their names coming up. So don't be surprised that their names do come up, and frequently, in *Tunes of the Twenties*.

I've included photographs of the sheet music covers for many of the songs. Prior to the 20s, sheet music sales were the primary indicator of a song's popularity. Typically, the covers were illustrated by an artist hired by the publishing firm to depict a scene expressing what the song meant. We have no way of knowing if the songwriters or publishers told artists what to draw, or if the artists were given carte blanche to let their imaginations soar. What we do know is that the covers played some part in telling the public what the song was about. I've also included snippets of the lyrics here and there when helpful. (The complete lyrics to most of the songs can be found in *The Real Dixieland Book*.)

Tunes of the Twenties assumes no prior familiarity with the songs, no training in music, and no particular knowledge of jazz and its practitioners. What it does assume is a fascination with the Jazz Age and the music it produced. Along with that, perhaps a bit of curiosity. Who was Aunt Hagar, Margie, or Rosetta? Why did "good friends always meet" on Basin Street? Where is the St. James Infirmary? Was there a real Baby Face? And just where did Robinson Crusoe go with Friday on a Saturday night? Let's grab some bathtub gin, crank up the Victrola and find out.

INTRODUCTION

Part of the charm of the music presented in this book is how it reflects a fascinating era of American history. The 20s saw the emergence of a then-stunning technology that brought music into the home, a development that propelled a vibrant expansion of the music industry. The music itself was revolutionary, pretty much in the literal sense of the word. At a time when the nation was beginning to chafe under the restrictive culture of the first years of the 20th century, jazz became the vehicle through which a new generation listened and danced its way into a era of wild abandon.

Before we get to the stories of the music, let's look at the story behind the story – the development of the phonograph, the music industry of the 20s, and the dance revolution.

The Phonograph

Turn it down! No, that's not my parents talking to me, it's my young friends when they hear my Victrola for the first time. They usually follow up with "I want one!" The mechanical phonograph really is a marvel to see and hear, and I think at some level we are just as astonished by its capabilities as people were a hundred years ago. How can such a simple apparatus produce such good sound—and so loudly—without electronics? What's the story behind this thing?

Thomas Edison gets the credit for its invention in 1877. As with the light bulb and several other innovations, he didn't come up with the concept, only the first practical working model. Others, including Alexander Graham Bell, soon went to work on improving it. Edison, who invented the light bulb two years later, was too busy supplying New York City with electricity to compete seriously in the phonograph industry. Besides, he had several strikes against him: First, he had initially envisioned his apparatus as a business dictation machine, not seeing its potential for recording music. Second, he had a serious hearing impairment. Third, he really didn't understand music, current trends, or popular tastes. When he did start recording music, he insisted on selecting the artists himself and wouldn't even allow their names to appear on the record labels. Subsequently, he fell behind in the game, and never did catch up to the competition.

Edison's system relied on a rotating cylinder with a vertically cut groove winding around the outside. Others found that it was easier to manufacture a disc, with a spiral groove running from the outside toward the center. Two major record companies began producing discs in 1901, Victor and Columbia, and they would dominate the field for decades to come. By the end of the decade their records would be recorded on both sides. Edison, for the time being, stubbornly stuck to his cylinders, which in some ways were superior to discs, but more expensive to make and less convenient to use and store.

The discs produced by Columbia and Victor were ten inches in diameter and meant to turn at a speed that eventually became standardized at 78 revolutions per minute. Thus, the advent of the "78." These discs were somewhat heavy and fragile, but remained the dominant medium for recorded sound until the early 1950s. They were cheap, convenient, and sounded pretty decent. Their main limitation was that they could hold just over three minutes of music. Song arrangements would have to be carefully timed to fill up this interval without going beyond it.

The record industry took some time to really get under way. At first, there was more money to be made by selling the phonographs themselves; the records were just something you bought to have something to play when you demonstrated your contraption to friends. The real way to make money in the music industry, at the time, was to sell sheet music. But all that began to change in the 20s. As mass marketing drove down the prices of phonographs and records, sales skyrocketed. By the end of the decade well over 100 million records were sold each year. If you had a hit in 1915 you were talking about sheet music sales. If you had a hit in 1925 you were definitely talking about record sales.

Whereas a few years before the piano had been a household necessity, now the phonograph was all the rage. This sounds a bit sad in a way, because it implies that people were no longer making their own music, but buying it prepackaged and ready to consume without effort. But there was an upside to this. In previous decades, songwriters and publishers were well aware that they were marketing songs primarily for amateur performance. With some exceptions, a tune had to be simple and predictable enough that ordinary people could sing and play it, otherwise they wouldn't buy it. But in the 20s their target audience shifted to professional performers. If a popular orchestra had a hit record with your song the royalties could be staggering. Composers were now free to write melodies, harmonies, and rhythms that would require real musicianship to pull off, and they did. What's more, professionally trained musicians now saw popular song as a fulfilling outlet for their talents, and one that might make them rich as well. By a strange quirk of Fate, mechanical reproduction of sound, which John Philip Sousa had denounced as "canned music," sparked an era of unprecedented creativity in American popular music.

Sheet Music and Tin Pan Alley

Among the many changes ushered in during the 20th century were higher wages, more leisure time, affordable pianos, and cheaper sheet music. The formula was perfect. A typical middle class family had the money to buy a piano, pay for lessons and music, and time to gather together to make music at home. When the family did go out together, it was often to a show in one of the newly built vaudeville theaters. This new venue offered entertainment for mixed gender audiences as an alternative to the saloons and variety halls patronized almost exclusively by men. A new song was likely to first be heard by the public in a vaudeville show, prompting people to go out and buy the music. Accordingly, the sheet music industry flourished.

Around the turn of the century, a songwriter wrote a series of articles for the New York Herald on this rapidly growing publishing business. There was one spot on West 28th Street where several of the publishing houses were based. Each had pianists busy writing or demonstrating songs, and their sounds simultaneously emerged through the open windows in a cacophony that sounded to him like the clanging of tin pans. Thus the phrase "Tin Pan Alley." Eventually the publishers moved on to other locations, but the term remained as a name for the popular music publishing industry itself.

At first publishers waited for performers and customers to come to them looking for new material, but soon they became more aggressive and the "song plugger" was born. This is simply a name for a salesman/pianist who aggressively promotes a song. Sometimes they demonstrated them in stores; often they would go out to theaters, vaudeville houses, saloons, or anywhere people gathered to badger orchestra leaders, entertainers, dancers, comedians, singers, managers, or anyone who would listen. Many famous songwriters started out as song pluggers, including George Gershwin, Jerome Kern, and Harry Warren.

Sheet music sales peaked in the 1910s, and have been in decline ever since, but the game wasn't over yet. In 1914 a group of composers got together and founded ASCAP, The American Society of Composers, Artists, and Publishers (note that performers are not included in that title). It all began when Victor Herbert noticed a band playing one of his songs, and began thinking about all the people across the country who were making money from his music but not paying him for it. The thrust of the organization, still very much alive and well today, is that they charge a licensing fee for those who play music composed by ASCAP members, and then return that money to their members as royalties. Fortunately for songwriters, when the recording industry took off, decimating their royalties from sheet music sales, they were then able to collect "mechanical" royalties from record sales. Publishing was still a lucrative business, even if people weren't directly buying the sheet music.

Dancing

Talk show host Merv Griffin once asked jazz drummer Buddy Rich if people ever danced to his music. Rich, a veteran smart aleck, quipped "I wish they wouldn't." The irony is that jazz first came into being as dance music. That was the whole point. Prior to 1910 or so, dancing in public was frowned upon, and dancing in private homes was confined to mostly waltzes and line dances (yes, even back then). But the peppy rhythms of the Ragtime Era proved too alluring, and a young couple named Irene and Vernon Castle were determined to do something about it.

Refined, elegant, fashionable, and amazingly talented, the Castles quickly became the most famous dance team in the country and the envy of New York City socialites. It was said that they sometimes asked $1,000 per hour for dance lessons and often got it. Not only were they respectable, they were even married. The Castles took advantage of their unblemished image to push their progressive ideas—they travelled with a Black orchestra, employed a lesbian manager, and most importantly, removed the stigma of vulgarity from close dancing. Among many other steps, the Castles introduced the foxtrot, which soon became and remained a staple of social dancing. The dance might have been associated with vaudevillian Harry Fox, but the Castles were the ones to define its movements, perform it in public, and teach it to the world.

The Castles intended many of their dances, including the foxtrot, to be danced to Ragtime. This style of music emerged a few years before the turn of the century and remained quite popular until around 1918, when the new sounds of jazz began to exert their influence. Ragtime takes its name from the syncopated or off-beat rhythms that sounded "ragged" to some ears. Ragtime was introduced by African-American musicians, and the influence of African-based complex rhythms can clearly be heard. In its formal structure, a rag is essentially a march set to Ragtime rhythm. Rags were generally published as piano pieces, but their influence permeated much popular song of the period. Additionally, small Ragtime orchestras were quite common, playing music for dancing and social functions.

The Castles' preferred musical ensemble was James Reese Europe and his Society Orchestra. Though not quite a jazz band, what Reese played was something more than Ragtime, something unlike any other band, and packed with energy and spirit. The country was listening. By 1920 every major hotel had a dance orchestra, and the ones playing the peppy new music called jazz were the most popular. For now, crooners would take a back seat. People wanted to dance, and they wanted hot, rhythmic instrumental numbers. A singer with a leading dance band could expect to sing one brief chorus on some of the numbers and sit quietly the rest of the time.

Rebounding from the horrors of World War I, and pushing ever further the freedoms from Victorian morality that the Ragtime Era brought, America was ready for a good time, and music was a main attraction. Americans would dance, drink, and party their way through the next decade, and they would do it to the new sounds of jazz. In *Tunes of the Twenties*, we'll take a look at the songs they listened to, the composers who wrote them, the publishers who promoted them, and the musicians who played them.

⇒ THE SONGS ⇐

Ace in the Hole (music: George Mitchell, lyrics: James Dempsey, 1909): (Not to be confused with the song of the same title written by Cole Porter for the 1941 show *Let's Face It*.) A typical story-telling gambling song, "Ace in the Hole" begins with the irresistible words, "This town is full of guys, who think they're mighty wise," and ends with a moral statement of sorts: "But their name would be 'mud' like a 'punk' playing 'stud' if they lost that old ace in the hole."

Despite its early copyright date, the song was a latecomer to the jazz scene. Very few recordings exist prior to 1944, when old-time New Orleans cornetist Bunk Johnson (1879-1949) recorded the song with the Yerba Buena Jazz Band in San Francisco. Johnson was an important figure in the Dixieland revival of the 1940s.

The Dixieland revival resulted in part from a series of record reissues and journalistic pieces that attempted to trace early years of jazz. Music at the height of the Big Band Era (1935-46) was certainly quite different from the jazz of the 20s and before, and an enthusiastic group of fans yearned for a return to the "real stuff." All of a sudden, old-time New Orleans musicians, such as soprano saxophonist Sidney Bechet, trombonist Kid Ory, bassist Pops Foster, and Bunk Johnson (who hadn't played in years, and no longer even owned a cornet) found themselves in demand again.

The revival was led by two factions. On the West Coast were musicians such as trumpeter Lu Watters and His Yerba Buena Jazz Band, who wanted to stay true to the authentic sounds of New Orleans, playing the old standards in a two-beat style. On the East Coast, guitarist Eddie Condon (1905-1973) championed the type of jazz that developed in Chicago in the 20s, playing the pop tunes of the day in a hard-driving four-beat style. These musicians included cornetists Wild Bill Davison and Muggsy Spanier, saxophonist Bud Freeman, and clarinetist Pee Wee Russell.

Bunk Johnson was retired and living in the vicinity of New Orleans when researchers tracked him down. They wasted no time pumping him for information (much of which turned out to be wrong!) and getting him in shape to play again. Johnson knew "Ace in the Hole." Evidently, musicians in New Orleans had been playing the song for years, while it remained relatively unknown in the North. But not for long. A slew of recordings followed in the late 1940s, and by the 1950s practically all of the Dixieland revival bands were playing the tune, including Turk Murphy, Bob Scobey, and the Dukes of Dixieland. Bunk's historic recording can be heard on a 2008 album entitled *The Roaring Forties*. I love that title!

After I Say I'm Sorry (music and lyrics: Walter Donaldson and Abe Lyman, 1926): By 1926, songwriter Walter Donaldson (1893-1947) was racking up an impressive collection of hit songs and within two years would resign his position as songwriter for the Irving Berlin Music Company to start his own publishing firm. Donaldson was working primarily with lyricist Gus Kahn at the time, but he teamed up with Abe Lyman for this one. Lyman (1897-1957) was not known as a lyricist, but rather as a bandleader. He was a great success in California where his band was hailed as "Los Angeles' most famous popular music organization." Having your song plugged by a well-known bandleader might not ensure success, but it couldn't hurt, and this time it worked. Lyman had a Number 6 hit record with the tune.

The song was introduced in vaudeville by Bee Palmer, but don't look for a recording by her. If she ever recorded "After I Say I'm Sorry," it didn't survive. An immensely popular and magnetic performer, Palmer was a main attraction through the 20s, but the few recordings she made were not released. (Fortunately, they were not destroyed, and have recently been issued on CD.) In addition to Lyman, both Ruth Etting and Jane Gray had very successful recordings. If you don't recognize the name "Jane Gray," you might try a different one. "The pseudonym girl" used at least 13 different names during her short but active recording career, among them Lillie Daltry, Nora West, Mae French, Dolly Prince, Sally Brown, and Marjorie Adams. Her real name was Marguerite Grace English (1893-1988). "Jane Gray" was the name she used when recording on the Harmony record label. During the same period she was recording for the Vocalion record label as Peggy English, which was the closest of her names to her real one.

Musicians liked "After I Say I'm Sorry." It has interesting chords and the melody lends itself to an instrumental. It quickly found its way into the jazz repertoire and stayed there. Recordings can be heard by Bobby Hackett (1940), Pee Wee Russell (1961), Wild Bill Davison (1977), and Maxine Sullivan (1984). The song appears in the 1955 film *Pete Kelly's Blues*, in which Jack Webb stars as a 20s cornet player, and also in the 1955 film *Love Me or Leave Me*, a biographical musical which tells the story of Ruth Etting.

"After You've Gone," by Turner Layton and Henry Creamer got off to a slow start but eventually became one of the most enduring songs they ever wrote. (Courtesy Lilly Library, Indiana University, Bloomington, Indiana.)

After You've Gone (music: Turner Layton, lyrics: Henry Creamer, 1917): Although the African-American songwriting team of Creamer and Layton produced some wonderful material together, their collaboration never found the success it should have, and the team split up after six years. But during that time they produced several fabulous songs, including "After You've Gone" (1917), "Strut Miss Lizzie" (1920), "Dear Old Southland" (1921), and "Way down Yonder in New Orleans" (1922). All of these songs have earned permanent places in the Dixieland repertoire.

"After You've Gone" is characterized by a broad-sweeping but repetitive melody and unique set of chord changes that have made it a favorite jam tune. (You might also notice that the first four notes are the same as those of "Peg o' My Heart," 1913.) "After You've Gone" spawned a few early hits, but didn't immediately enter the jazz repertoire. That changed with Bessie Smith's rediscovery of the tune in

1927. Shortly after, hits followed by Sophie Tucker (1927), Paul Whiteman (1930), and Louis Armstrong (1932). Soon jazz bands across the country were playing and recording it. A 1927 recording by the Charleston Chasers features an outstanding alto saxophone solo by young Jimmy Dorsey. (Read more about this fabulous reed player in the entry on "Sweet Sue.")

The Charleston Chasers was a "name-only" ensemble. In the jazz world of the 20s, as in today's jazz world, band personnel can be somewhat fluid. Unlike classical or rock ensembles that rely on set, well-rehearsed routines, jazz musicians, by the very nature of their craft, very often "wing it." That is, they rely on the listening instincts, common background, and musical abilities of fellow band members to present a tight but largely improvised performance. Music executives were aware of this, and in the case of the Charleston Chasers, they simply drew from the top 20 or so jazz musicians among their signed bands and pieced together ensembles for a various recording sessions, dubbing them all the Charleston Chasers. Between 1925 and 1930 dozens of records were made under this name, several of them top hits, but the personnel was never fixed and they never performed as a unit outside of the studio.

Ain't Misbehavin' (music: Fats Waller, lyrics: Andy Razaf, 1929): Thomas Wright "Fats" Waller (1904-1943) was a pianist, composer, singer, and comedic entertainer famous both for his musical genius and effusive personality. Razaf called him "a bubbling bundle of joy" and all accounts seem to agree that wherever he went, at whatever time of day, it was "happy hour." As a pianist, his abilities were unsurpassed in his field, leading composer and fellow pianist Oscar Levant to call him the "Black Horowitz." His hundreds of published compositions include some of the musical gems of the era, not to mention the countless songs he recklessly sold outright for which he didn't receive credit. And his singing and clowning made him one of the most popular entertainers of the 20s and 30s.

The continuous wild party that was his life includes this fantastic story, told by his son Maurice:

> Dad was playing solo piano at the Hotel Sherman, not very far from East Cicero, the home of Chicago's "second mayor," Al Capone.... Suddenly someone shoved a revolver into his paunchy stomach and ordered him into a car. He did what he was told. The gunman ordered the driver to take them to East Cicero, and Dad began to sweat it out.... The car pulled up in front of what appeared to be a hotel or fancy saloon. It was the headquarters of Al Capone. Dad's four escorts ... led him to a piano, and

told him to play. It was a surprise birthday party. Capone, who had heard Dad play at the hotel, was delighted when he saw the present the boys brought him sitting at the piano.... After the birthday party was over, three days later, the mugs returned him to Chicago several thousand dollars richer.

"Ain't Misbehavin'" is perhaps the most beloved of all of Waller's songs. It has been a popular favorite since its debut in 1929 in the extremely successful show *Hot Chocolates*. Within weeks of its release, hit versions of the song began to appear, including recordings by Gene Austin, Ruth Etting, and Louis Armstrong. Waller himself had great success with his 1929 recording for Victor, and sang the song in the 1943 musical film *Stormy Weather*. In 2004, the National Recording Registry named the original Fats Waller stride piano version of "Ain't Misbehavin'" as one of the 50 most significant recordings in U.S. history. ("Stride" piano was a style developed by Harlem pianists characterized by a sweeping left-hand motion that alternates deep bass notes with middle-register chords.)

Following the song's initial success, musicians seem to have left it alone for a few years. But in 1933 Duke Ellington recorded "Ain't Misbehavin'" as an instrumental, a solid jazz version leaving plenty of solo space for his men. Two years later Paul Whiteman recorded the song. But he recorded everything, so why is that special? Because the performance showcases the legendary Jack Teagarden with both a vocal chorus and a trombone solo. At a time when most musicians of Teagarden's caliber were striking out on their own, Teagarden was confined by an exclusive five-year contract with Whiteman, which he regretted signing. Whiteman was aware of Teagarden's talent and featured him prominently. What's more, they became serious drinking buddies. Nevertheless, the very day his commitment was fulfilled, at the end of 1938, Teagarden walked out, leaving an astonished Paul Whiteman without a lead trombone player.

Ain't She Sweet (music: Milton Ager, lyrics: Jack Yellen, 1927): The songwriting team of Milton Ager and Jack Yellen is responsible for several treasures in the traditional jazz repertoire, including "Hard Hearted Hannah," "Happy Days Are Here Again," "I May Be Wrong," and "I'm Nobody's Baby." "Ain't She Sweet" is a typical light-hearted Roaring Twenties tune that sold over a million copies of sheet music. The melody doesn't stray very far for the opening line, nor do the lyrics. Yet for all its simplicity, the song has an enduring charm that has kept it going for all these years. An early hit by Gene Austin sent the tune on its way, and dozens of notable recordings have followed, including a top-twenty hit by The Beatles in 1961.

A fine early jazz version was recorded by guitarist Eddie Lang and violinist Joe Venuti with the Jack Pettis band in a particularly inventive arrangement. Lang and Venuti were recognized as the finest performers on their instruments in the jazz world. When they played together, Lang's powerful rhythmic pulse coupled with Venuti's fluid improvisations worked magic.

"Ain't She Sweet" was featured in the films *You Were Meant for Me* (1948) and *The Eddy Duchin Story* (1956). It can also be heard in the background in *Margie* (1956).

A popular vaudeville number, "Alabama Jubilee," by George Cobb and Jack Yellen, fell out of favor with 20s audiences, but was revived successfully in the 1950s. Like many of her era, entertainer Elizabeth Murray, who introduced the song, was well known on the stage but not as a recording artist. With the decline of vaudeville her name was all but forgotten. (Courtesy Lilly Library, Indiana University, Bloomington, Indiana.)

Alabama Jubilee (music: George L. Cobb, lyrics: Jack Yellen, 1915): Before teaming up with Milton Ager to write some of the classic songs of the 20s (see "Ain't She Sweet"), lyricist Jack Yellen had his earliest hits with George Cobb. Cobb is perhaps best remembered as the composer of "Russian Rag," which he loosely based on Rachmaninoff's Prelude in C-sharp minor (1892). "Alabama Jubilee" is a novelty song about some down-home folks having a dance party. The chorus begins, "You ought to see Deacon Jones when he rattles the bones."

Introduced on vaudeville by Elizabeth Murray, it was a hit for the comic duo of Arthur Collins and Byron Harlan in 1916. However, the song's feel and rural sentiment were not in step with the Roaring Twenties, and it went underground for a number of years. "Alabama Jubilee" was revived in the 1950s, with hits by Red Foley (1951), the Ferko String Band (1955), and successful recordings by many others. Although most treated it as a novelty or country song, jazz renditions also began to appear, especially among revivalist bands. Recommended recordings include those by Muggsy Spanier (1950), the Firehouse Five Plus Two (1954), the Dukes of Dixieland (1957), and Teresa Brewer and the Dixieland Band (1959). Although Brewer might seem an unlikely interpreter of jazz material, her recordings with this ensemble are generally solid and swinging, although somewhat over-arranged.

Alabamy Bound (music: Ray Henderson, lyrics: Buddy DeSylva and Bud Green, 1924): (Not to be confused with "I'm Alabama Bound," the 1909 rag composed by Robert Hoffman.) Both the music and lyrics conjure railroad images, and this fact was not lost on the various arrangers of this song. (What orchestrator could resist the lyric "Just hear that choo-choo sound"?) Fletcher Henderson's 1925 recording is not the only one to open with a train whistle.

The sheet music cover reads "As successfully introduced by Al Jolson," which says it all. The song had several notable recordings in 1925, including a big seller by bandleader Isham Jones, and has remained a jazz standard ever since. It has been used in several films, including *Show Business* (1944) and *The Great American Broadcast* (1941).

The opening eight bars of the tune share the same chords as "Limehouse Blues," and melodic similarities can be heard as well. In any case, it has had longstanding appeal for many audiences. Plentiful Dixieland and country recordings can be heard, a few pop versions (such as those of Ray Charles and Bobby Darin), and even a handful of bebop interpretations, such as a 1956 recording by Sonny Criss.

The Alcoholic Blues, by Albert Von Tilzer and Edward Laska, expresses how many Americans felt about Prohibition. (Courtesy Lilly Library, Indiana University, Bloomington, Indiana.)

Alcoholic Blues (music: Albert Von Tilzer, lyrics: Edward Laska, 1919): This song is a comical lament to the onset of Prohibition (just as Arthur Johnston's "Cocktails for Two" would celebrate the end of Prohibition 15 years later). The lyrics actually require explanation for contemporary audiences, particularly the phrase "When Mister Hoover said to cut my dinner down, I never even hesitate, I never frown." Yes, the song is referring to Herbert Hoover, but not as President Hoover, since he would not occupy that office until 1929. Instead, the lyrics refer to Hoover as Woodrow Wilson's appointed head of the U.S. Food Administration in the war effort. His motto was "food will win the war," and he encouraged citizens to reduce consumption of foods that were needed for soldiers' rations. The protagonist of the song is willing to do this, but when the government now restricts his drinking he complains, "Now they dug deep in my soul!"

The song is a basic blues with a 16-bar verse (with two sets of lyrics) in front. The appeal is in the lyrics, which contain some charmingly bad rhymes: "whiskey, you used to make me frisky," "so long gin, when you comin' back again?" and the wonderfully cringe-worthy "I've got the blues, since they amputated my booze."

There are relatively few recordings of "Alcoholic Blues." Billy Murray (1919) recorded it as a novelty number, the Louisiana Five Orchestra (1919) recorded an instrumental version, and Pianist Pete Wendling made a QRS piano roll (1919). As was often the case, it was the revivalist bands of the 1940s and 50s who brought the song back. Perhaps the best recording from this era is that by Lu Watters with Clancy Hayes on the vocals (1956). A relatively recent recording by pianist Steve Pistorius (1994) seems to get the balance of jazz and hokum just about right.

"Alexander's Ragtime Band, the song that catapulted Irving Berlin from a poor Jewish immigrant to a songwriting celebrity, was based on lyrics salvaged from an earlier song to which Berlin provided a new melody. (Courtesy Lilly Library, Indiana University, Bloomington, Indiana.)

Alexander's Ragtime Band (Irving Berlin, 1911): This was the gigantic hit that launched Berlin's career. And what a career it was. Irving Berlin (born Israel Isidore Baline, 1888-1989) is generally recognized as the father of the American Songbook. With tunes like "White Christmas," "Easter Parade," and "God Bless America" to his credit, Berlin is arguably more a part of American culture than any composer in history.

How odd that the most popular Ragtime song ever written isn't a rag at all—it's a simple 32-bar pop song in ABAC form. (In discussing song form, capital letters are used to indicate different sections. The same letter means the same material repeats.) But it is about Ragtime, and the song's title, syncopated spirit, and enticing lyrics provided a winning formula for the times. The first line of the chorus implores the audience to "Come on and hear," and they did. Arthur Collins, Billy Murray, Prince's Orchestra, and the Victor Military Band, some of the most popular artists of the day, all had hit recordings of the song shortly after its publication.

In the long run, it was better that "Alexander's" was not strictly a rag, for when the jazz era arrived, the song fit perfectly, as can be heard in the interpretations of Bessie Smith (1927) and Louis Armstrong (1937). Bing Crosby and Connee Boswell charted at Number 1 with the song (1938) and hit versions were still appearing in the 1950s. "Alexander's" is a supplication to "get with" the Ragtime spirit, and blatantly quotes "Old Folks at Home" in the last section to the lyrics, "And if you care to hear the Swanee River played in Ragtime."

One of Berlin's work habits was to hold on to a song or lyric that didn't quite work at a particular time and try again sometime in the future. A classic example was "God Bless America," which Berlin wrote in 1918 but decided to cut from his own show. Exactly 20 years later, he pulled the song out again, and the time was right. Berlin used this strategy from the start. He had actually written the lyrics to "Alexander's" a year before, to a melody by his publisher Ted Snyder entitled "Alexander and his Clarionet." (I have no idea why he spelled clarinet that way.) The song went nowhere. When Berlin tried again the following year with a melody he composed himself, he struck gold. "Alexander's Ragtime Band" became so popular that some 65 performers at one time or another were successful enough with the song to have sheet music printed with their picture on the cover. But Berlin's strategies didn't always work. A year after penning "Alexander's Ragtime Band," he published a follow-up called "Alexander's Bagpipe Band." Never heard it? Neither have I.

"Alice Blue Gown," by Harry Tierney and Joseph McCarthy, was introduced in Irene, which set the record as the longest-running Broadway show of its day. (Courtesy Lilly Library, Indiana University, Bloomington, Indiana.)

Alice Blue Gown (music: Harry Tierney, lyrics: Joseph McCarthy, 1919): The Alice referred to is Alice Roosevelt Longworth, daughter of President Teddy Roosevelt. While he was in office, she became the darling of the press (and embarrassment to the family) because of her headstrong personality and daring antics, such as smoking in public, gambling, and staying out at late-night parties. The song title derives from the fact that she preferred a tint of azure in her dress that became a fashion rage across the country and inspired the color name Alice Blue. It became the official color used by the United States Navy for insignia on vessels named after Theodore Roosevelt.

The lyrics to the song begin with "I once had a gown, it was almost new, Oh, the daintiest thing, it was sweet Alice Blue." Edith Day introduced the number in the *Irene*, which became the longest-running Broadway musical up to that time, holding that record for 28 years. Day also had a Number 1 hit with "Alice Blue Gown" in 1920, and the Original Dixieland Jazz Band recorded it in 1921. An excellent record by Red Nichols and his Five Pennies (1929) features strong solos by Jimmy Dorsey on alto saxophone, Red Nichols on cornet, and Adrian Rollini on bass saxophone. Other hot versions were recorded by Ben Pollack (1937), Teddy Wilson (solo piano, 1938), Muggsy Spanier (1944), and Eddie Condon (1945).

More recent recordings include those by cornetist Ed Polcer from his album *Coast to Coast* (1994), clarinetist Dan Levinson from his album *Dan Levinson's Roof Garden Jass Band Salutes the ODJB and the Beginning of Recorded Jazz* (1998), and Drew Nugent and the Midnight Society from his album *Alice Blue Gown* (2013). But one of the most fascinating recordings of "Alice Blue Gown" dates from a 1999 album entitled *Lars Edegran presents Lionel Ferbos and John Robichaux*. Featuring two long-time New Orleans musicians, the result is guaranteed to be authentic, as trumpeter Ferbos was 88 at the time of the recording while drummer Robichaux was 84. Robichaux was killed in Hurricane Katrina and Ferbos died in 2014 at the age of 103.

By the time Irving Berlin wrote "All By Myself" he had formed his own publishing company, Irving Berlin, Inc. (Courtesy Lilly Library, Indiana University, Bloomington, Indiana.)

All By Myself (Irving Berlin, 1921): By the 20s Irving Berlin was operating his own publishing house and his career was in full stride. An unassuming song with a catchy lyric, "All By Myself" got off to a good start with at least six hit records in 1921, including a Number 1 record for Ted Lewis. It was his biggest hit since "When My Baby Smiles at Me." In just over a year "All by Myself" had sold more than a million records, a million copies of sheet music, and some 160,000 piano rolls.

Berlin wrote the song a year before his mother died and meant the song to express the sadness and loneliness of growing old. He continued this concept in the following years with the songs "What'll I Do" (1923) and "All Alone" (1924). Incidentally, the original lyric to the second eight-bar section reads, "I sit alone in a cozy Morris chair," not, "with a table and chair," as it is often sung. The Morris chair was an early type of recliner sold by the William Morris Company. The term appears in several pop song lyrics of the day, such as "My Honey's Lovin' Arms" and Berlin's "You'd be Surprised." The original sheet music to "All By Myself" depicts a pretty young girl reading a book and not looking sad at all, sitting in a chair that is certainly not a Morris chair. So much for historical accuracy!

Bob Crosby and the Bob Cats made a fine recording in 1940. This excellent band distinguished itself by playing the traditional jazz repertoire in a big-band swing setting, and generally the results were excellent. More recently, clarinetists Bobby Gordon and Bob Wilber teamed up to record the number on their 2002 album *Yearnings*. Wilber (born 1928) had been Sidney Bechet's protégée, while Gordon (1931-2013) was the only clarinetist of his generation to successfully follow in the footsteps of Pee Wee Russell. For an excellent solo piano version of "All By Myself" listen to Neville Dickie (2004).

Angry (music: Henny Brunies, Merritt Brunies, Jules Cassard; lyrics: Dudley Mecum, 1925): The tune was a joint effort by members of the New Orleans Rhythm Kings from Chicago. Young Bix Beiderbecke idolized this band and loved this song. According to cornetist Paul Mares, "Bix—he was in school at Lake Forest Academy then—used to sneak down and pester us to play 'Angry' so he could sit in. At the time, it was the only tune he knew." Alas, Bix's time at Lake Forest was limited. One night in the spring of 1922, as he was returning from making his all-night rounds of the Chicago jazz clubs, he was caught climbing into his dormitory window via the fire escape and subsequently expelled. Today he is considered one of the school's most distinguished alumni.

Although the New Orleans Rhythm Kings had been playing the song for quite some time, they didn't record it until 1923 and it wasn't published until 1925, when both Ted Lewis and Art Gillham had hit records with it. Years later, it would chart once again, with hits by Tiny Hill (1939) and Kay Starr (1951). Hill adopted the tune as his signature song. "Angry" is also a staple in the barbershop quartet repertoire, probably because of the lighthearted lyrics that conjure images of an earlier era. The lyric to the chorus begins, "Angry, please don't be angry, 'Cause I was only teasing you." Notable jazz renditions include those by Earl Hines (1934), Bob Crosby (1939), and Muggsy Spanier (1944). More recently, New Orleans clarinetist Tommy Sancton included the song on his 1999 album *Louisiana Fairytale*.

As much as he loved the song, Bix never recorded it. But this problem has been solved, well, as much as that is possible. There's a cornetist active today who sounds remarkably like Bix, and has pretty much devoted his life to doing just that. On the album *Bix off the Record: Original Re-creations of Unrecorded Performances* (2015), Andy Schumm performs 15 of the songs Bix often played in the 1920s but never recorded. The result is spectacular, with fellow band members Josh Duffee (drummer/leader), Kristoffer Kompen (trombone), Mauro Porro (clarinet), David Boeddinghaus (piano), and Frans Sjostrom (bass saxophone) all sounding like they just stepped out of the Jazz Age.

As Long as I Live (music: Harold Arlen, lyrics: Ted Koehler, 1934): The song was written for the 1934 *Cotton Club Parade*, the fifth and final show that the famous songwriting team provided the music for. Each season had produced songs that have become enduring standards in the American Songbook: "Between the Devil and the Deep Blue Sea," "I Love a Parade," "I've Got the World on a String," "Stormy Weather," and "Ill Wind" among them.

"As Long as I Live" was to be sung and danced by a male-female duo, which included a fellow named Avon Long, who was making his Cotton Club debut. Long was a fine singer, but his dancing was considered traditional and out of date. The female singer wasn't happy with her assigned partner, and disappeared shortly before the show opened. To take her place, management chose a 16-year-old girl from the chorus named Lena Horne.

Horne's spectacular performance with the number attracted favorable attention, prompting the star of the show, Adelaide Hall, to take her under her wing. Lena soon had a small part in a Broadway show, and within a few years she became a main attraction as a singer, dancer, and actress. She can be heard singing "As Long as I Live" on a recording from 1944. Benny Goodman and Jack Teagarden made a fine recording together in 1934, with Jack on vocals, and they each kept the song in their repertoire for the rest of their careers.

And what became of the famed Arlen/Koehler songwriting team? They broke up. Arlen received an offer to do a full-length Broadway show, a dream come true, but the offer was for him and Yip Harburg, not Ted Koehler. Arlen felt so bad that he couldn't even face Koehler, so he wrote him a letter. There was no breach in their friendship, but their collaboration was over, and the team of Arlen and Harburg was firmly established. A few years later they were chosen to write the score to *The Wizard of Oz*.

"As Long as I Live" (as well as several other songs discussed in this book) can be heard on the 2005 album *As Long as I Live*, featuring cornetist Randy Reinhart and a line-up of some of the top musicians currently playing this repertoire.

At a Georgia Camp Meeting, by Kerry Mills, is one of the few tunes in the traditional jazz repertoire that was written as a Cakewalk. (Courtesy Sandy Marrone, Cinnaminson, NJ.)

At a Georgia Camp Meeting (Frederick Allan "Kerry" Mills, 1897): This is one of the few songs in the Dixieland repertoire that is actually a Cakewalk. Intended as music for a dance of the same name, a Cakewalk is a syncopated piece of music that was popular around the turn of the century and may be thought of as halfway between a march and a rag. The term inspired the expression "take the cake," meaning to prove victorious or win the prize. In the Old South, the slaves would sometimes gather together to make music and dance. Supposedly, they performed steps with exaggerated grace and elegance to satirize the dances they saw the White people do. At the end of the affair, the master would award a cake to the couple that danced the best. The dance, along with the accompanying song form, became quite popular in the late 1800s.

Frederick Allen "Kerry" Mills (1869-1948) was a concert violinist who encountered the Cakewalk during his tours around the country. He became fascinated with the form, and began to compose in the idiom. When he could not find publishers willing to publish his songs, he founded his own company. He met with limited success with his first compositions, but made his mark with "At a Georgia Camp Meeting." The song was an instant success, ignited a Cakewalk craze in America, and established F.A. Mills as a leading New York music publisher. "At a Georgia Camp Meeting" became a staple of the Dixieland repertoire and was performed by most of the leading musicians. Notable recordings include those by Sidney Bechet (1950) and Kid Ory (1955). It was a particular favorite of the revivalist bands, such as the Firehouse Five and Lu Watters.

The Bechet recording is particularly interesting because it teams up Wild Bill Davison, a fiery, aggressive cornet player, with Sidney, a musical extrovert if there ever was one. Efforts to include Louis Armstrong and Sidney Bechet in the same band had failed, as personalities clashed and both men attempted to take command. But the formula clicked with Bechet and Davison, and they produced some inspiring recordings together. Davison told British journalist Russell Davies, "I was smart enough to know when he was playing the lead to play the second part. I didn't try to step on his toes, and when I had solos he let me go."

Probably the best rendition of "At a Georgia Camp Meeting" to hear is one of the most recent. A 2014 album entitled *The New John Robichaux Society Orchestra* presents a collection of numbers that date from the late 1800s, just prior to the advent of Ragtime. John Robichaux (1866-1939) led the premier dance orchestra in New Orleans from 1893-1927. New Orleans pianist/bandleader Tom Hook gained access to the original Robichaux arrangements and orchestrated them for a modern ensemble in an attempt to faithfully re-create the original sound.

At Sundown (Walter Donaldson, 1927): One of relatively few Walter Donaldson songs for which he wrote his own words, "At Sundown" sold a million copies of sheet music and more than two million records. Introduced by Cliff Edwards at the Palace Theater in NYC, the song had several hit recordings, including a Number 1 hit for George Olson in 1927.

Its place in the jazz repertoire was assured when cornetist Muggsy Spanier included it as one of the "Great Sixteen." This nickname refers to a group of recordings made by Muggsy in 1939. At the height of the Big Band Era, and just before the first Dixieland revival, Muggsy put together a group called Muggsy Spanier's Ragtime Band. The band was phenomenal, and included a well-rehearsed four-horn front line with cornet, clarinet, trombone, and tenor. Unfortunately, the public was not yet ready for a return to traditional jazz at this time, and the band broke up after just nine months. Before they did, they recorded 16 sides for RCA-Victor that jazz fans have since referred to as the "Great Sixteen."

"At Sundown" can be heard in several movie musicals, including *Glorifying the American Girl* (1930), *This is the Life* (1944), *Music for Millions* (1944), *Margie* (1946), *The Fabulous Dorseys* (1947), *Love Me or Leave Me* (a musical biography in which Doris Day plays Ruth Etting, 1955), and *The Joker Is Wild* (1957).

"Aunt Hagar's Blues" appeared at the onset of the "blues craze." Around 1920, it became a fad to use the word "blues" in a title, even for ordinary pop songs. But when W.C. Handy wrote a blues, it was a blues. (Courtesy Lilly Library, Indiana University, Bloomington, Indiana.)

Aunt Hagar's Children Blues (music: W.C. Handy, lyrics: J. Tim Brymn, 1921): There is some inconsistency as to the exact title of this song, since two versions were issued—an instrumental called "Aunt Hager's Blues" and a vocal edition with "children" in the title. The reference is a Biblical one. "Hagar" was the mother of Abraham's son Ishmael, who founded Africa, thus making Blacks "Aunt Hagar's children."

This classic Handy blues depicts a church service in which the deacon's restrictions against Ragtime singing are vociferously opposed by Aunt Hagar. "Why all this razzin' about the jazzin'? My boys have just come home, With the latest music, They play it on the saxophone." When he hears the music, the deacon is soon persuaded, declaring, "If the devil brought it, the good Lawd sent it right down to me," and encouraging his flock to join in.

Convincing interpretations can be heard by Jack Teagarden (1947), Louis Armstrong (1954) and, more recently, the Grand St. Stompers (2011).

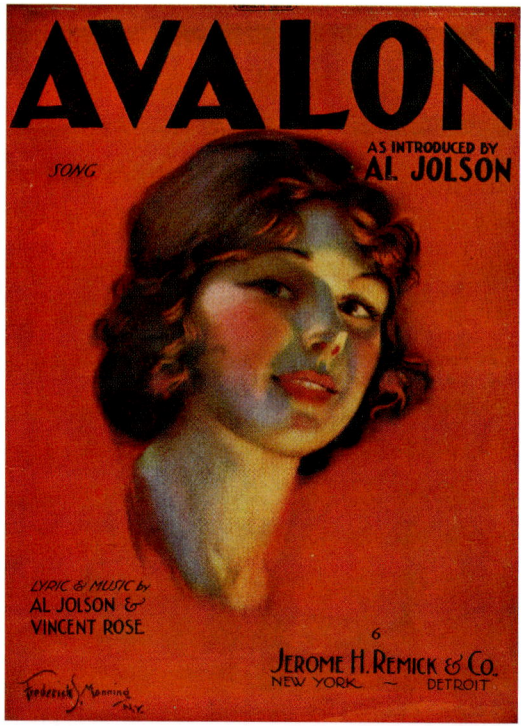

"Avalon", by Al Jolson and Vincent Rose, is a charming song about a charming place, but ironically initiated a nasty law suit. (Courtesy Lilly Library, Indiana University, Bloomington, Indiana.)

Avalon (music: Vincent Rose, lyrics: Al Jolson, Buddy DeSylva, 1920): A longtime favorite of jazz musicians, the song is closely associated with Benny Goodman. In addition to Goodman's several recordings (including the 1938 live performance at Carnegie Hall), of particular interest are Cab Calloway's 1934 version, a 1935 session with Coleman Hawkins and Django Reinhardt, and the 1960 recording by Louis Armstrong with the Dukes of Dixieland. The song can also be heard in *The Jolson Story* (1946), *The Benny Goodman Story* (1956), and (at least part of it) in *Casablanca* (1942). (It is the song Sam was playing just before Ilsa asks him to play "As Time Goes By.") Bria Skonberg and Gary Mazzaroppi recorded a crisp, swinging version on the 2012 album *Timeless Melodies*.

"Avalon" bears a vague similarity to Puccini's aria "E lucevan le stelle" from *Tosca*. The resemblance was close enough to spark a lawsuit for copyright infringement, which Puccini and his publishers won. Rose and his publishers were forced to pay 25,000 dollars and concede all future print royalties to the song. Fortunately for Rose, it was agreed that he would retain mechanical royalties—that is, payment for record and piano roll sales. Puccini's advisors had badly miscalculated, as sheet music was on its way out and records were on their way in—not to mention radio and movie musicals which were just on the horizon. In the long run, $25,000 was a small price to pay for the lucrative royalties that Rose would eventually receive from the song.

Incidentally, the "Avalon beside the bay" referred to is Catalina Island in California, not the seaside resort in New Jersey.

Baby Face (music Harry Akst, lyrics: Benny Davis, 1926): No, we're not talking about the famous gangster "Baby Face" Nelson. (Besides, he didn't rob his first bank until 1930). But was there an original "Baby Face"? Probably. In the mid-twenties, Clara Bow, "The It Girl," was a box office draw and one of the leading silent film stars of the era. ("It girl" is a 20s phrase for a young woman who seems to have a perfect blend of all the qualities men are looking for.) As the foremost sex symbol of her time, she was known for her youthful appearance and child-like innocence, and was influential in the creation of the character "Betty Boop." Adding to the "Baby Face" association, Bow was chosen by the Western Association of Motion Picture Advertisers as the "foremost baby" of 1924. It is certainly reasonable to believe that Benny Davis had her in mind when writing the lyrics to his song. Evidently, the illustrator of the sheet music cover had similar sentiments—the young girl depicted certainly looks like Bow.

"Baby Face" is a simple tune with an unassuming lyric that captured the public's attention from the start. A string of early recordings soon appeared, including a

Number 1 record by bandleader Jan Garber. The song was successfully revived in 1948, spawning several additional hits, and lived on to see versions by Little Richard (1958), Bobby Darin (1962), Julie Andrews (1967), and Paul McCartney (1974). Although usually sung as a pop tune, a few jazz interpretations can be found, such as a 1957 recording with trombonist Kid Ory and clarinetist Darnell Howard.

The sheet music cover to this edition of "Baby Won't You Please Come Home," by Clarence Williams and Charles Warfield, references Manzie Campbell, a highly respected drummer of early jazz history whose name unfortunately is largely forgotten today. (Courtesy Sandy Marrone, Cinnaminson, NJ.)

Baby Won't You Please Come Home (Clarence Williams, Charles Warfield, 1919): Williams was an all-round musician who found success as a pianist, composer, promoter, vocalist, theatrical producer, and publisher. He was an important contributor to the core repertoire of Dixieland Jazz, including "I Wish I Could Shimmy like My Sister Kate" (as publisher—not composer), "Royal Garden Blues," "Tain't Nobody's Business If I Do," "Everybody Loves My Baby," "West End Blues," and "I Ain't Gonna Give Nobody None of This Jelly Roll." Although he and Warfield wrote "Baby Won't You Please" in 1919, Williams didn't get around to publishing the song until 1923, by which time his publishing business was thriving and had adequate resources to plug a song. Moreover, by then he had married Eva Taylor, a premier performer in Harlem nightspots. Taylor introduced the song, and her picture appears on the original sheet music, but it was Bessie Smith who had the hit (accompanied by Williams at the piano) in 1923.

But early sheet music often appeared in several editions, mentioning or depicting various performers that might appeal to potential buyers. The cover shown above doesn't reference Eva Taylor. Instead, it states, "Featured by Manzie Campbell." This African-American stage actor and comedian is largely forgotten today, except, curiously enough, among drummers with a keen knowledge of the instrument's history. It seems that Campbell was primarily a drummer before turning to the stage, and none other than Jo Jones, the celebrated drummer with the Count Basie band, called Campbell the greatest drummer he ever heard. As Abbott and Seroff proclaim in their book about Black travelling shows: "Manzie Campbell had been the drummers' drummer of African-American minstrelsy for more than a decade." What a shame to know that his talents were heard by thousands of theatergoers but never recorded for posterity.

"Baby Won't You Please" was taken up by musicians right from the start, and is a reliable standard in the category of "bluesy ballads." Most of the legendary jazz musicians have recorded it, including Bix Bciderbecke (1929), Louis Armstrong (1939), Sidney Bechet (1949), and Jack Teagarden (1954). A spirited big-band version by Jimmie Lunceford (1939) is considered one the finest renditions of the song.

Back in Your Own Backyard (music: Dave Dreyer, lyrics: Billy Rose, 1927): Al Jolson's name also appears in the credits for this song, but it was most likely a "cut-in," meaning that a performer will promote a song in return for a percentage of the royalties. Jolson frequently made such deals. He recorded the song in 1928, and Ruth Etting also made a popular record with it that same year. With its angular but predictable melody and inviting harmonic background, jazz musicians took to the song immediately. The "no-place-like-home" theme resonated with audiences, with lovely rhymes such as "You'll find your happiness lies right under your eyes."

Lyricist Billy Rose was an interesting fellow. Before turning to songwriting he was a stenographer. A student of John Robert Gregg, inventor of the famous shorthand system, Rose could take some 200 words of dictation per minute and was considered the fastest in the world. He became head of the clerical staff of the War Industries Board during World War I. After the war he determined to become a song lyricist, and prepared by spending long hours in the New York Public Library analyzing past hits. Through the 20s and 30s Rose had a long list of hit songs, including "Clap Hands! Here Comes Charlie," "Me and My Shadow," "I Found a Million Dollar Baby in a Five and Ten Cent Store," and "It's Only a Paper Moon." He was also a highly successful producer and theater owner. Rose was known for being somewhat miserly. (Richard Rodgers called him a man "who never parted with a dime if he didn't have to.") By the time he died, in 1966, Rose had amassed a fortune of $42 million.

Paul Whiteman recorded "Back in Your Own Backyard" in 1928 with a splendid Bill Challis arrangement that featured Bix Beiderbecke on cornet and Jimmy Dorsey on alto saxophone. Fortunately, two takes of this have survived, and as was generally the case, Bix's solos are completely different. Ten years later, another legendary trumpet player, Bunny Berigan, recorded a hard-swinging version with lots of solo space featuring himself and tenor man Georgie Auld. Other notable versions include those by Eddie Condon (with Max Kaminsky on cornet, 1945), Pee Wee Russell (with Wild Bill Davison and Vic Dickenson, 1954), and guitarist/vocalist Marty Grosz and the Orphan Newsboys (1996).

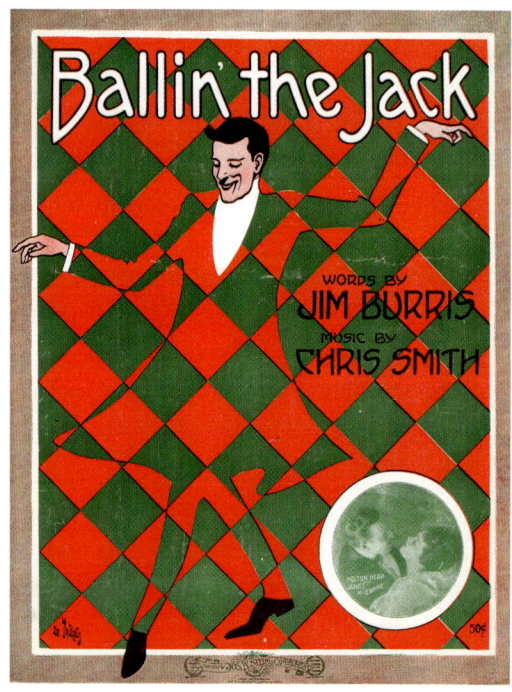

"Ballin' the Jack, by Jim Burris and Chris Smith, is representative of a category of songs that describe the steps to be danced to a song.

Ballin' the Jack (music: Chris Smith, lyrics: James Henry Burris, 1913): The African-American composer Chris Smith (1879-1949) was one of the best songwriters of the teens. Capitalizing on the dance craze that was then sweeping the country, Smith and Burris wrote a song that describes a new dance step, giving specific instructions on how to do it:

> First you put your two knees close up tight,
> Then you sway 'em to the left, then you sway 'em to the right,
> Step around the floor kind of nice and light,
> Then you twis' around and twis' around with all your might,
> Stretch your lovin' arms straight out in space
> Then do the Eagle Rock with style and grace
> Swing your foot way 'round then bring it back,
> Now that's what I call "Ballin' the Jack."

The dance step's name has a rather convoluted origin: There was a railroad signal used in the 1800s that consisted of a red ball on a pole. When the ball was lifted high, the engineer understood that the track was clear ahead and he was free to go at full speed. Since railroad workers often referred to the engine as the "jack," the expression "ballin' the jack" soon took hold, meaning "full steam ahead." Hence the significance of the Ragtime dance step that shares the name. Presumably, the alcoholic beverage known as the "high ball" derives from the same railroad reference.

The song is cleverly assembled, with a verse beginning in another key that builds tension and anticipation as it modulates several times, finally leading smoothly into the opening chord of the main part of the tune. The middle of the chorus features a built-in two bar break, aptly set to the phrase "Then you twis' around and twis' around with all your might."

Prince's Orchestra had a Number 1 hit with the song in 1914, but it is anything but a jazz version. Since the song predates the Jazz Age, early recordings treat the song with a strict Ragtime feel. From the 20s on, numerous jazz interpretations can be heard, such as those by clarinetist Johnny Dodds (1927), cornetist Red Nichols (1930), trombonist Miff Mole (1944), and pianist Art Hodes (1946).

"Basin Street Blues" by Spencer Williams, celebrates the district's flourishing jazz scene, which was already long gone by the time of the song's composition. (Early 20th-century postcard, public domain, via Wikimedia Commons.)

Basin Street Blues (Spencer Williams, 1929): Louis Armstrong recorded the song in 1928, without verse or lyrics, a year before the publication date. The words were reportedly added by Jack Teagarden and Glenn Miller the night before a February 1928 recording session featuring Jack, accompanied by the Charleston Chasers under the leadership of Benny Goodman. According to Nat Shapiro and Nat Hentoff, Teagarden recalled: "After we had worked out a first draft of verse and chorus, Glenn sat on the piano bench and I leaned over his shoulder. We each had a pencil, and as he played, we'd each cross out words and phrases here and there, putting in new ones. We finally finished the job sometime early in the morning." The recording, with Jack on the vocals, was a hit, and the tune became a signature song for him. He would go on to record it several times, often tinkering with the lyrics. In 1934, Benny had a hit with his own band, and recordings by Bing Crosby with Connee Boswell (1937) and Louis Armstrong (1938) were also very successful.

Basin Street takes its name from a "turning basin" at the end of a canal that once linked Lake Pontchartrain to the French Quarter of New Orleans. There were plans to extend the canal up Basin Street and down Canal Street to the Mississippi, but that project was never carried out. Nevertheless, because of those plans, Basin Street and Canal Street are remarkably wide, with expansive "neutral grounds" (as residents call them) in the middle.

In the mid 1800s, Basin Street was one of the finest residential streets in the city, but by century's end had become a red light district. In an ill-fated attempt to control and confine prostitution, the city defined a specific area where prostitution would be legal, with Basin Street serving as the dividing line between Storyville (as the district came to be called) and the French Quarter.

Basin Street featured a row of lavish establishments run by well-known madams who catered to a wealthy clientele. Reportedly, some of the most prominent men in Louisiana were regular customers. The active nightlife on Basin Street was an important part of the early jazz scene in New Orleans and is vividly described by pianist Jelly Roll Morton in his memoirs. This era of legalized prostitution lasted from 1897 until 1917, when Storyville was shut down. Evidently the temptation for a sailor on shore leave was more than the U.S. Navy could tolerate.

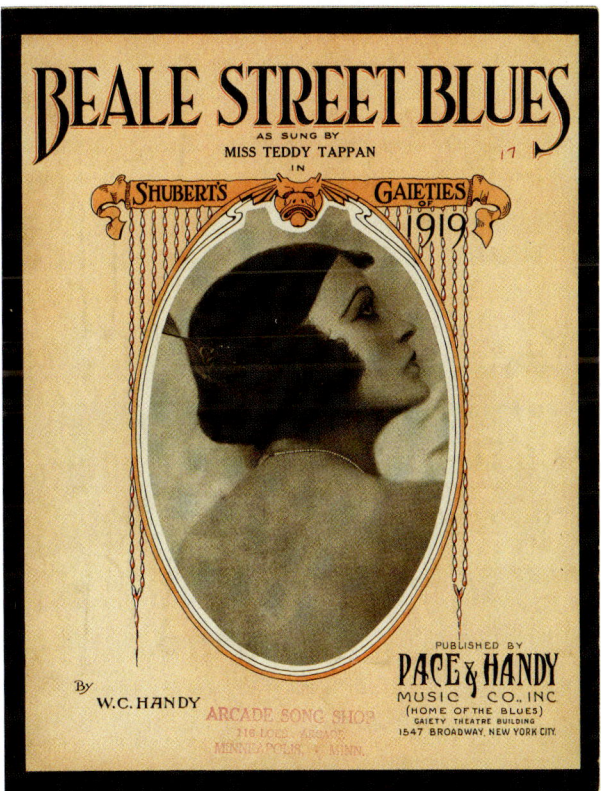

W.C. Handy was cheated out of the royalties for his first published blues, "Memphis Blues," but he went on to write others, including "Beale Street Blues," which became an even bigger hit. (Courtesy Lilly Library, Indiana University, Bloomington, Indiana.)

Beale Street Blues (W.C. Handy, 1916): W.C. Handy's "Memphis Blues" (1914) became such a famous composition that it was only appropriate that he write a song named after Beale Street, the hot spot for music and nightlife in the city. "Beale Street Blues" was one of the big hits of 1917 and would go on to become Handy's second most recorded song after "St. Louis Blues." During the years around 1920, Handy's blues classics (the fourth one being "Yellow Dog Blues") were played by practically every dance band in New York City. At first, they were mainly performed as instrumentals, as Handy's down-home lyrics found little favor with big-city audiences. But with time, the public took to the words as well.

An excellent 1930 recording by Jack Teagarden, set to a curious arrangement with snippets of *Rhapsody in Blue* worked in here and there, features a young Teagarden working out the singing and playing pattern that would make him famous. A year later he can be heard as an increasingly confident vocalist with Joe Venuti and Eddie Lang. Other notable recordings include those by Jelly Roll Morton with the Red Hot Peppers (1927), a more mature Jack Teagarden (1939), Henry "Red" Allen (1952), and Wild Bill Davison (1955).

Bei Mir Bist Du Schon (Means That You're Grand) (music: Sholom Secunda, Yiddish: lyrics Jacob Facobs, English lyrics: Sammy Cahn and Saul Chaplin, 1937): The song was originally written in 1933 for a Yiddish theater production called *I Would If I Could*. When Sammy Cahn, who understood Yiddish, heard the song, he fell in love with it and bought a copy of the sheet music. One day, the Andrews Sisters happened to see the music while visiting with Sammy, became interested in the song, and decided to record it. Decca records asked for a set of English lyrics, which Sammy and Saul Chaplin provided. The song turned out to be one of the biggest hits of 1938. Benny Goodman's 1937 recording is perhaps the definitive jazz rendition.

Regarding the spelling and pronunciation of the title: While spelled as if it were German, the lyric is actually in Yiddish, and the original title was spelled "Bay mir bistu sheyn." (There is no standard spelling of Yiddish with Latin letters.) Therefore, "schon" is properly pronounced "shane" in this context. The direct translation of the title is "To Me You're Beautiful."

"Bei Mir" can be heard in the films *Swing Kids* (1993) and *Being Julia* (2004). For a great jazz recording in the right spirit, hear the New Orleans-based Hot Club of New Orleans on their 2004 album *More!* featuring Matt Rhody on violin and Christopher Kohl on clarinet.

Between the Devil and the Deep Blue Sea (music: Harold Arlen, lyrics: Ted Koehler, 1931): Standing on the corner of 142nd Street and Lenox Ave, the Cotton Club was the pearl of New York City nightlife from 1923 to 1935—in other words, during the greater part of Prohibition. The Whites-only establishment featured the top African-American talent of the day in an ongoing series of revues that featured dancers, singers, comedians, variety acts, and a famous house band.

Performers had to be Black, but the songwriters and arrangers didn't. The White songwriting team of Harold Arlen and Ted Koehler wrote the music for the Cotton Club revues from 1930 through 1934. "Between the Devil and the Deep Blue Sea" was written for *Rhythmania* (1931), the second of five shows that the team would write for the Cotton Club. It was introduced by Aida Ward backed by Cab Calloway and his Orchestra. (Cab had recently become the Cotton Club house band, replacing the Duke Ellington Orchestra, which had left to go on tour.) This was the same show in which Cab premiered his famous "Minnie the Moocher."

The expression "between the devil and the deep blue sea" is an old one, entering the English language at least by the 17th century. Okay, the first appearance in print is so quaint that I have to share it. A Scottish General, Robert Monro, recalling his experiences during the Thirty Years War, wrote in his memoirs of 1637, "I, with my partie, did lie on our poste, as betwixt the devill and the deep sea." Perfect! Now we just have to set it to music.

"Between the Devil and the Deep Blue Sea" is built on a melody that skips around quite a bit and works best as a medium-tempo swing number. The up-and-down motion of the notes aptly complements the lyrics, which reveal the lament of a lover going back and forth between why she wants this relationship and why she doesn't. Cab Calloway, Louis Armstrong, and Connee Boswell all had early hits with the song, and many other versions followed. Varying interpretations can be heard by trombonist Dicky Wells with guitarist Django Reinhardt (1937), singer Lee Wiley (1942), Eddie Condon (1943), and pianist Willie "The Lion" Smith (1944, 1960). Former Beatle George Harrison included the number on his last album, *Brainwashed*.

Bill Bailey (Hughie Cannon, 1902): Ragtime pianist Hughie Cannon (1877-1912) and vaudeville singer/trombonist Bill Bailey were drinking buddies in Jackson, Michigan, a wild railroad town during the early years of the 20th century. The downtown area had nearly 75 saloons, and Bailey and Cannon were familiar faces in several of them. Bailey was married to a girl named Sarah, and his hard drinking and all-night carousing didn't sit well with her. As she explained many years later, "Bill was my sweetheart, but he was everybody else's, too. He lied to me all the time, but I was too young to understand much then. I was a country girl." At some point, Bailey's conversations about his marriage inspired Cannon to write a song. It became an instant success, and went on to become one of the best-known popular songs of the century. But Cannon was to enjoy few rewards for his effort—he sold the copyright for $350 and died penniless in 1912 at the age of 34. As for Bailey, somehow he and Sarah managed to keep their marriage going for another dozen years or so, but ultimately divorced, though they remained friends. Bill died in 1954 and Sarah in 1978, at the age of 104.

"Bill Bailey" found a permanent place in the jazz repertoire when Kid Ory recorded it in 1921, making it one of the earliest jazz recordings by a Black musician. Among the numerous excellent recordings of the song, Sidney Bechet's 1950 version (recorded in Paris with French musicians) is particularly spirited.

"Bill Bailey" also happens to be among the early popular songs employing the 32-bar format. Although a song can be any length, the ear expects to hear multiples of four or eight measures, and around the turn of the century 32 bars became the norm. The basic harmonic structure of "Bill Bailey" is the same as "Washington and Lee Swing," "Bourbon Street Parade," "Beer Barrel Polka," and a section of "Tiger Rag." But "Bill Bailey" predates them all.

Birth of the Blues (music: Ray Henderson, lyrics: Buddy DeSylva and Lew Brown, 1926): These three men comprised a very successful songwriting team in the 20s, turning out hits such as "I'm Sitting on Top of the World," "Button Up Your Overcoat" and "You're the Cream in My Coffee." "Birth of the Blues" was written for *George White's Scandals of 1926*. These annual revues produced by George White had little to offer in the way of plot or storyline, but introduced some of the best songs of the era. (George Gershwin's early work was largely written for the *Scandals* of 1920-24.)

Paul Whiteman had a Number 1 hit with "Birth of the Blues" in 1927; Harry Richman and the Revelers each had top records as well. Whiteman's version features a creative arrangement by Ferde Grofè, which contains some subtle allusions to *Rhapsody in Blue*. As with many songs from the 20s, "Birth of the Blues" was revived in the 1950s and Frank Sinatra had a successful 1952 version. Overall, there have been more pop and country versions of the song than jazz recordings, but solid swing renditions can be heard by Wild Bill Davison (with Eddie Condon, 1952) and Buck Clayton (1952). Coleman Hawkins and Roy Eldridge give the tune a slower, bluesier feel (1959) and Teddy Wilson's solo piano version (1956) is not to be missed. Jack Teagarden performed the song when he appeared in the 1941 movie *Birth of the Blues* and the song remained in his repertoire for the rest of his career.

Black and Blue (music: Fats Waller, lyrics: Harry Brooks and Andy Razaf, 1929): The blockbuster hit from the 1929 show *Hot Chocolates* was "Ain't Misbehavin'," but the song "Black and Blue" made quite an impression as well. Allegedly, Waller and Razaf were asked to write a comic song about a dark-skinned girl lamenting how she lost her beau to a lighter-skinned girl. While the verse fulfills the comic element to some extent, the rest of the song is anything but that. What Razaf presents is a powerful statement on racism with poignant lyrics that elaborate on the intended pun of the title with devastating effect, with lines such as "I'm white inside, it don't help my case" and "why was I born?" The producers had not gotten exactly what they asked for, but they knew a hit when they heard one and nobody complained.

Edith Wilson introduced the song, Fats Waller performed it regularly, and Ethel Waters made the classic recording (1930). Louis Armstrong recorded the song several times, and it can be hard on his well-known album *Satch Plays Fats* (1955). Because of its sensitive subject matter, the song was not recorded very often, nor did it appear in film musicals, but it was again brought to public attention in the Broadway show *Ain't Misbehavin'* (1978).

Black Bottom (music Ray Henderson, lyrics: Buddy DeSylva and Lew Brown, 1926): Not to be confused with Jelly Roll Morton's "Black Bottom Stomp" (1926), this tune was written for *George White's Scandals of 1926*. In the mid 20s the Black Bottom overtook the Charleston to become the most popular new dance in the country. The step had actually been around for decades and was well known to Southern Blacks, but when dancer Ann Pennington introduced it to New York audiences in *Scandals* it became a national craze. Although the lyrics do not describe the dance, they reference it directly ("They call it black bottom, a new twister … they clap their hands and do a raggedy trot"), while the halting syncopations of the melody imitate the movement of the dance.

Just to clarify, the term "Black Bottom" does not reference an African American's derriere, in case that thought crossed your mind. Rather, the dance takes its name from the Black Bottom district of Detroit, named by the French to describe the rich soil of the region. When Southern Blacks migrated north early in the century, Black Bottom became a thriving African-American community, and nightlife flourished during the 20s.

Johnny Hamp's Orchestra had the hit on the tune in 1926, while Annette Hanshaw (with Red Nichols and Miff Mole) released a spirited version that same year. Since then, more novelty versions than jazz renditions have been produced, but Eddie Condon's 1950 recording with Wild Bill Davison retains the original spirit while adding some real Chicago-style punch.

"Blue and Broken Hearted," by Lou Handman, Grant Clarke, and Edgar Leslie. The contrasting sheet music covers show how much separate editions of the same song could vary. Sometimes photographs of recording artists were inserted to promote their records. The musician on the right is Ross Gorman, who led a popular band called The Virginians, and who would later become a featured member of the Paul Whiteman Orchestra. He is shown here with a curious array of instruments, some of which even I can't identify. (Both photographs courtesy Sandy Marrone, Cinnaminson, NJ.)

Blue and Broken Hearted (music Lou Handman, lyrics: Grant Clarke and Edgar Leslie, 1922): Songwriter Lou Handman had a series of hit songs between 1919 and his death in 1956, including "My Sweetie Went Away," "Puddin' Head Jones," and his biggest, "Are You Lonesome Tonight?" He was accompanist to Marion Harris, one of the most popular singers of the 20s, who had a hit with "Blue and Broken Hearted" in 1922. In Dixieland circles, the song is perhaps best known as a signature ballad for cornetist William "Wild Bill" Davison, who recorded the song many times. There are also film clips of him performing the song with Eddie Condon (1962, 1964). Wild Bill was a hot and powerful trumpet player who was associated with Eddie Condon from the 1940s through the 1960s. His rough and ragged, no-nonsense approach might seem an unlikely treatment for a tender ballad, but his interpretation of this song must be heard.

Blue Room (music: Richard Rodgers, lyrics: Lorenz Hart, 1926): How do you begin to explain who Richard Rodgers was in one paragraph? One of the "big six" who produced the canon of great musical compositions known as the "Great American Songbook," Rodgers wrote some 900 songs for 43 Broadway musicals. (The other "members" of this exclusive club are generally considered to be Irving Berlin, Jerome Kern, George Gershwin, Cole Porter, and Harold Arlen.) Rodgers has won the Emmy, Grammy, Oscar, and Tony Awards, in addition to the Pulitzer Prize. It has been said that his musicals are so popular and enduring that every day, somewhere in the world, at least one of them is in production somewhere. He worked primarily with two lyricists throughout his life: Lorenz Hart, from 1919 until 1943, and Oscar Hammerstein, from 1943 until 1959.

"Blue Room" was an early tune by the team of Rodgers and Hart, written for their second hit show, *The Girlfriend* (1926). Rodgers created a fascinating melody that keeps returning to the same note, with a bridge that begins with a simple scale in the home key. Hart took the unusual melody and worked his own legerdemain: The recurring lower note gets the rhyme, while the gradually ascending upper note always gets the word "room." The lyric demonstrates how Hart could be silly, charming, and amazingly clever at the same time. ("We'll have a blue room, A new room, For two room ...")

Bill Challis wrote a fine arrangement of the song, which was played, but not recorded, by the Jean Goldkette Band with Bix Beiderbecke and Frankie Trumbauer. It can be heard on *The Goldkette Project*, an album released by Vince Giordano and the Nighthawks in 1987 in collaboration with Bill Challis. Other jazz versions include those of Eddie Lang and Joe Venuti (1928), Sidney Bechet (1952), and Wild Bill Davison with Ralph Sutton (1977).

Blue Skies (music and lyrics: Irving Berlin, 1926): The words to the song contrast former "blue days" with the present "blue skies" that come with being in love. Berlin cleverly weaves the harmony into the lyric to achieve a similar effect—with a minor key yielding to major throughout the tune.

The song was introduced as a last minute interpolation into a 1926 show by Rodgers and Hart called *Betsy*. Evidently, the singer Belle Baker was unhappy with the songs Rodgers and Hart had supplied, so she requested this one from Irving Berlin. The show was a flop, and produced no notable numbers by Rodgers and Hart, but Berlin's "Blue Skies" was a sensation. The audience asked for several encores and producer Flo Ziegfeld had a spotlight put on Irving Berlin, who was in the audience. Not a happy moment for Rodgers and Hart.

"Blue Skies" was also a last minute insertion into *The Jazz Singer*, the first talking film, starring Al Jolson, and would appear again and again in Hollywood productions. It can be heard in *Alexander's Ragtime Band* (1938), *Blue Skies* (1946) and *White Christmas* (1954).

More than half-a-dozen hit recordings of "Blue Skies" appeared in 1927 alone. Notable jazz recordings include those of Maxine Sullivan (1937), Mary Lou Williams (1944), and Django Reinhardt (1949).

Blue Turning Grey Over You (music Fats Waller, lyrics: Andy Razaf, 1930): In 1930 publisher Joe Davis hired Waller with a weekly salary and offered Razaf an exclusive contract. Waller was set up in a little cubicle from ten o'clock to five o'clock and supplied with two bottles of liquor a day. Waller's "day job" lasted less than a year, but he did write "Blue Turning Grey" during this time. Razaf's clever lyrics portray the lament of an abandoned lover whose hair is turning grey from heartache. The song is not in a minor key, but has a mournful air about it because of chromatic alterations in the melody and a distinctive descending chord sequence at the opening. Louis Armstrong introduced the song on record, followed by Fats himself as well as numerous versions by other jazz musicians. Especially notable are versions by Ralph Sutton (1950), Earl Hines (1956), Bobby Hackett with Vic Dickenson (1969), Yank Lawson with Bob Haggart (1991), and pianist Jeff Barnhart (2012).

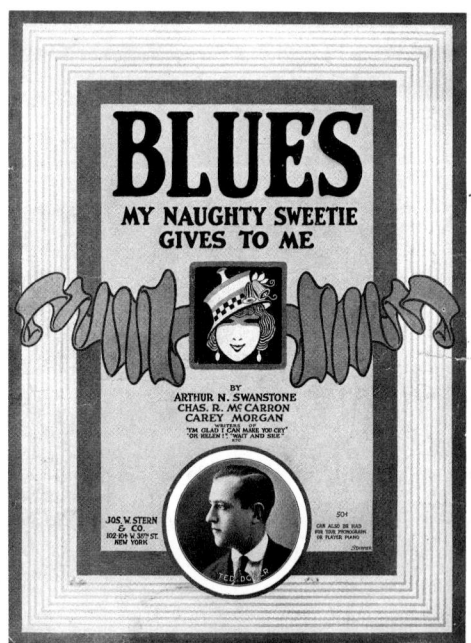

"Blues My Naughty Sweetie Gives to Me" by Arthur N. Swanstone, Charles R. McCarron and Carey Morgan, is a romping, minor-key number with a famous "patter" chorus. (Courtesy Sandy Marrone, Cinnaminson, NJ.)

Blues My Naughty Sweetie Gives to Me (music and lyrics: Charles McCarron, Carey Morgan, Arthur N. Swanstone, 1919): This is a fascinating tune, squarely in a minor key, but with a distinctive blues quality that lends itself to various treatments. Early vocal versions displayed Ragtime settings, but Ted Lewis's instrumental version of 1920 (one of his first hits) clearly sounds like the Original Dixieland Jazz Band (which is exactly what Columbia had in mind when they signed him). His 1926 remake has an exotic feel to it (and Ted could get some exotic sounds out of the clarinet!), sounding almost Klezmer at times.

Through the years, the tune settled into its niche as a fast, driving, minor blues number, as can be heard on the Firehouse Five's 1949 recording, or Matty Matlock's more polished studio version of 1957. Sidney Bechet (who could drive hard and fast when he wanted to) keeps the tempo and intensity in check on his 1952 recording, as does Earl Hines (1975). For a good rendition of the tune's extensive lyrics, including the patter chorus, listen to Clancy Hayes (1966). Essentially, a patter chorus is a section of rapid-fire lyrics in stop time, often humorous, where the band plays short hits allowing the singer to present the words lyrics unaccompanied. Here is an example from "Blues My Naughty":

> There are blues you get from wimmin
> when you see 'em goin' swimmin'
>
> And you haven't got a bathing suit yourself.
>
> There are blues you get much quicker when you
> hide a lot of liquor
>
> And your lady goes and swipes it off the shelf.
>
> There are blues that come from waitin' on the dock,
> wondering if the boat is gonna rock,
>
> And there's blues that come from gettin' in a taxicab and frettin'
>
> Everytime you hit a bump and jump the clock.
>
> There are blues you get from tryin'
> when you save a guy from dyin'
>
> And he afterwards forgets you in his will.
>
> But the blues much worse than this is when you're walkin'
> with the missus
>
> And some chorus lady shouts, "Hello there Bill!"
>
> But the blues that make me crazy mad and
> sorer than a bunion
>
> 'Till I feel like goin' out and stabbin'
> someone with an onion
>
> Are the blues my naughty sweetie gives to me.

Bluin' the Blues (Henry Ragas, 1918): Although credited to pianist Henry Ragas, this early hit by the Original Dixieland Jazz Band, as with most of their originals, was most likely a collaboration by the entire ensemble. For their 1917 recordings, credit was generally given to the whole band, but by 1918 they began to take turns in receiving composer's credit (and royalties) by drawing names out of a hat! Unfortunately, this was to be Ragas' last recording session with the band—he came down with the Spanish influenza in late 1918, dying in February, 1919.

As with most of their tunes, "Bluin' The Blues" became a jazz standard. It features a hard-driving melody to a 12-bar blues structure with some added chords in the middle section that keep the tension building through to the end. The song's stature in the jazz repertoire was forever established when Muggsy Spanier included the tune in his famous Ragtime Band recordings of 1939, often referred to as "The Great Sixteen." "Bluin' the Blues" is also heard in the 2000 film *The Legend of Bagger Vance*."

Borneo (music and lyrics: Walter Donaldson, 1928): This is one goofy tune. Yes, the reference is to the Asian island, but the rest is all nonsensical fantasy. If you're wondering what rhymes Donaldson could have found for "Borneo," how about "corneo," "dawneo," "torneo," "horneo," and "pawneo"? The lyrics are set to an equally exotic melody and simply tell of a hot new dance from Borneo Bay. There's plenty of fun to go around, and executives thought well enough of the tune to use it on *The Muppet Show* in November 1977.

The tune is quite good. You can hear from the first three notes that there is something unusual about the melody, and it clearly conjures images of some far-away land. Its construction is deliberately plain and repetitive in order to give a primitive effect, which Donaldson keeps going through some clever harmonic shifting. There's even a verse, seldom sung, which makes a wonderful contrasting section when inserted in the middle of the tune. (I've never heard it done up front.)

The tune never charted, but that didn't prevent the recording of some fine records. At the top of that list is a 1928 recording by Frankie Trumbauer with Bix Beiderbecke. Trumbauer (1901-1956) was one of most influential saxophonists of the 20s. He played what is now a rare instrument, the C-melody saxophone, which is larger than an alto, but smaller than a tenor. He did his best work with Beiderbecke (1903-1931). Bix was a cornetist, pianist, and composer of such originality, that his short, tragic life has become legendary, and his recordings have been revered by generations of musicians. "Borneo" demonstrates Bix's uncanny abilities, particularly when he trades two-bar phrases with Trumbauer. The two of them, often referred to as

"Bix and Tram," recorded frequently and the results were generally spectacular.

The vocalist on the Bix/Trumbauer recording is a fellow named Scrappy Lambert. He recorded hundreds of records, but he was mainly a "studio" musician, hired for specific recordings with various bands. For example, he also recorded "Borneo" with Ben Bernie and His Hotel Roosevelt Orchestra that same year.

Other fine recordings of "Borneo" were made by the British bandleader Jack Hylton (1928), and Milt Shaw and His Detroiters (1928).

Breezin' Along with the Breeze (music and lyrics: Haven Gillespie, Seymour Simmons, Richard Whiting, 1926): If you're not acquainted with these songwriters, you certainly are familiar with their work. For example, Gillespie (along with Fred Coots) wrote "Santa Claus is Comin' to Town," while Simmons (along with Gerald Marks) wrote "All of Me," one the most often-performed standards in the American Songbook. Prior to his untimely death in 1938 at the height of his career, Whiting had penned a number of well-known tunes, among them "The Japanese Sandman," "Sleepy Time Gal" and "Ain't We Got Fun." Since his career spanned the 1920's and 1930's, it is not surprising that many of his tunes have entered the Dixieland repertoire. Richard was the father of Margaret Whiting, one of the great jazz stylists of the 20th century.

"Breezin'" was a hit for Al Jolson and frequently recorded by pop and jazz musicians. Not unexpectedly, it became the theme song for orchestra leader Lou Breese. The song can also be heard in the 1953 film *The Long, Long Trailer*, staring Lucille Ball and Desi Arnaz, as well as the 1955 film *Pete Kelly's Blues*.

Bugle Call Rag (music and lyrics: Jack Pettis, Billy Meyers, Elmer Schoebel, 1923): For those who are only familiar with Benny Goodman's romping big-band version of the song, it might seem hard to believe that it was written some 15 years earlier. Members of the New Orleans Rhythm Kings, an important early jazz band that modeled itself after Black New Orleans jazz, originally recorded the tune in 1922 as "Bugle Call Blues." Other performers, including Ted Lewis (1926), Red Nichols (1927), and the Mills Brothers (1932) had successful recordings of the song. One of the hottest of the early recordings is an excellent 1929 side with guitarist Eddie Lang as leader, featuring some fantastic solo work by Jimmy Dorsey on clarinet and Tommy Dorsey on trombone.

The Mills Brothers recording is noteworthy not just because it was a Number 2 hit, but also because is exemplary of their early style. Many who know the famous quartet only from their later pop hits do not realize that they started out as an a cappella jazz band, imitating instruments--generally two trumpets, a trombone, and tuba. As this recording reveals, this was not a novelty routine–they are actually performing hot instrumental jazz without instruments (except for a single guitar). They phrase, improvise, and articulate like instruments, and the result is almost unbelievable, as can be heard on their "instrumental" version of "Bugle Call Rag."

The distinguishing feature of the "Bugle Call Rag" is that two of its three sections actually begin with bugle calls (Reveille, Assembly, and Taps are three often used), intended to be played by solo cornet. Other recommended recordings of the tune include those by Django Reinhardt and Dicky Wells (1937), Adrian Rollini (1938), Sidney Bechet (1942), and Eddie Condon (with Muggsy Spanier on cornet, 1945).

Of particular interest is a recording from 1949, featuring the all-star cast of Tony Parenti on clarinet, Wild Bill Davison on cornet, Jimmy Archey on trombone, Art Hodes on piano, Pops Foster on bass, and Arthur Trappier on drums. The re-release of the session on CD contains five complete versions of "Bugle Call Rag"! It was not uncommon in the days before tape splicing and audio editing to record multiple versions of the same song and select the best one for release. Considering the built-in breaks in "Bugle Call," it can be expected that some notes will be flubbed here and there and that musicians would want to select the cleanest version possible. However, over time, the "out" takes have become valuable as well, since they contain improvised music that hasn't been heard before.

By and By (music and lyrics: Charles Albert Tindley, 1906): (Not to be confused with "In the Sweet By and By" [1868] by Sanford F. Bennett.) Since gospel music is a precursor to jazz, it isn't surprising that some of the oldest Dixieland tunes are hymns. Rev. Dr. Charles Albert Tindley (1851-1933) was an American Methodist minister and one of founding fathers of gospel music. In the 1960s, his hymn "I'll Overcome Someday" was adapted to become "We Shall Overcome," the anthem of the U.S. civil rights movement.

Hymnals list the tune by its full title, "We'll Understand It Better By and By," but jazz musicians refer to the song as "By and By," the opening words of the refrain. The spelling "Bye and Bye" will be found as frequently as the one given here.

Of the many recordings of this song, Turk Murphy's from 1950 and Eddie Condon's from the 1956 Newport Jazz Festival stand out. But Louis Armstrong seems particularly comfortable with the song, perhaps owing to his early childhood familiarity with gospel music. He recorded it four times (1938, 1954, 1959, and 1964), and each recording seems even better than the previous one. My favorite is by far the 1964 version, recorded the same year as his huge hit recording of "Hello Dolly." While Armstrong no longer displays the trumpet range and virtuosity his earlier work did, the recording captures a solid New Orleans feel and swings hard all the way through.

The Biltmore Hotel, where Bert Lown led his famous orchestra.(Author's personal collection.)

Bye Bye Blues (music and lyrics: Fred Hamm, Dave Bennett, Bert Lown, Chancey Gray, 1930): The number is loosely based on the 1911 song "The Star" by James H. Rogers, but the character of the tune is entirely different. The melody is quite simple, and is driven by a chord sequence strongly characterized by the move to an unexpected key in the third bar. The chord is actually built on the flatted sixth scale, which is not found in the major scale, and the jarring motion is very effective. (Yes, "The Star" used the same chord with the same melody note, but in a different place and with a different feel.)

"Bye Bye Blues" became the theme song for Bert Lown, who led the orchestra at the Biltmore (a luxury hotel in New York City). Although picked up early on by jazz artists, most of the hits of the song (and there were several) came in the 1950s and 1960s by non-jazz artists. Traditional jazz versions of the song include those by Frankie Trumbauer (1930), Doc Evans (1950), Al Hirt (1965), and trumpeter Duke Heitger (2015).

Cakewalking Babies from Home (music and lyrics: Chris Smith, Henry Troy, Clarence Williams, 1924): Chris Smith (1879-1949) was without a doubt one of the top African-American songwriters of the 1910s, turning out such hits as "Ballin' the Jack" (1913) and "Down in Honky Tonk Town" (1916). By the mid-20s he had adapted well to changing tastes and was turning out some fine blues numbers, but was not achieving the success he had in the previous decade.

The words to the song describe a prize-winning cakewalking couple (see entry on "At a Georgia Camp Meeting") in vivid detail. The chorus begins with "Here they come, Look at 'em syncopatin'," and clever rhymes in African-American dialect occur throughout.

"Cakewalking" was almost certainly written by Smith with lyrics by Troy and a cut-in by Williams—that is, a cut of the royalties in return for agreeing to publish and promote. He did his part. Clarence Williams' Blue Five had a decent hit with "Cakewalking" in 1925, with a historic recording that featured Louis Armstrong and Sidney Bechet on the same session. Although the results were excellent, the formula was volatile. During the 20s, Armstrong and Bechet were arguably the two outstanding soloists in the jazz world, and there were few if any who could challenge either of them. Armstrong was known as a gentle, amiable musician, as long as he was in charge. Bechet was known as a fiery, sometimes dangerous personality, who took charge on the bandstand whether it was his band or not. They produced some fine music on the occasional dates that Williams put together for them in 1925, but did their best to avoid each other for the rest of their lives.

California Here I Come (music and lyrics: Al Jolson, Buddy DeSylva, 1924): Often called the "unofficial" state song of California, this melody has been ubiquitous throughout the 20th century, turning up in countless guises, such as cartoons, movies, television shows and, of course, musical performances. The melody is contagiously catchy and, while often performed (or at least quoted) as a romping hell-raiser, the tune is quite adaptable in many contexts. Several versions appeared in 1924, each with a different interpretation. Paul Whiteman and the California Ramblers (who adopted the tune as their theme song) each recorded dance arrangements with exotic interpretations of the verse. Cliff Edwards delivers it as a clever novelty tune, while Al Jolson sounds like, well, Al Jolson. It was a Number 1 record for him.

Through the years many other interpretations have appeared. Banjo players often play it as technical tour de force. Modern jazz players have also recorded the tune, a good example of which is Bill Evans' marvelous 1967 version. (On hearing Evan's interpretation, a Dixieland musician once said to me "That's not 'California Here I Come.' That's Bill Evans. 'California Here I Come' just got in the way.") Even Ray Charles left his mark on the tune with a swinging big-band arrangement from 1960.

Traditional jazz versions can be heard from Fats Waller (1935 piano solo), Eddie Condon (1938), violinist Stephane Grappelli (1982), trumpeter Duke Heitger (2000), and, if clarinet is your thing, a charging live recording with Bob Wilber and Buddy DeFranco from 2003.

Canal Street, New Orleans, is the widest "main street" in the country. (Canal Street in 1921. By Ewing Galloway, public domain, via Wikimedia Commons.)

Canal Street Blues (music by Joe Oliver, 1923): This is one of many Dixieland tunes with a place name reference. Canal Street is, of course, the main street in New Orleans, named for a canal that was never built. After the Louisiana Purchase (1803), Canal Street became the dividing line, and neutral territory, between the original residents of French descent and the newly arriving Americans. A century later, Joe Oliver would have known the street as the dividing line between the formally schooled Creole musicians downriver and the self-taught Black musicians upriver from the French Quarter.

By 1923, Joe "King" Oliver had left New Orleans and was leading the hottest jazz band in Chicago. With Louis Armstrong playing second cornet, King Oliver's Creole Jazz Band was the envy of local musicians, both Black and White. Fortunately, their marvelous playing was captured on a series of recordings for Gennett Record Company that are now considered the first masterpieces in recorded jazz. At their first session, in April of 1923, the band recorded "Canal Street Blues" along with four other titles.

The early version of the tune is of historical significance because of the two-cornet work between Oliver and Armstrong. Their interaction on the bandstand was legendary, and people wondered how it was possible for them to play together so well on their improvised breaks. Few other recordings were made of "Canal Street Blues" prior to the tune's revival in the 1950s, but Henry "Red" Allen, a trumpet player who sounds a lot like Louis Armstrong—as much as that's possible—recorded an excellent rendition with Buster Bailey on clarinet (1940). Armstrong recorded the song again himself in 1957, 1962, and 1966.

Careless Love (Anonymous): One of the oldest tunes in the jazz repertoire, this song was regularly played by Buddy Bolden and other New Orleans jazz musicians during the early 1900s. The lyrics varied according to the performer, but all dealt with the woes of an abandoned lover. For an eclectic interpretation that reflects his New Orleans roots, hear Harry Connick, Jr. on his 2007 album *Oh, My Nola*.

In 1921, W.C. Handy wrote a verse and his own lyrics to the melody, publishing the tune as "Loveless Love." Some sources also credit Spencer Williams and Martha Koenig as co-writers of that song, but Handy gave no indication that he received any help with the song's composition. Unlike Handy's other adaptations of traditional melodies, this one did not become a permanent fixture in the jazz repertoire.

Due to the straightforward simplicity of the song's melody, chords, and structure, "Careless Love" has found its way into many contexts other than jazz. Versions that preserve the early jazz feel of the song include those by Bessie Smith and Louis Armstrong (1925), Sidney Bechet and Bunk Johnson (1945), and George Lewis (1953).

Chicago Breakdown (Stratford Hunch) (Jelly Roll Morton, 1926): Ferdinand Joseph LaMothe, better known as Jelly Roll Morton (1890-1941), was an early jazz pianist, composer, and bandleader of indisputable importance in the evolution of early jazz. Among his incredible musical talents was an astonishing capacity for musical invention. "He could go home and produce overnight," said his publisher, Walter Melrose. His output was not only staggering in terms of numbers, but also in terms of quality; dozens of his tunes are revered as among the finest in the jazz repertory. When asked where his tunes came from, he replied, "You mean the music, the melody? I don't know. It's one of those things just roamin' around in my head. Sometimes I, I just start, and get at the piano and say, I think I'll write a tune, and something'll just bob up in my head, and I, out it comes on my fingers."

An example of this phenomenon is revealed in a story that dates from 1923: A couple of members of the New Orleans Rhythm Kings were experimenting with a riff, trying to come up with a tune. Jelly Roll asked if he could sit in. He sat down at the piano, began to play, and ten minutes later "Milenberg Joys" had been composed.

Along with this gift for invention was his amazing stamina in performance: "Stratford Hunch" was one of 11 original solo piano compositions that Jelly Roll recorded on June 9, 1924 for the Gennett Record Company in Richmond, Indiana. Few pianists in jazz history have recorded that many tunes in one day. Jelly Roll seemed to have a limitless supply of original music in his head ready to play at any given moment. And he wasn't shy about saying so and proving it.

Three months later, Jelly Roll made a piano roll of "Stratford Hunch" for the Vocalstyle Music Company, located in Cincinnati, Ohio, just 65 miles from Richmond. The choice of companies was obviously one of convenience, but unfortunately, Vocalstyle rolls were significantly inferior to those of QRS, the leader in the field. The poor paper quality resulted in rhythmic irregularities, which were difficult to correct. However, in 1997 the Nonesuch label released a CD produced by Artis Wodehouse that uses modern technology to create a convincing recording of all of Morton's 1924 piano rolls. It is especially interesting to hear Jelly Roll stretch out his arrangements, unrestricted by the time limits of 78 rpm records.

"*Chicago, That Toddlin' Town*," by Fred Fisher, celebrates the wild times of Chicago in the 20s. (Courtesy Lilly Library, Indiana University, Bloomington, Indiana.)

Chicago, That Toddlin' Town (music and lyrics: Fred Fisher, 1922): Fred Fisher (1875-1942) was from an earlier generation of songwriters who are largely forgotten, though their music lingers on. Fisher was the composer of many successful tunes, including "Peg o' My Heart," "And the Band Played On," "Dardanella," "Your Feet's Too Big" (popularized by Fats Waller), and "Come Josephine in My Flying Machine."

Fisher's lyric certainly captured the fast-paced wild ride that Chicago took during the 20s, while the bouncing melody is very much in keeping with the flourishing jazz scene. With the onset of Prohibition, Chicago gangsters lost no time in supplying the city's public with all the booze they wanted, and the demand certainly was huge. Fisher refers to the "town that Billy Sunday [famous evangelist and proponent of Prohibition] could not shut down," and "I saw a man he danced with his wife."

The timing was just perfect for jazz musicians, as the closing of Storyville in 1918 somewhat dampened the music scene in New Orleans, prompting many jazz musicians to move up north to Chicago. Commenting on the plentitude of music he heard in the city in the mid 20s, Eddie Condon wrote in his 1948 autobiography, "You could hold an instrument in the middle of the street [near the corner of 35th and Calumet, on Chicago's South Side] and the air would play it." By far, there are more pop and modern jazz recordings of "Chicago" than there are Dixieland ones, but traditional treatments can be found. Recommended are recordings by Django Reinhardt (1937) and Bob Scobey (with Clancy Hayes on vocals, 1959).

Chimes Blues (music by Joe Oliver, 1923): Although it is little more than a simple blues riff, this tune is hugely important in jazz history. Louis Armstrong played his first recorded jazz solo on this number in April, 1923 (the same session that produced "Canal Street Blues"). "Chimes" refers to the use of the percussion instrument called the chimes in the course of the tune, though later versions often use the piano to mimic the effect. At this point in the development of jazz, solo improvisation was generally confined to short "breaks" of just a few measures. It was highly unusual for a musician to play a full chorus alone. Armstrong plays two choruses on "Chimes Blues," displaying a sense of swing and command of the idiom that no one had heard before. As jazz scholar Gary Giddons said, when you heard this solo "you heard the future."

Without a doubt, Louis Armstrong (1901-1971) was the future of jazz. Sometimes known as "Pops" or "Satchmo" (short for "Satchel-mouth"), Armstrong made his mark as a trumpeter, singer, comedian, and entertainer. He was the most influential figure in the history of jazz, and one of the most recognizable personalities of the 20th century. His prowess on the trumpet was unsurpassed during the 20s and 30s, and his vocal enunciation and phrasing introduced an entirely new approach to singing.

As a curious follow-up, Jelly Roll Morton recorded the tune in 1928 with his celebrated recording ensemble The Red Hot Peppers. He changes the title to "Mournful Serenade," uses the melody and chords nearly verbatim, but credits Joe Oliver as the composer. Since the song is so closely aligned in character to the very early years of jazz, the best recordings are probably the ones that preserve this spirit. Recommended versions include those by Art Hodes (1940), George Lewis (1954), Louis Armstrong (1959, from the LP entitled *Satchmo Plays King Oliver*), and *Sweet Emma and her Preservation Hall Jazz Band* (1964).

"China Boy," by Phil Boutelje and Dick Winfree, was written as a lullaby, but is generally performed as an up-tempo swing number. (Courtesy Sandy Marrone, Cinnaminson, NJ.)

China Boy (music: Phil Boutelje, lyrics: Dick Winfree, 1922): The song was intended as a lullaby, with a smooth lilting melody that complements the words:

> China Boy, go sleep
>
> Close your eyes, don't peep
>
> Sandman soon will come
>
> While I softly hum

So much for intentions. Jazz musicians took to the tune from the start, and preferred it as a rousing instrumental. It was a favorite song of Benny Goodman, in particular, who never fails to show a dazzling display of technique and melodic invention.

Composer Phil Boutelje received his musical training at the Philadelphia Musical Academy, one of the oldest conservatories in the United States, which still operates today as the School of Music within the University of the Arts. He played piano and arranged for Paul Whiteman and later became an accomplished film composer. He was twice nominated for an Academy Award.

Bandleader/guitarist Eddie Condon once claimed that he met pianist Jess Stacy through "China Boy," while playing a club date in Chicago:

> The band was one of those salt-mine combinations and I was planning to spend a very miserable evening, until I heard the piano player. It was a case of love at first sight. He was showing me some new chords on "China Boy," and I asked him his name. His name turned out to be Jess Stacy.

Stacy quickly became one of Condon's favorite piano players, and they worked and recorded many times together over the years.

Outstanding recordings of "China Boy" are too numerous to mention, but they seem to start with Paul Whiteman's 1929 recording featuring Bix Beiderbecke. Red Nichols and his Five Pennies recorded a fine version the following year showcasing Benny Goodman, and Goodman himself had a hit with the song in 1936 with his trio. He would continue to play and record this number throughout his career, and it can be heard in the 1956 film *The Benny Goodman Story*.

Like several songs of the era, "Chinatown, My Chinatown," by Jean Schwartz and William Jerome, didn't enter the jazz repertory until Louis Armstrong demonstrated what could be done with it. (Courtesy Lilly Library, Indiana University, Bloomington, Indiana.)

Chinatown, My Chinatown (music: Jean Schwartz, lyrics: William Jerome, 1910): Chinatown, located in Lower Manhattan just below Little Italy, developed over the last decades of the 19th century, harboring a population of 7,000 by 1900. The culture fascinated Americans, inspiring a spate of Chinese-themed songs, with titles such as "China Boy," "China Moon," "In China," "Under the Golden China Moon," "My Dreamy China Lady," and many others. "Chinatown, My Chinatown," one of few songs specifically about the district, was introduced in the show *Up and Down Broadway* (1910). Several hit recordings followed in 1915, including a Number 1 hit by the American Quartet, but the song seems to have pretty much dropped out of sight during the 20s. Louis Armstrong's 1932 revival of the number sparked a string of additional hits and "Chinatown" quickly became a staple of the jazz repertoire. It has a solid, comfortable chord sequence that makes it appealing for improvisation. Among many noteworthy recordings is a 1938 version by Tommy Dorsey and his Clambake Seven. Dorsey was of course famous for his big band and his lyrical trombone playing, but he was also a fine Dixieland trombonist and featured a smaller ensemble playing traditional jazz selections on many of his engagements and recordings.

"Clarinet Marmalade," by Larry Shields and Henry Ragas, was one of several early hits by the Original Dixieland Jazz Band. They had so many popular recordings that their publisher used the same cover for several tunes--listing the various titles at the bottom. (Courtesy Sandy Marrone, Cinnaminson, NJ.)

Clarinet Marmalade (music and lyrics: Larry Shields and Henry Ragas, 1918): The song was introduced by the Original Dixieland Jazz Band, the ensemble that is credited with having made the very first jazz recordings. Since most of their compositions were group efforts by the entire band, it's hard to identify who wrote what. The record label credits this one to clarinetist Larry Shields and pianist Henry Ragas, which seems appropriate for this number.

The band's 1918 recording did not reach the charts (a somewhat meaningless term prior to the 20s), but became one of the most esteemed recordings in jazz history. Although Shields does not contribute a clarinet "solo" to the recording (Louis Armstrong would lead the way toward solo improvisation a few years later), his ensemble improvisations and clarinet "breaks" were copied and imitated by other clarinetists for years. In 1923, the New Orleans Rhythm Kings, probably the most significant White jazz ensemble to come after the Original Dixieland Jazz Band, recorded "Clarinet Marmalade" with Leon Roppolo on clarinet. As can be heard on the recording, musicians were taking actual solos by that time, but still not straying very far from the melody, except for unaccompanied break sections.

The Fletcher Henderson Orchestra, generally hailed as the greatest among the large African-American jazz bands prior to Duke Ellington, made a fine recording of "Clarinet Marmalade" in 1926, featuring Buster Bailey on the clarinet. On this recording we can hear further development in the jazz solo—Bailey is clearly improvising a new melody—not just embellishing the original. The following year Frankie Trumbauer recorded the tune, featuring fine solos by Bix Beiderbecke, Trumbauer on C-melody saxophone, and Jimmy Dorsey on clarinet. In just under ten years, the art of solo improvisation had reached its first maturity, and its progress can be traced through "Clarinet Marmalade."

For a recent recording of the number, check out the Jim Cullum band on their 2002 album *The Real Stuff*.

Come Back Sweet Papa (music and lyrics: Paul Barbarin, 1926): Paul Barbarin (1899-1969) came from an important New Orleans musical family and developed into one of the finest early jazz drummers. He was very much involved in the New Orleans musical scene throughout his life. Although he toured and spent time in Chicago and New York, he always returned to New Orleans. In 1960 he re-created his father's Onward Brass Band and remained active until his death in 1969. His compositions also include "Don't Forget to Mess Around" (1926) and "Bourbon Street Parade" (1949).

Louis Armstrong recorded "Come Back" on the second Hot Five recording session in February 1926. It has been cited as an example of how far ahead of his band mates Armstrong was in honing the art of swing and improvisation. As with many of the Hot Fives and Hot Sevens, it was many years before other musicians recorded their own versions. The tune was brought back into the repertoire with the revival bands of the post-World War II Era.

Copenhagen (music: Charlie Davis, lyrics: Walter Melrose, 1924): You might imagine that the song is named after the city in Denmark, but in fact it refers to the brand of tobacco preferred by Charlie Davis' bass player. Charlie Davis had a very successful jazz band in Indiana during the 20s. Bix Beiderbecke heard Davis' composition in 1924 and was granted permission by the composer to record the song with the Wolverines. A session was scheduled for Gennett records and the recording took place on May 6, 1924. Walter Melrose, a successful music publisher from Chicago, heard Bix's recording and contacted Davis offering to write lyrics for the song and publish it. Successful recordings followed by the Benson Orchestra, the California Ramblers, and others, and the tune remained in the jazz repertoire (though usually without the lyrics). Significant jazz versions include those by Fletcher Henderson with Louis Armstrong (1924) and Bud Freeman (1940). "Copenhagen" is on the flip side of Teresa Brewer's 1950s hit song "Music, Music, Music" and her interpretation is solid and swinging. A fine recent version can be heard by clarinetist Dan Levinson on his 2008 album *At the Codfish Ball*.

Cornet Chop Suey (music: Louis Armstrong, 1924): This number is famous as a tour-de-force for the cornet (or trumpet). It was truly revolutionary for its time, raising the bar exponentially as to what could be done by a jazz trumpet player. In his autobiography, Louis said he remembered writing the song on Lil Hardin's back steps. (Lil was the pianist in King Oliver's band when Louis was with that unit.) That certainly seems plausible, since the song is copyrighted January 24, 1924 and they married on February 4. The title probably derives from Louis's love for Chinese food, and most likely is a bit of word play with "Clarinet Marmalade."

If leader and first cornetist Joe Oliver even allowed Louis to play this bravura piece with his band, he certainly wasn't going to allow him to record it. Louis's chance came two years later, with his own Hot Five ensemble, on February 26, 1926. A curious aspect of the song is that it was not improvised—every note he plays on the recording is indicated in the 1924 sheet music. Louis apparently forgot about the song for the next 20 years (or else was intimidated by his own spectacular recording), but repeated his performance at his famous Town Hall Concert of May, 1947.

This concert is said to have inspired Louis to drop the big-band accompaniment he had been working with and return to the traditional New Orleans format. Shortly after the concert, he assembled the Louis Armstrong All Stars, the ensemble he fronted for the rest of his life.

Clarinetist Barney Bigard recalls the band's first engagement: "I went to work not even knowing who else was in the band.... I got there real early and Sid Catlett came in with his drums. I knew 'Big Sid' just casually and then in came Dick Cary (who, incidentally, was the original pianist with the band before Earl Hines joined) followed by Arvell Shaw with a bass violin and Velma Middleton, our female vocalist.... In came Louis and Jack Teagarden.... That was the band."

Cottage for Sale (music: Willard Robison, lyrics: Larry Conley, 1929): This song has endured since its publication, largely due to the folksy but haunting metaphor of the lyrics: "Our little dream castle, With every dream gone." Although the subject of the song is never stated directly, the words reveal that the relationship has ended and "no one is waiting anymore." The melody, too, wanders and sinks in a dreamy way. Robinson was in fact noted for the down-home, unassuming quality of his tunes. For that reason he is often compared to fellow Midwesterner Hoagy Carmichael. While Robison didn't write his own lyrics, his tunes seem to invoke a similar spirit, with titles such as "Old Folks," "Round My Old Deserted Farm," and "Don't Smoke in Bed."

Robison recorded the song with his own band in 1930, but both Guy Lombardo and the Revelers each had hits with their versions. Through the years, the song remained an essential recording item for pop artists, and interpretations can be heard by, well, everybody you'd expect, including Billy Eckstine, Nat "King" Cole, Peggy Lee, Tony Bennett, Lou Rawls, Johnny Mathis, Judy Garland and all the rest. Perhaps the most well-known version is from Frank Sinatra's 1959 album *Who Cares?* Interesting jazz versions begin with several 1930 recordings (Jack Hylton's is notable) and include those by Jack Teagarden (1962), Ruby Braff (1968), and Joe Venuti (1977).

Crazy Rhythm (music: Joseph Meyer, lyrics: Irving Caesar, Roger Wolfe Kahn, 1928): Meyer ("California Here I Come," "If You Knew Susie") was one of the most successful songwriters of his era, while Caesar ("Sometimes I'm Happy," "Tea for Two") would ultimately be inducted into the Songwriters Hall of Fame. Roger Wolfe Kahn, however, was a much more colorful character. Roger Wolfe Kahn was the son of Otto Kahn, a successful banker who became one of the most influential patrons of the arts in U.S. history. Roger shared his father's love for music and is said to have learned to play 18 musical instruments before launching his own successful orchestra in 1923 at the age of 16. Both father and son appeared independently on the cover of *Time* magazine, Otto in 1925 and Roger in 1927. Roger's musical career flourished until the 1930s, when he became fascinated with aviation. He disbanded his orchestra and ultimately became a test pilot and technical manager for an aviation company.

"Crazy Rhythm" was written for the Broadway show *Here's Howe*, for which Kahn was co-composer. Kahn's orchestra had a hit record with it and the song's popularity never waned. The catchy rhythm and melody have made it a favorite jazz standard for both traditional and modern players. No fewer than a dozen jazz albums that include the song are entitled *Crazy Rhythm*. And does "Crazy Rhythm" really use a crazy rhythm? Somewhat. A syncopated figure is introduced in the first two bars and dominates the rest of the song. What's crazy about it is that once you get it in your ear it's hard to forget it, which is exactly what the composer had in mind.

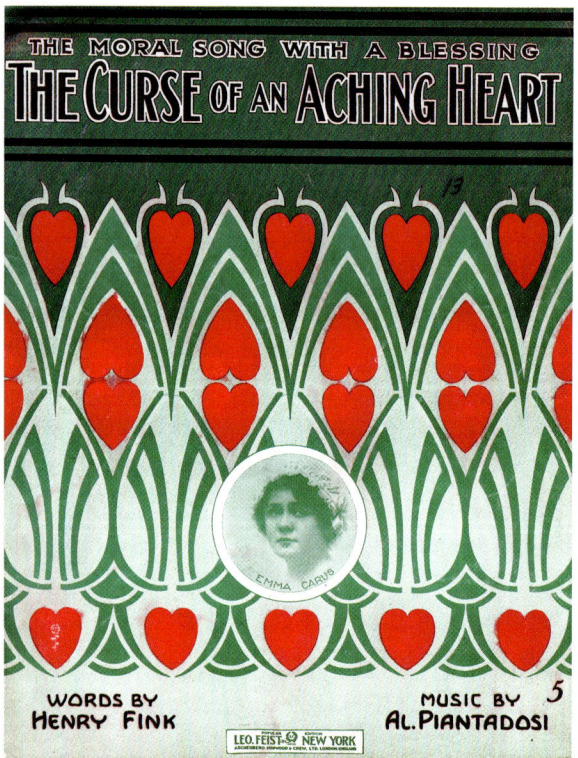

"The Curse of an Aching Heart, by Henry Fink and Al Piantadosi, was intended as a melodramatic tearjerker. It was Fats Waller who revealed its potential as a jazz number. (Courtesy Lilly Library, Indiana University, Bloomington, Indiana.)

The Curse of an Aching Heart (music: Al Piantadosi, lyrics: Henry Fink, 1913): Songwriter Al Piantadosi is not much remembered today, but he achieved quite a bit of notoriety in his time, exerting an unexpected influence that far exceeded that of the average composer. It seems that he penned a song in 1915 called "I Didn't Raise My Boy to Be a Soldier." That song became a huge Number 1 hit for both the Peerless Quartet and Morton Harvey, charting for nearly four months. More importantly, it became the anti-war cry that helped to create the pacifist movement and galvanize those who were opposed to the United States entering World War I. As could be expected, the song inspired both praise and scorn, leading to several imitations and parodies, such as "I Didn't Raise my Dog to be a Sausage" (a comic song written in 1915 by Herman Paley and Charles McCarron).

Written two years earlier, "Aching Heart" has no such lofty ambitions. It is a simple song in waltz meter about a jilted lover who blames his former partner for making him a total wreck, beginning with "You made me what I am today, I hope you're satisfied." Early versions had nothing to do with jazz, but the tearful lyrics lived on in popular culture, even inspiring a hilarious scene in Laurel and Hardy's *Blotto* (1930). As a strolling musician sings "Aching Heart" at their table, Ollie becomes increasingly irritated and impatient, while Stanley breaks down sobbing.

Fats Waller had the first successful jazz version of "Aching Heart" in 1936 (at a bouncy swing tempo of course!). The Dixieland revival bands of the 1940s (such as Turk Murphy) took up the song and it has remained in the traditional jazz repertoire ever since. Banjoist Clancy Hayes sings a solid version of the number with Bob Scobey's Frisco Jazz Band (1957). For a recent recording, listen to Meschiya Lake and the Little Bighorns on their 2010 album *Lucky Devil*. An innovative singer in the traditional blues style, Meschiya has been a significant presence in the New Orleans music scene in recent years.

52 | THE SONGS

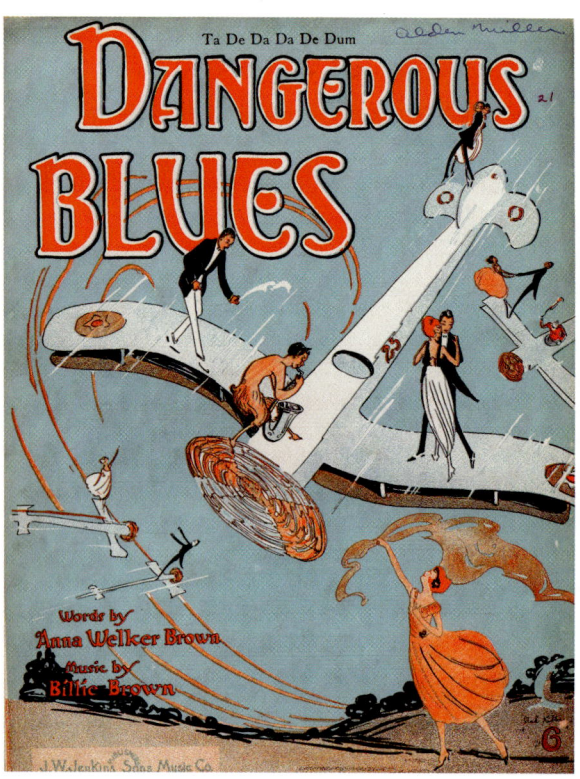

"Dangerous Blues," by Billie Brown and Anna Welker Brown, exemplifies the whimsical creativity of sheet music covers of the era. (Courtesy Lilly Library, Indiana University, Bloomington, Indiana.)

Dangerous Blues (music: Billie Brown, lyrics: Anna Welker Brown, 1921): Billie Brown (pseudonym for Irene W. Anderson, 1894?-1921) lived a short tragic life shrouded in mystery. She was born in Arkansas to a Swedish father and Illinois-born mother who gave her up for adoption. Billie was taken in by William B. Brown, a saloon keeper in Eureka Springs, Arkansas, and his wife Anna Welker Brown. Most likely, she received an early music education and was influenced by the Ragtime music she heard in the saloon. Anna left William at some point, and by 1915 mother and daughter were living in Kansas City, Missouri. By this time, the daughter was going by the name of Billie Brown and was working as a professional pianist.

Brown's first professional publications began to appear that year. She continued to work and compose in collaboration with her mother, and her age seems have been deliberately falsified to give the impression that she was much younger than she was. (Her death certificate claims she was born in 1903.) The mother-daughter team achieved limited success for several years, but gained nation-wide attention with

"Dangerous Blues." It caught on quickly, prompting recordings by Mamie Smith, The Original Dixieland Jazz Band, and Eubie Blake. But her promising future was cut short when she contracted small pox that same year, dying in December 1921. After her death, a few pieces were published posthumously, including the popular "Lonesome Mama Blues" in 1922.

Singer Mamie Smith (1883-1946), "Queen of the Blues," had a hit recording of "Dangerous Blues" in 1921. Although overshadowed by Bessie Smith in subsequent years, Mamie was in fact the first African American to make a vocal blues recording. Her million-seller "Crazy Blues" of 1920 was largely responsible for the "blues craze" of the early 20s and did much to convince record companies that the African-American market was worth considering. Many labels quickly added the category "race records" to their offerings, with Okeh Records referring to Mamie Smith as their "race artist." "Dangerous Blues" was clearly intended to follow up on the tremendous success of "Crazy Blues" the year before.

The fantastic cover of the music to "Dangerous Blues" demonstrates sheet music illustration art at its best. Ilah Kibbey (1888-1958) was an artist who was active in Kansas City, MO, specializing in genre and landscape. Kibbey also illustrated the cover to "Lonesome Mama Blues," which was also a hit for Mamie Smith.

"Dardanella," by Johnny Black and Fred Fisher, incorporated several unusual musical techniques, yet became one of the biggest hits of its day. (Courtesy Lilly Library, Indiana University, Bloomington, Indiana.)z

Dardanella (music: Johnny Black, Felix Bernard; lyrics: Fred Fisher, 1919): One of the most popular numbers of 1919, "Dardanella" initially was a Ragtime composition called "Turkish Tom Tom." Vaudevillian Felix Bernard reworked the piece into popular song form, and Fred Fisher supplied the lyrics. It was an instant success. Sheet music sales topped one million, but Ben Selvin's Novelty Orchestra had a hit record that sold five million copies, making "Dardanella" the best selling record prior to Gene Austin's "My Blue Heaven."

Evidently the publishers thought the success of "Dardanella" was big enough to warrant a tune whose subject was the song itself. In 1920 the writers published a song called "The Dardanella Blues," which was written "about the little fellow who wrote Dardanella." The sheet music cover actually included an image of the original song to assure readers that it was written by the same people. The number was introduced by Sophie Tucker and both Billy Murray and Ed Smalle had hits with the song, though it never came close to rivaling the popularity of "Dardanella."

"Dardanella" has an unusual melody—a combination of tightly compacted chromatic runs offset by wide leaps. Another curious and innovative aspect to "Dardanella" is the incorporation of a bass line that very much resembles what would later be called "boogie woogie." Undoubtedly, this had a lot to do with the song's immediate success. When Jerome Kern composed a tune with a similar bass line two years later, Fisher sued him and won the case, collecting $250 in damages.

Johnny Black was responsible for another famous song, but did not live to reap the rewards. In 1915 he wrote "Paper Doll" but it went unpublished until 1930 and was neglected until the Mills Brothers turned it into a gigantic hit in 1943. Black had died several years earlier.

"Dardanella" was widely recorded during the 1920s, including a 1928 session with the Paul Whiteman band featuring Bix Beiderbecke. Bix deftly navigates the unusual song, interjecting traces of the melody between his own lyrical inventions. After the 20s, few recordings of "Dardanella" appear. In fact, the tune is more often quoted during jazz solos then it is actually played. New Orleans stride pianist John Royen includes the number on his 1996 album *Solo Tradition*.

"The Darktown Strutters' Ball," by Shelton Brooks, with its simple but clever design, has remained a favorite in traditional jazz circles. (Courtesy Lilly Library, Indiana University, Bloomington, Indiana.)

The Darktown Strutters' Ball (music and lyrics: Shelton Brooks, 1917): Shelton Brooks (1886-1975) was one of the most distinguished Black songwriters of the teens. He started out as a cafe pianist in Detroit and Chicago. Before long, he began to gain a reputation in vaudeville as an imitator of Bert Williams, who saw the act and thought well of it. (Williams [1874-1922] was arguably the most popular Black entertainer prior to the 20s and one of the greatest comedians of all time.)

Brooks made some attempts at publishing songs about this time, and achieved notoriety when Sophie Tucker enthusiastically embraced his "Some of These Days" (1910), making it her theme song. Several other successful songs followed, and then came "Darktown" in 1917. Millions of copies of sheet music were sold and numerous bands recorded the song, including The

Original Dixieland Jazz Band, The Brown Brothers, and some years later Ted Lewis (1927), and the Coon-Sanders Original Nighthawk Orchestra (1929). The Coon-Sanders arrangement is both hot and inventive and showcases the band at the height of its popularity.

This ensemble, led by drummer Carlton Coon and pianist Joe Sanders is known as one of the first jazz orchestras to achieve national recognition through radio broadcasting. They first went on the air in 1922, and took the name "Nighthawks" because they broadcast late at night. Radio was new at the time, and Coon-Sanders started on the ground floor. Being based in Kansas City was a definite asset, since network broadcasting was still in the future, and their central location over the as yet nearly empty air waves allowed them to be heard throughout the continental United States. As radio gained in popularity, so did the Nighthawks. Their name lives on today through the currently active orchestra Vince Giordano and the Nighthawks, perhaps best known for providing the soundtrack for the *Boardwalk Empire* HBO Series.

"Darktown" is a typical song of the period about dancing, but unlike most, which describe the steps to be danced, this one talks about going to the dance. "I'll be down to get you in a taxi, honey, You better be ready about half past eight. . . ." The song is simple in both melody and harmony, and at 20 measures, it's just over half the length of the average song (32 measures). But it moves along at a fast pace, with an effective tag at the end set to the lyrics: "Goin' to dance out both my shoes, When they play the "Jelly Roll Blues,' Tomorrow night at the Darktown Strutters' Ball."

In 1964, ASCAP (the American Society of Composer, Authors and Publishers) named "Darktown" as one of the 16 best songs in the organization's 50 year vhistory. At Brooks' memorial service in 1975, a 13-piece band paid him something of a New Orleans funeral tribute, performing a slow rendition of "Just a Closer Walk with Thee," followed by up-tempo versions of "Some of These Days" and "Darktown Strutters' Ball."

"Dear Old Southland," by Turner Layton and Henry Creamer, combines the melodies of two well-known hymns. (Courtesy Sandy Marrone, Cinnaminson, NJ.)

Dear Old Southland (music: Turner Layton, lyrics: Henry Creamer, 1921): This catchy song has earned a solid place in the Dixieland repertoire, but cannot be listed as one of Creamer and Layton's most creative efforts for the simple reason that they didn't write the song. The composition is a direct patching together of two Negro Spirituals: "Deep River" and "Sometimes I Feel Like a Motherless Child," with only a few rhythmic adjustments. True, Layton's lyrics are original, but offer nothing beyond obvious rhymes and clichés about the old South (e.g.: "How I long to roam back to my old Kentucky home"). Nevertheless, the song caught on, probably because people knew and liked the melodies it was based on.

Creamer and Layton recorded the song in 1921 and Paul Whiteman had a hit with it the following year. Whiteman's recording, like others of its era, plows through the song marching-band style as just another dance vehicle. Red Nichols' recording of 1928 makes some attempt at sensitivity, going back and forth between slow, expressive tempos and upbeat, hot sections. But Louis Armstrong's 1930 recording treats the song nearly as operatic recitative, not going into tempo until the very end. His performance is expressive and heartfelt, but the expected gags and banter are there throughout, both on the trumpet and in his comments, such as when he says to his pianist "watch the chord there Satchelmouth." On the other end of the spectrum, Al Hirt (1963) romps through the tune like he's trying to catch a train. There may be nothing spiritual about his performance, but he sure could swing and play the trumpet.

Deed I Do (music: Fred Rose, lyrics: Walter Hirsch, 1926): If some of Fred Rose's early songs (such as "Red Hot Mamma," and "Flamin' Mamie") have a down-home feel to them, it might be expected, considering that in the 1940s he turned to country music. He became extremely successful in this field, becoming one of the three charter members of the Country Music Hall of Fame when it opened in 1961, and later being inducted into the Nashville Songwriter's Hall of Fame in 1970 and the Songwriters Hall of Fame in 1985.

The words to "Deed I Do" contain a direct answer to the question "Do I love you?" couched in simple melody and predictable rhythm. What the tune might lack in complexity it makes up for in its charm and logical structure. Benny Goodman recorded the song in his first studio session with Ben Pollack in December 1926. Ruth Etting and Johnny Marvin both had hits with the song in 1927, and Lena Horne revived the tune with a personal touch in 1948. The harmonic structure of the tune has found appeal with jazz musicians and many outstanding recordings can be found in both traditional and modern settings.

Diga Diga Doo (music: Jimmy McHugh, lyrics: Dorothy Fields, 1928): A fortunate moment in show business history occurred when Jimmy McHugh asked the young Dorothy Fields to write some lyrics for his *Blackbirds of 1928*. The show was the idea of impresario Lew Leslie (see entries on "Mandy Make Up Your Mind" and "Memories of You") who had already had significant success in presenting African-American talent on stage. The tremendous success of the show, as well as the songs they wrote together, cemented a partnership between McHugh and Fields that would last until 1935. Among the well-known songs from *Blackbirds* are "Diga Diga Doo," "I Must Have That Man," and the smash hit "I Can't Give You Anything but Love." In coming years they would contribute standards such as "Don't Blame Me," "Exactly like You," "On the Sunny Side of the Street," and many others.

"Diga Diga Doo" is a sprightly jump number in a minor key, with the nonsense "diga diga doo" syllables finishing off each phrase. Reversing the more common pattern of songs in major going to minor for the middle section, this one starts in minor and goes to major. Duke Ellington had a hit with his clever arrangement of the song in 1928. The band swings like mad, and features James "Bubber" Miley on the cornet. Bubber specialized in using the plunger mute. (Plunger mutes are simply sink or toilet plungers with the stick removed. The player manipulates the placement of the mute with his or her hand to achieve the desired effects.) Bubber was a featured soloist with Ellington during the 20s and stayed on with the band until shortly before his early death in 1932. The recording contains a vocal chorus, which might sound a bit out of character with the rest of the performance. That's Ellington's White manager, Irving Mills, who worked wonders with Ellington's career, but often tried to get himself into the act with his limited singing and composing abilities.

Another recording of "Diga Diga Doo" worth mention was made by Frankie Trumbauer and his Orchestra in 1936. Among several fine soloists that are featured, Jack Teagarden stands out with a spectacular chorus using the half trombone/water-glass technique. This bizarre method of playing the trombone, probably invented by Teagarden, involves removing the bell of the trombone (essentially half of the instrument), and placing a hand-held water glass over the tubing. The slide functions normally, but the resulting sound is muted, having a timbre something like that of a cornet.

"Dill Pickles," by Charles L. Johnson, was the most famous rag to follow "Maple Leaf Rag." The composer considered it his favorite among his own compositions. (Courtesy Lilly Library, Indiana University, Bloomington, Indiana.)

Dill Pickles (music: Charles L. Johnson, 1906): Music seldom makes a drastic change from one style to another, and the transition from Ragtime to jazz was a gradual one with much overlapping of material. Consequently, the Ragtime numbers that were very well known when jazz came into its own stayed in the repertoire. "Dill Pickles" was one of the most popular rags of the era. "Maple Leaf Rag" was the first rag to sell a million copies, and "Dill Pickles" was the second. In fact, by 1906 Ragtime was beginning to fade, and it is believed that "Dill Pickles" was in part responsible for reviving the movement.

The word "Ragtime" takes its name from the jagged syncopations of the rhythm that sounded "ragged" to some people. "Dill Pickles," though rather simple by Ragtime standards, popularized the "three-over-four" syncopation that was taken up by many other composers in subsequent years. As for the meaning of the title: Johnson was working one afternoon at his publisher's when the bookkeeper came in and asked him what the name of his new rag was going to be. The man happened to be carrying a container of pickles, so Johnson said "Dill Pickles Rag." Among all his published works, this remained Johnson's personal favorite.

Dinah (music: Harry Akst, lyrics: Sam M. Lewis and Joe Young, 1925): Harry Akst was working as a staff pianist/songplugger for Irving Berlin's publishing company when he wrote the tune "Dinah," which launched his songwriting career. He soon became one of the leading composers on Tin Pan Alley, turning out such classics as "Am I Blue," "Baby Face," and "Travelin' Light." Several hit records of "Dinah" appeared in the years following its publication, including those by Ethel Waters (1926), The Revelers (1926), Cliff Edwards (1926), Fletcher Henderson (1926), Ted Lewis (1930), Bing Crosby (1932), the Mills Brothers (1932), The Boswell Sisters (1935), and Fats Waller (1936).

When auditioning for jobs, fledgling singer Frances Rose Shore sang the song so frequently that people started to refer to her as "the Dinah girl," prompting her to change her name to Dinah Shore. Indeed, it is almost impossible to overestimate the popularity of this song, which today remains at the core of the traditional jazz repertory. The tune is usually done as a romper, as can be heard and seen on a famous film by Louis Armstrong from 1933, but for a more sensitive treatment hear Joe Venuti's Blue Four (1927). More recently, cornetist Andy Schumm performs the song on the album *Bix off the Record* (2015).

When researching this tune, one troubling piece of information cropped up. Sigmund Spaeth, in his classic 1948 book *A History of Popular Music in America*, says that

"Dinah" "came into existence through Sam Lewis, Joe Young and Harry Akst, with some question as to the identity of its original creator." He says nothing more about it. Just before going to press with *Tunes of the Twenties*, additional information came my way through Steve Brecker, who relates that his grandfather, Sam Brecker had always claimed that he wrote the melody to "Dinah" in 1914 to a tune he called "Chow Mein."

Samuel Brecker (1893-1977) was a pianist/composer with a handful of published tunes to his credit. His story was that when he first experienced chow mein (Chinese food did not become popular among Americans until the 20s), he was so delighted that it inspired him to write a song about it. A New York resident, Brecker took the song down to Tin Pan Alley, playing and singing it for several publishers in an attempt to get interest. No one accepted his song, so he abandoned it and went on to other projects. However, it's reasonable to suppose that the melody remained in someone's ear. Akst, Lewis, and Young were all active musicians with close ties to the publishing industry at the time, and one of them might have remembered it. In any case, Brecker's quaint lyrics, which are very much a product of the teens compared to the snazzier words to "Dinah," fit the melody nearly perfectly.

> Chow mein, did you ever eat chow mein
> How I love to eat chow mein
> on Saturday night, in China Town

> Oh, Chow Mein, can't do without chow mein
> Yes, I love to eat chow mein
> On a Saturday night,

> A bowl of rice
> Oh so nice
> Vegetable & spice
> And crisp noodles
> What a delight

> Oh, chow mein, I love to eat chow mein
> Crazy about chow mein
> Down in Chinatown

Dippermouth Blues (music: Joe Oliver, 1923): Joe "King" Oliver was Louis Armstrong's teacher and mentor. When he left New Orleans in 1918, he told Louis that when he became successful he would send for him. That moment came in 1922 when Armstrong joined Oliver's band in Chicago for a steady job at the Royal Gardens Cafe. In the spring of 1923, the band made a series of memorable recordings for the Gennett Record Company. Among the many jazz classics introduced on these records was "Dippermouth Blues," the title referring to one of Armstrong's nicknames. It is likely that Armstrong had a hand in writing the song.

Oliver was known for his creative use of mutes on the cornet as can be heard on this recording. In fact, his "wah-wah" solo on "Dippermouth Blues" became so famous that it would be re-created verbatim by generations of cornet players yet to come. Benny Goodman included it in his arrangement of the song ten years later, and it can also be heard on Muggsy Spanier's 1939 recording. (King Oliver had given Muggsy the very mute that he used for the original solo.) Another tradition that pertains to the performance of this song is an open break near the end where someone in the band shouts "Oh play that thing!" According to the musicians who were there in 1923, drummer Baby Dodds, who had been drinking whiskey during the recording session, forgot to play a short solo that was worked out for him. Hearing the silence, banjoist Bill Johnson screamed, "Play that thing!" The tradition continues to this day.

Do You Know What It Means to Miss New Orleans (music: Louis Alter, lyrics: Eddie De Lange, 1946): The song was written for the movie *New Orleans* (1947), which starred Louis Armstrong and Billie Holiday. As with many Hollywood musicals of the period, the film offers little in the way of drama or reality, but more than compensates for its weaknesses through its strong musical content. In addition to Armstrong and Holiday, several other jazz greats appear in the film, including Woody Herman, Barney Bigard and Kid Ory.

Lyricist Eddie De Lange (who provided the lyrics to such classics as "Moonglow," "Darn That Dream," and "Solitude") wrote a quaint and apt lyric (including plenty of moss-covered vines, magnolias in bloom, and moonlight on the bayou), while Alter contributed a broadly sweeping melody with a lilting rhythm and unexpected harmonic effects. Amazingly, jazz critic Al Rose tells the story of attending a jazz brunch with Alter in 1976 and learning that it was his first time in New Orleans! According to Rose, Alter wrote him a letter after returning to New York, proclaiming, "Now I know what it means to miss New Orleans."

The tune remains in the repertoire of practically every traditional jazz band, and it took on an especially poignant meaning in the years following Hurricane Katrina (2005), when it was used in various documentaries and television shows alluding to the tragedy.

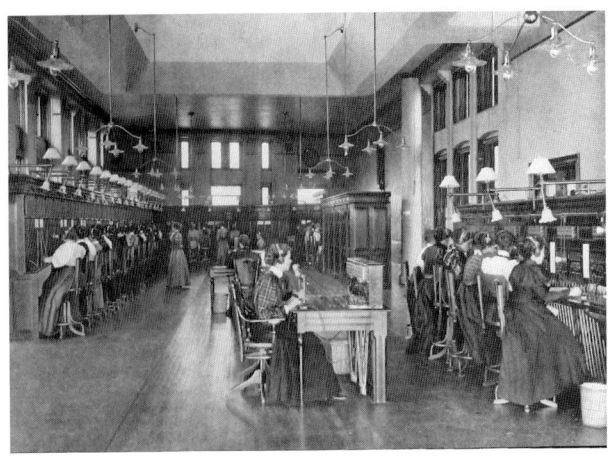

The early fascination with the telephone inspired many song references, including "Hello Central, give me Dr. Jazz." (Montreal Telephone Exchange, photographer unknown, public domain, via Wikimedia Commons.)

Doctor Jazz (music: Joe Oliver, lyrics: Walter Melrose, 1926): Original publication information lists Oliver and Melrose as co-composers, but it is likely that Oliver wrote the tune with Melrose supplying the lyrics. Walter Melrose, who published compositions for Oliver, Jelly Roll Morton, Duke Ellington, and other jazz writers, typically added lyrics to instrumental songs so he could collect half the royalties. While many of his lyrics seem perfunctory, the words to "Doctor Jazz" are at once playful, catchy, and reminiscent of an era long gone: "Hello Central, give me Doctor Jazz."

Jelly Roll Morton made his recording debut as a singer with this song in December 1926, on one of his early Red Hot Pepper recordings. Composer Joe Oliver didn't record the song until March 1927. Since Jelly Roll's recording became much more widely known, many assumed he wrote the tune, and even some books and recordings give false attribution.

Both recordings are carefully arranged, while still allowing for breaks and solo improvisation. Jelly Roll's intention with the Red Hot Pepper recordings was to depict the New Orleans sound the way he remembered it; accordingly, he wrote out ensemble parts that would ordinarily have been improvised. In 1927, Oliver was leading a band called the Dixie Syncopators, which, following trends at the time, used expanded instrumentation and fully written-out arrangements. Oliver is very much in form on this recording, but the Syncopators would be his last successful band, and his playing days were numbered. By the late 20s he began to experience difficulty performing because of gum disease, eventually quitting the music business altogether.

"Doctor Jazz" can be heard in a powerfully swinging version by the Dutch Dixie All Stars on their 1997 album *At the Jazz Band Ball*.

Don't Get Around Much Anymore (music: Duke Ellington, lyrics: Bob Russell, 1942): Although it's hard to imagine it now, in the early days of jazz (say, before 1922), dancers were reluctant to accept a vocalist, preferring instrumental versions of their favorite tunes. (Paul Whiteman was one of the first popular dance bands to add a vocal chorus.) Again, in 1935, when Benny Goodman initiated the swing movement, the emphasis was on dancing and hot instrumental numbers. But by the 1940s things had turned around and singers were getting most of the attention.

"Don't Get Around Much Anymore" is a case in point. Originally written by Duke Ellington as an instrumental number called "Never No Lament," the song received little attention following its 1940 release. Always the opportunist, Duke had no objections when lyricist Bob Russell added words to the song in 1942, changing the title to "Don't Get Around Much Anymore." Both the Ink Spots and Glen Gray recorded the song and had big hits in 1943. With all the attention his song was now getting, Duke decided to re-release his earlier recording of "Never No Lament" as "Don't Get Around Much Anymore." Nothing was changed. It was the very same recording that went nowhere three years before. But this time it became a hit, reaching Number 8 and remaining on the charts for 14 weeks. There is just no way of predicting the public.

Although the song falls more into the category of "swing" than "traditional jazz" (for those who wish to make a distinction), that didn't stop Eddie Condon (1945) or Earl Hines (1974) from recording it. For something delightfully in between, listen to Harry Connick, Jr. on the soundtrack to the 1989 motion picture *When Harry Meets Sally*.

Down by the Riverside (1865): One of the oldest songs in the Dixieland repertoire, this traditional Negro spiritual is pretty much an anti-war song, and is sometimes referred to as "Ain't Gonna Study War No More." In Black-American culture of the time, "study" includes the meaning "to engage in, or turn one's attention to." It was adapted into a Tin Pan Alley song sometime after 1900 and recordings began to appear after 1920. Though popular as a gospel number, "Down by the Riverside" was not performed often by jazz musicians prior to World War II. Dixieland revival bands took up the tune (for example, Bunk Johnson, 1942) and it became immensely popular in the 1950s after it had become a hit for the Four Lads (1953) and Bing Crosby (1954). Eventually, it became part of the repertoire of most traditional jazz bands.

"Down Home Rag," by Wilber Sweatman, who played a key role in the transition from Ragtime to jazz. (Courtesy Lilly Library, Indiana University, Bloomington, Indiana.)

Down Home Rag (Wilbur Sweatman, 1911): Wilbur Sweatman (1882-1961) was an extremely important figure in the transition from Ragtime to jazz and one of the most successful of early African-American musicians. Primarily a clarinetist,

Sweatman played several instruments, soon finding early success as a composer and bandleader. He toured with major vaudeville circuits and gained attention with an act in which he played three clarinets at once. A good friend of Scott Joplin, Sweatman also composed rags, "Down Home Rag" being one of his best. His 1916 recording of this number could arguably be considered the first jazz record in history, since there are elements of improvisation in his performance, though the feel is still Ragtime. His recordings were quite successful for a few years, but sales began to wane after 1920 when newer jazz styles began to prevail. Although he would continue to perform through the years, Sweatman turned his attention increasingly toward the publishing business.

"Down Home Rag" follows the standard model for its genre, but contains some nuances that make it interesting. The opening refrain employs a device called hemiola, meaning that a short rhythmic pattern repeats in such a way that the first note alternates between falling on the downbeat and the upbeat. The technique is often used in rags, but Sweatman keeps it going for a long time in this one. The next section repeats a two-bar riff, similar to the kinds of background rhythms swing musicians would improvise behind soloists some 25 years later. Then comes a dogfight (a short strain in the latter half of the march in which groups of instruments alternate statements, building suspense prior to the start of another section). And finally a trio section, which consists entirely of a pentatonic scale—the same five notes supply the entire melody.

"Down in Jungle Town," by Edward Madden and Theodore Morse, is representative of a bizarre category of novelty tunes called "monkey songs." (Courtesy Lilly Library, Indiana University, Bloomington, Indiana.)

Down in Jungle Town (music: Theodore Morse, lyrics: Edward Madden, 1908): A glance at various other titles written by these early Tin Pan Alley songwriters gives an idea of the broad scope of subjects that captured American tastes in the early years of the 20th century. Morse was the composer of "M-O-T-H-E-R" and "Hail, Hail the Gang's All Here," while Madden supplied the lyrics to classics such as "By the Light of the Silvery Moon," and "Moonlight Bay." Although hard to imagine now, there was an entire category of novelty numbers referred to as "monkey songs" that achieved popularity at this time, with titles such as "Monkey Doodle Dandy," "On a Monkey Honeymoon," "Moonlight in Jungleland," and "All Aboard for Monkeytown."

"Down in Jungle Town" was a follow-up on Morse's "In Monkeyland" (1907), and these two songs did much to establish the genre. As with other fad songs of the period, the subject matter is whimsical and totally inaccurate, fraught with exotic islands, jungles, coconuts, along with an attempt by the composer to provide jungle sounds and music, whatever that might mean. "Down in Jungle Town" follows a common storyline for the genre—the courtship and marriage of a monkey couple, this time with the monkey king as the groom. In spite of the novelty lyrics, the chorus to the song is quite good—a well-constructed melody that would stand on its own in any context.

The comedy team of Arthur Collins and Byron Harlan made a 1909 recording of "Down in Jungle Town" that sold very well for its day. Not surprisingly, the tune's potential as a jazz number is not at all evident in this rendition. "Jungle Town" really didn't gain momentum in the jazz world until after 1940. A hard-swinging rendition by Henry "Red" Allen from 1940 demonstrates that he was one of the few trumpeters in jazz who could keep up with Armstrong. A recording from 1949 by the Castle Jazz Band features some nice trombone work by George Brunies. Before long, all the jazz bands were doing the number. One of the most convincing interpretations of the tune I've heard was recorded by Vince Giordano and the Nighthawks (2014) for the *Boardwalk Empire* HBO Series, Volume 2. At the opening, the musicians do a remarkable job of imitating jungle sounds with their instruments over a steady tom-tom beat, then joining together in a driving swing arrangement.

East St. Louis Toodle-oo (music: Duke Ellington and Bubber Miley, 1927): One of Duke's compositions from his "jungle period," this was his first charting single. (Ellington's jungle style was very much responsible for his initial success. It involved the evocation of primitive imagery through exotic sounds and sonorities, including blue notes, growls, and vocalized instrumental sounds.) "East St. Louis" was released in 1927, Ellington's last year at the Kentucky Club before moving to the Cotton Club, where he became famous. (Amazingly, the Cotton Club job was first offered to Joe Oliver, who turned it down!) Ellington explains the origin of the song's title: "We started out calling it the "Todalo," and, of course, the printer obviously made a mistake and put another 'o' in it or something.... Todalo, you know, is a broken walk... We were walking up Broadway one night after playing the Kentucky Club, and we were talking about this old man, after a hard day's work in the field, where he and his broken walk are coming up the road. But he's strong, in spite of being so tired, because he's headed [home] to get his feet under the table and to get that hot dinner that's waiting for him. And that's the 'East St. Louis Todalo.'"

Trumpeter Bubber Miley apparently first thought of the opening melody. Writing in 1940, Roger Pryor Dodge reports: "Miley told me that the inspiration for the East St. Louis Toodle-O came one night in Boston as he was returning home from work. He kept noticing the electric sign of the dry-cleaning store Lewando's. The name struck him as exceedingly funny and it ran through his head and fashioned itself into 'Oh Lewandos, oh Lewandos'" (which fits the rhythm of the opening theme).

Whatever its origin, the piece became Duke's signature song for a number of years, and was a showcase for Miley's growling, plunger-mute style. Miley died in 1932, but the tune stayed in Ellington's book, Miley's part going to first Cootie Williams, then Ray Nance. As was his custom, Ellington rewrote his arrangement several times over the years.

"Toodle-oo" is unlike any other song in the traditional jazz repertoire, and will perpetually bear the stamp of Duke Ellington. It opens with an eerie ostinato bass line, which continues as the trumpet enters with the blues-inflected, minor-key theme—just the outline of a melody, with space for the special effects of the cornet. The solo section goes to major, and the cornet returns with the theme at the end to wrap up the tune.

Duke recorded "Toodle-oo" more than 10 times, and, for the most part, other musicians have steered clear of it. An exception is a notable version by Steely Dan on their 1974 album *Pretzel Logic*. Jeff "Skunk" Baxter used a wah-wah pedal to imitate Bubber Miley's trumpet on the electric guitar.

Everybody Loves My Baby (music: Spencer Williams, lyrics: Jack Palmer, 1924): Spencer Williams (1889-1965) is a relatively unknown but central figure in jazz history, having penned some of the core tunes of the Dixieland repertoire, including "Basin Street Blues," "Royal Garden Blues," "I've Found a New Baby," "Mahogany Hall Stomp," "Shimmy-Sha-Wobble," "I Ain't Gonna Give Nobody None of My Jelly Roll," and "Tishomingo Blues." Born in New Orleans, Williams has the fascinating distinction have having been raised (and pampered) by Lulu White, the famed madam who owned and operated the glorious Mahogany Hall on Basin Street. With music in his head and passable skills as a pianist, Williams found his way to Chicago by his late teens, where he joined up with publisher Clarence Williams (also from Louisiana but no relation). A string of hit songs followed, launching a successful career as a composer, performer and singer.

"Everybody Loves My Baby" is a minor key romp with a catchy riff that became an instant favorite among jazz musicians. The tune was so successful that Spencer followed up with a sequel, "I've Found a New Baby" (1926), also with words by White lyricist Jack Palmer. The songs are very similar and both are Dixieland standards.

Exactly like You (music: Jimmy McHugh, lyrics: Dorothy Fields, 1930): Although the 1930 Broadway show *International Review* achieved little success and was soon forgotten, two of its songs became megahits: "Exactly like You" and "On the Sunny Side of the Street." By this time, the McHugh/Fields partnership was in full stride and turning out a string of fabulous tunes. McHugh's deceptively simple melody is the perfect complement to Fields' charming lyrics, with lines such as: "Now I know why Mother taught me to be true," which, of course, sets up a rhyme with the title words of the song.

Several popular recordings soon followed (Ruth Etting's had the biggest hit), but jazz musicians were a little slower in embracing the song. Although Louis Armstrong recorded "Exactly like You" in 1930, it wasn't until Benny Goodman's 1936 recording (featuring Lionel Hampton) that jazz musicians joined the bandwagon. Django Reinhardt and Stephane Grappelli laid down a classic recording the following year, and others soon began recording their own versions. Teddy Wilson made a smooth instrumental version in 1939 and Lester Young recorded the number the same year with Glenn Hardman and his Hammond Five. This unusual ensemble consisted of Hardman on organ, Lee Castle on trumpet (see entry on "June Night"), Jo Jones on drums, Freddie Green on guitar, and Lester on tenor. The results are odd—the technique of jazz organ as we know it today had not yet been developed, and the result sounds like swing musicians jamming with a theater organ. Nevertheless, the rhythm is solid and the solos are excellent.

But a large part of the attraction of "Exactly like You" lies in the lyrics. Among the scores of recordings made in recent years in many genres, an especially swinging yet accurate treatment of Dorothy's words can be heard by Michael Feinstein on his 2008 album *The Sinatra Project*. Michael has pretty much become the guardian of the American Songbook of our generation, and he never fails to treat the music with artistry and respect.

Farewell Blues (music: Paul Mares, Leon Roppolo and Elmer Schoebel, 1922): Mares, Roppolo, and Schoebel were the cornetist, clarinetist, and pianist, respectively, of the famed New Orleans Rhythm Kings, the most acclaimed of the early White jazz bands that followed the Original Dixieland Jazz Band. Like the Original Dixieland Jazz Band, NORK wrote much original material, often as a collective effort with shared publishing rights. They recorded their classic version of this song in August, 1922, and Roppolo's clarinet solo became famous as one the first examples of a full-chorus improvised jazz solo. Over the years, many instrumentalists copied and performed this solo note-for-note.

As with many early songs entitled "blues," "Farewell Blues" does not follow the standard 12-bar blues structure; rather, it is based on a 16-bar structure in AABA form. Nevertheless, there is a distinctive blues quality throughout, supporting the thesis that "the blues is a feeling, not a form."

Reportedly, it was the NORK recording of "Farewell Blues" that inspired a group of students from Austin High School in Chicago to become musicians. That group included clarinetist Frank Teschemacher, saxophonist Bud Freeman, cornetist Jimmy McPartland, and several others who would go on to become some of the hottest jazz musicians of the day. After school they would gather at a local ice cream parlor which had a phonograph and some records. As reported by Nat Shapiro and Nat Hentoff, McPartland recalled: "One day they had some new Gennett records on the table, and we put them on. They were by the New Orleans Rhythm Kings, and I believe the first tune we played was 'Farewell Blues.' Boy, when we heard that—I'll tell you we went out of our minds. Everybody flipped. It was wonderful…. Right then and there we decided we would get a band and try to play like these guys." Today the "Austin High Gang" are considered among the pioneering musicians of Chicago Style Jazz.

Five Foot Two, Eyes of Blue—Has Anybody Seen My Gal? (music: Ray Henderson, lyrics: Sam M. Lewis and Joseph Young, 1925): A cutesy novelty song typical of the 20s, the lyrics are mostly about a description of the missing girl. Fortunately, we have her picture, complete with "turned up nose" and "turned down hose," at least according to illustrator Sidney Leff who depicted her for the sheet music cover. Unfortunately, the sheet music, though long out of print, is still under copyright and could not be included here.

Unlike sheet music of later decades, which often had a photograph of the recording artist on the front cover, prior to the mid 1930s publishers hired an illustrator to convey the emotional content of the song. The illustrators worked free-lance only and received no recognition other than the possible inclusion of their initials in the picture. Sidney Leff drew some two thousand of these covers, including such songs as "Stormy Weather," "Sophisticated Lady," "Ain't Misbehavin'," and "Yes, Sir, That's My Baby." The work of Leff, as well as many other contributors, was artistic in its own right, and it is not unreasonable to think that their depictions had an impact on how performers and the public perceived the intentions of the song.

The California Ramblers had one of the first of many interpretations of the song by jazz bands. The Ramblers, one of the top White jazz-inspired bands of the 20s, did not come from California, nor were they based there. Like many organizations of the period, they simply chose the name because they thought it sounded good. "Five

Foot Two" was a Number 1 hit for Gene Austin in 1926, and many pop, big-band, and country hits appeared in the coming decades. "Five Foot Two" can be heard in *The Great Gatsby* (1974).

The Fish Man (Le Marchand de Poissons) (music: Sidney Bechet, lyrics: Fernand Bonifay, 1956): Although not as famous as Louis Armstrong, Sidney Bechet (1897-1959) also pioneered the art of solo improvisation in jazz, and must be ranked among the greatest of New Orleans musicians. Coming from a middle-class Creole family, he was formally trained as a clarinetist, but soon turned to jazz, eventually adopting the soprano saxophone as his primary instrument. He was known for his inventive solos, intense sound, and boundless musical energy. He was among the earliest jazz musicians to seek opportunities abroad, eventually settling in France. While his absence from the U.S. jazz scene caused him to be nearly forgotten, he became quite famous in his new homeland.

An American tourist in the 1950s once remarked, "Sidney could have become mayor of Paris if he wanted to. Crowds of people followed him through the streets. I was never so surprised in my whole life as when I discovered that a compatriot, whom I had barely heard of, had become the darling of the French." While enjoying his pop-star status, Bechet continued to compose songs in the New Orleans tradition, recognizable by their French titles, such as "Dans Le Rue D'Antibes," Petite Fleur," and "Si Tu Vois Ma Mere."

"Le Marchand" is a cheerful number about a boy named Gaston who sells fish on the street. It has a bouncy melody start to finish, and a change to habanera rhythm in the middle—a technique that Jelly Roll Morton referred to as the "Spanish tinge." Bechet recorded the tune with French musicians in Paris in 1952. Other recordings are scarce, as Bechet's tunes tend to have such a personal stamp on them that other musicians sometimes avoid them. An exception is a fine recording of "Le Marchand" (titled "The Fish Vendor" on the CD) by New Orleans clarinetists Tim Laughlin and Jack Maheu (1995).

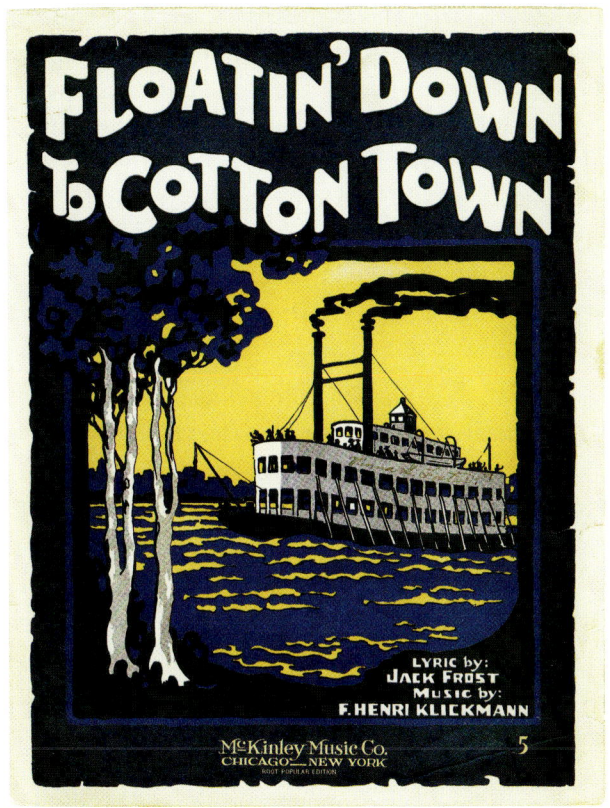

"Floatin' down to Cotton Town," by Frank Henri Klickmann and Jack Frost, is one of many tunes of the era that incorporate nostalgic imagery of the South. (Courtesy Lilly Library, Indiana University, Bloomington, Indiana.)

Floatin' down to Cotton Town (music: Frank Henri Klickmann, lyrics: Jack Frost, 1919): Frank Henri Klickmann (1885-1966) was a successful musician out of Chicago who started out as a Ragtime composer and then expanded into popular music. He published more than 100 works, many of which were quite good, but few of which have endured. Harold G. "Jack" Frost (1893-1959) was a competent lyricist who teamed up with Henri in the 1910s and 20s, when they turned out dozens of catchy tunes. Frost's songs reflected the playful spirit of the day, with numbers such as "I'm Going to Bring a Wedding Ring," "Finders Is Keepers and I Found You," and "You Can't Afford to Marry if You Can't Afford a Ford."

"Floatin' down to Cotton Town" builds on the stereotypical "Gone with the Wind" image of the South, replete with steamboats, cotton blossoms, sugar cane, and banjos, all sung to "my little honey lamb." The well-constructed melody is actually a perfect fit for the lyrics, and despite the hackneyed imagery, the song hangs together quite well. Early jazz versions of song are rare, but both Wingy Manone and Fats Waller each recorded the song in 1936, and by the 1950s most traditional jazz bands included the song in their repertoire, usually as a rousing stomper. For a sparkling rendition that remains true to the song's era (complete with harmonized vocals), listen to Dan Levinson and his Canary College Jazz Orchestra on their 2005 album *Crinoline Days*.

Gee Baby Ain't I Good to You (music: Don Redman, lyrics: Andy Razaf, 1929): Saxophonist Don Redman (1900-1964) was a highly influential arranger, introducing much of the style that led to the Big Band Era. He pioneered the technique of having the various sections of a big band play contrasting figures that complemented one other. During the 20s, he wrote most of the arrangements for the Fletcher Henderson band. From 1927 to 1931 he was with McKinney's Cotton Pickers. During his tenure with the organization this Detroit-based ensemble was one of the most popular African-American bands in the country. Redman left the Cotton Pickers in 1931 to form his own band. He is also the composer of "Cherry" and "Save it Pretty Mama."

Redman introduced "Gee Baby" with McKinney's Cotton Pickers in 1929, singing the vocals himself in a half-spoken, half-sung style of delivery. The song has a winding, haunting melody and unusual chord progression that seems to begin in one place and end up in another. Perhaps this explains why the song was pretty much ignored by other musicians for more than ten years. Recordings began to appear in the 1940s, and Nat "King" Cole's 1944 hit record of the song stimulated a strong revival. The tune soon became common for both pop singers and jazz musicians of all styles.

Georgia on My Mind (music: Hoagy Carmichael, lyrics: Stuart Gorrell, 1930): Of all the musicians whose parents wanted them to be lawyers, Hoagy actually listened. He graduated from the Indiana University School of Law in 1926 and passed the bar in 1927, but he just wanted to write songs. He wrote "Stardust" that same year, which pretty much guaranteed that his wish was going to happen. "Stardust" went on to become one of the most recorded songs of the 20th century.

By 1930, Hoagy had hit his stride. With songs like "Riverboat Shuffle," "Stardust" and "Rockin' Chair" under his belt, he settled down to write a string of great tunes with an unmistakable sound. "Georgia," one of his best-known songs, typifies his style with its lazy, lilting, winding melody that seems in no hurry to get anywhere. C-melody saxophonist Frankie Trumbauer had a respectable hit with the song in 1931, while Mildred Bailey had a huge one, but it was Hoagy's own rendition that has become of particular historical interest. Hoagy was a fine singer in his own right, and the outstanding lineup of musicians on the date included Joe Venuti, Jack Teagarden, and Bix Beiderbecke. This was to be Bix's last recording session, and fittingly, he plays the closing bars of the song as a muted cornet solo. In 2014, the recording was inducted into the Grammy Hall of Fame.

Hoagy wrote "Georgia" with his sister in mind, but everyone associates the song with the state. Not surprisingly, following hits by Ray Charles (who was from Georgia) in 1960 and Willie Nelson (1978), the tune was declared the official state song of the state of Georgia. (Never mind that Hoagy had never even been to Georgia when he wrote the song.) Michael Bublé sings a beautiful rendition of "Georgia" on his 2009 album *Crazy Love*.

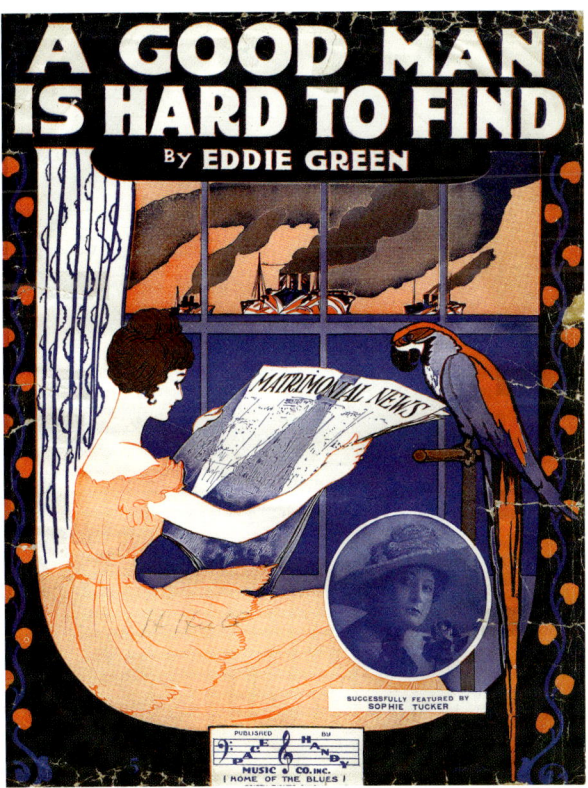

"A Good Man is Hard to Find," by Eddie Green, was a favorite among blues singers. (Courtesy Lilly Library, Indiana University, Bloomington, Indiana.)

A Good Man is Hard to Find (music and lyrics: Eddie Green, 1918): A lyric-driven song with a nondescript melody, this bluesy number made quite a splash in its day. African-American songwriter Eddie Green published only a few tunes in his lifetime, but this one was enough to give him a place in history. Pioneer jazzman Wilbur Sweatman had a small hit with the number in 1919, but it was Sophie Tucker's adoption of the song in her act that stimulated sheet music sales. (Some say Sophie was responsible for the gag of reversing the adjectives in the title; others say Mae West.)

The song came along at a good moment for W.C. Handy, who had just moved his publishing house (Pace and Handy) from Chicago to New York, gambling big on his good fortune with "Beale Street Blues." The proceeds from "A Good Man" ensured the success of their company, at least for the time being. The illustration for the sheet music cover was done by William and Fredrick Starmer (who drew, possibly, a quarter of all sheet music covers prior to 1920). Their British upbringing evidently inspired a more, let's say, Currier-and-Ives interpretation of the song's meaning. A young woman is pictured reading a newspaper entitled "Matrimonial News," while outside the window can be seen warships steaming on the water. Probably not what Sophie Tucker had in mind.

The song has cleverly imbedded "breaks" that provide open spaces for singers to deliver the punch lines. The chorus begins "A good man is hard to find, You always get the other kind, Just when you think that he is your pal [BREAK] You look for him and find him fooling 'round some other gal." Bessie Smith's 1928 recording is excellent—she tweaks the words to suit her style and pretty much replaces the melody with her own blues-laced lyricism. But singers weren't the only ones to have fun with this number. A 1951 recording under the leadership of drummer George Wettling with some of the Eddie Condon boys features some gutsy plunger work by cornetist Wild Bill Davison.

Goodbye (music and lyrics: Gordon Jenkins, 1935): Jenkins had written the song in 1934 to express his loss when his wife died in childbirth. Jenkins, a staff arranger for Isham Jones at the time, presented the number to his boss, but Jones rejected it as being "too sad." Later that year, while talking with his friend Benny Goodman, the latter mentioned that he was looking for a theme song for a radio show he was about to begin called "Let's Dance," scheduled to premier on December 1, 1934. When Jenkins showed "Goodbye" to Benny, he liked it, requested an arrangement, and adopted it as his closing theme. The song was soon known by listeners from coast to coast.

"Goodbye" is arguably one of the saddest and eeriest melodies in the American Songbook. The opening bars (supported by a dissonant obbligato figure in the Jenkins arrangement), have a funeral-march quality, while an unusual harmonic structure moves the song steadily forward. The form of the song is also unusual, in that the middle section sugar cane, yielding a symmetrical ABA form. This is so unexpected that some performers repeat the A section anyway.

Goodman's September 1935 recording (an instrumental number) became a hit, reaching Number 20 on the charts in 1935. Andy Kirk's band introduced the first vocal recording of the song in 1938, and it wasn't until 1955 that Goodman (with Rosemary Clooney) finally recorded a vocal version. For a recent version hear clarinetist Joe Barrett on his 2012 album *Memories of You*.

Grandpa's Spells (Jelly Roll Morton, 1923): The copyright was filed a few weeks after the first recording, but this composition probably dates from early in Jelly Roll's career. For one thing, his original manuscript indicates a time signature of two-four, which was typical of rags, not jazz compositions. Moreover the piece actually sounds like a rag, particularly the first strain, more so than any of his other compositions. Jelly Roll's performances, however, are anything but Ragtime. Not only does he swing and improvise, but on the piano roll he actually repeats sections with variations made up on the spot in order to extend the overall length of the piece. He frequently did this when making piano rolls, indicating that he had complete control of his materials, and was far beyond reproducing memorized pieces by rote.

There are many interesting aspects to "Grandpa's Spells," including the three contrasting melodies (Ragtime, lyrical with bass counterline, and riff chorus), left hand rhythmic patterns that seem to turn the beat around, and, of course, the famous "crashes" in the third strain. Presumably, Grandpa's "spells" were moments when he nodded off, which the pianist demonstrates by descending upon the keyboard with hands, elbows, head, or whatever body part is presently available. Jelly Roll made a solo piano recording in July 1923, a piano roll in 1924, and a band recording with the Red Hot Peppers in 1926.

For a long time, the number was usually only performed by pianists, but revivalist bands changed that, with recordings by Lu Watters (1949) and Turk Murphy (1957). An excellent recording by a smaller ensemble was made by New Orleans clarinetist Tom Fischer (2006), and among the finer solo piano versions is a 2014 recording by Stephanie Trick.

"Grizzly Bear," by George Botsford and Irving Berlin," dates from Berlin's early days as a lyricist only. Soon after he would write his own melodies as well. (Courtesy Lilly Library, Indiana University, Bloomington, Indiana.)

Grizzly Bear (music: George Botsford, lyrics: Irving Berlin, 1910): The Grizzly Bear dance originated in San Francisco around 1909 and soon spread across the country. The motions were meant to imitate the clumsy movements of a bear, thus the dance step was anything but graceful. Not missing a beat, Florenz Ziegfeld put the dance in his *Follies of 1910*, introduced by Fanny Brice. Moral watch guards and civic leaders were not amused by the Grizzly Bear, and by 1912 New York, as well as several other cities, banned it along with other "degenerate" dance movements. The public responded, of course, by completely ignoring the ban and the dance appeared regularly on Broadway and in various vaudeville and cabaret acts.

George Botsford, a well-known rag composer of the day, wrote "Grizzly Bear Rag" as a wordless piano composition. As luck would have it, the yet-unknown Irving Berlin had just signed on with the Ted Snyder publishing company, which issued "Grizzly Bear Rag." The song was republished with lyrics by Irving Berlin, and it soon became a hit, with top selling recordings by both the American Quartet and Arthur Collins in 1911. It's insightful to have a glimpse of Irving Berlin's early efforts at songwriting (this was a year prior to "Alexander's Ragtime Band," the song that ensured his success), and note how in step with the times he was (and would remain throughout his career), with lines such as: "Talk about yo' bears that Teddy Roosevelt shot, they couldn't class with what old San Francisco's got."

"Grizzly Bear" is a shortened version of the multi-part rag it derives from, with the trio relabeled as the "chorus" and the C section eliminated. Traditional jazz bands generally play the entire number as it appeared in the rag, though without adhering strictly to the form. George Botsford can be heard playing his own number on a 1925 piano roll.

Hard Hearted Hannah, the Vamp of Savannah (Jack Yellen, Milton Ager, Bob Bigelow, and Charles Bates, 1924): Jack Yellen and Milton Ager were the heavyweights on this group songwriting effort. Yellen (1892-1991) was an immensely successful lyricist and screenwriter, while Ager (1893-1979) wrote the melodies to dozens of well-known tunes. Their collaborative efforts also include "Ain't She Sweet" and "Happy Days Are Here Again."

"Hannah" is a comic song about a gal "who likes to see men suffer." The melody opens up with several "breaks" allowing the punch lines to come through, such as "Brother, she's the polar bear's pajamas" and "there was Hannah pouring water on a drowning man." It's not a blues in terms of form, but is absolutely laced with blues harmony and melody throughout.

At least three hit recordings followed the tune's publication, the one by Cliff Edwards (1924) probably being the most jazz-flavored. "Hannah" has proven to be quite adaptable to many types of treatment, and artists as diverse as Jim Croce, Bobby Darin, Carol Burnett and Toni Tennille have all had a whack at it. The song is performed by Ella Fitzgerald (playing the character of Maggie Jackson) in the 20s-inspired film *Pete Kelly's Blues* (1955). More recently, Nikki McKibbin won third place with the number in the debut season of the television series *American Idol*.

Heebie Jeebies (Boyd Atkins, 1926): This was Louis Armstrong's second recorded vocal, and his first commercial hit with his Hot Five band. The song created quite a sensation in its day because of Armstrong's scat chorus. The far-fetched story, but one that Armstrong repeated throughout his life and which fellow band members corroborated, was that he dropped his music during the recording session and had to make up nonsense syllables to finish the vocal chorus. In any case, while it cannot be said that Armstrong invented scat singing, it is reasonable to claim that this recording made it popular.

Business interests moved quickly to capitalize on this success. Since the song is about a dance called the "Heebie Jeebies," which in reality didn't yet exist, nationally known producer Floyd Du Pont was engaged to provide steps to the song, and a professional dancer was photographed demonstrating the new dance. (All of this was following closely on the heels of the previous dance craze, the "Black Bottom.") Soon newspapers across the country were running the illustrations meant to teach readers how to perform the step. Ethel Waters recorded her version of the song that fall (and if anybody could give Louis a run for his money as a singer, she could), and the rage continued. The sheet music was published shortly after, entitled "Dance Called Heebie Jeebies," with pictures of Atkins, Waters, and the Hot Five ensemble on the front cover.

High Society (Porter Steele, 1901): New Orleans bassist Wellman Braud (1891-1966) remembered, "It wasn't a dance in New Orleans until they played 'High Society.'" This beloved classic of New Orleans jazz is a high-spirited march, complete with introduction, dogfight, and trio. Early on it became and remained one of the core compositions in the traditional jazz repertoire. Its success and popularity were largely due to New Orleans clarinetist Alphonse Picou (1878-1961). Picou came from a wealthy Creole family and received early training in music. He became a professional musician at a young age, playing in both classical and jazz orchestras. Recognized as one of the earliest of jazz practitioners, Picou's style, like that of fellow jazz musicians at the time, involved embellishment of the melody rather than improvisation.

Accordingly, Picou adapted the piccolo part in "High Society" into a decorative clarinet solo, which he repeated every time he performed the number. Right from the start, other clarinetists learned his solo, and to this day it is common for clarinetists to quote either a few bars or Picou's entire solo before embarking on their own creations. In the late teens, Picou moved to Chicago for a while, but didn't like the north and returned to New Orleans, where he lived a long life as one of most venerated musicians in the city's history. He died in 1961 at the age of 82, and his funeral procession was said to be one of the largest the city had ever seen.

The first well-known recording of "High Society" was made by Prince's band in 1911. Charles Adams Prince (1869-1937) had several dozen best-selling records between 1905 and 1923. As musical director for Columbia Records, it was his charge to assemble bands to record the most popular tunes of the day. Chances are the public didn't even know what he looked like, let alone the names of the musicians in his band. All they knew was that they could depend on him for solid renditions of their favorite songs. But Prince recorded the number as a standard march, as jazz was still unknown to most of the country.

Joe Oliver had the first notable jazz recording of "High Society" in 1923, featuring Baby Dodds on the clarinet solo, and the record sold quite well. But that was about it. Jazzed-up marches might have provided the foundation for jazz, but audiences up north weren't flocking to the New Orleans classics just yet. Recordings of "High Society" are scarce during the 20s and 30s. But there is one special session from 1939 that merits attention.

By the late 1930s, Jelly Roll Morton was on the ropes. Ridiculed for calling himself the creator of jazz, though he was more worthy of the title than anyone, and practically unknown to the general public, he was having trouble earning enough to survive. Aware that some of his compositions were now becoming top swing hits, such as "King Porter Stomp," the song that Benny Goodman himself claimed started the Swing Era, Jelly Roll attempted to get back into the action. He prepared arrangements of three of his compositions and brought them to Benny Goodman. Goodman wouldn't see him. He then approached a record dealer associated with RCA Victor asking for a recording session. He had been getting some press in *Down Beat* magazine lately (largely due to some exaggerated claims he was making out of shear desperation), and he got the okay. In September 1939 Jelly Roll Morton and his New Orleans Jazzmen went into the studio.

Morton prepared arrangements and asked for the best New Orleans men in New York. He got five of them: Sidney Bechet and Albert Nicholas on reeds, Wellman Braud on bass, Zutty Singleton on drums, and himself on the piano. Local musicians filled out the rest of personnel. On the first day in the studio Bechet was the last to arrive. What would this encounter be like? The three giants of New Orleans jazz were Armstrong, Bechet, and Jelly Roll. The pairing of Armstrong and Bechet didn't go so well. How would Bechet and Jelly Roll work together? To make matters worse, Bechet could not read, and Jelly Roll had composed written arrangements.

When Bechet arrived, before he ever had a chance to see the music stand with his part on it, Jelly Roll put his arm around him, walked him to the piano, and said, "You remember this one, Sid." He then proceeded to play through each arrangement on the session, all the while telling stories, laughing, and joking with Bechet, while

Sidney's astounding ear heard and remembered everything he was expected to do. Jelly Roll then had the boys play a run-through of "High Society" as a warm-up. The band proceeded to record more than half-a-dozen New Orleans classics, including a superb rendition of "High Society."

There are many recordings of "High Society," but the song's link to the past is so distinctive that it works best in a traditional New Orleans setting. Picou himself recorded the number in 1940, and there is actually a film clip of him playing his famous solo in 1959 at the age of 80. For a recent recording in the New Orleans tradition, listen to New Orleans clarinetist Tommy Sancton on his album *City of a Million Dreams* (2012). Sancton was a student of another legendary clarinetist, George Lewis (1900-1968), and plays with the warm, resonant sound of the old jazz masters.

"Hindustan," by Oliver Wallace and Harold Weeks. It seems that the illustrator included every stereotype of India that he could think of. (Courtesy Lilly Library, Indiana University, Bloomington, Indiana.)

Hindustan (music: Oliver Wallace, lyrics: Harold Weeks, 1917): Harold Weeks (1893-1967) was active as a songwriter in the years around 1920, producing titles in keeping with the fashionable topics of the day, especially those involving faraway places, such as "Siren of a Southern Sea," "Tropical Moonlight," and "Chong: He Came from Hong Kong." Oliver Wallace (1887-1963) initially worked as a conductor and organist, but his career skyrocketed after he joined Disney Studios in 1936. Over the coming decades, Wallace would supply the scores to some 150 Disney productions, including such well-known titles as *Dumbo*, *Cinderella*, *Alice in Wonderland* and *Peter Pan*.

"Hindustan" (referring to the geographical area in northern India) is an innocent little ditty that captured the right spirit at the right moment and became a blockbuster hit. The lyrics speak of love that sparked in the exotic land of Hindustan, and Weeks provides some vivid imagery and clever rhymes on the word "Hindustan." The tune is carefully constructed so as to start with utter simplicity at the beginning, saving the dissonant intervals and surprise chords until the end. The sheet music cover depicts the silhouette of an Indian city, against a red sky, with an elephant in the foreground (of course!).

Of the countless version of "Hindustan," a must-hear in my book is a sparkling recording by Jon-Erik Kellso on his 2007 album *Blue Roof Blues*. Kellso is one of finest Bix-inspired cornet players to ever play the horn and can be heard as a sideman on dozens of recordings.

Home, When Shadows Fall (music: Peter van Steeden, lyrics: Harry Clarkson and Geoffrey Clarkson, 1931): Peter van Steeden led a successful orchestra in the 1930s and was prominent on radio broadcasts throughout the 30s and 40s. Geoffrey Clarkson (who probably wrote the melody to the song) was a pianist who worked with various bands, including a long stint with Les Brown. "Home" was his most successful composition by far. Although he continued to write songs throughout his life, few received attention. He wrote the theme for the 1940 *Abbott and Costello Show*, and collaborated with Johnny Mercer on a song called "Time to Smile" (1966). (The latter song was included on Tony Bennett's 2004 album *The Art of Romance*.)

The early history of "Home" reveals much about the popular music industry of the day. The release of the song was delayed until a radio broadcast on the night before Thanksgiving, executives thinking that people would be in a receptive mood for the content matter of the song at that time. It worked. Also, as was the custom of the day, the 1931 sheet music issue has an illustration on the cover, showing a setting sun and a house with smoke rising from the chimney to form the letters "Home." The 1943 printing, however, has a picture of the Andrews Sisters on the cover, with no illustration.

The song has endured through the decades, and was recorded by Paul McCartney in 2012 on his album *Kisses on the Bottom*. Recommended jazz versions include those by Mildred Bailey (1933), Jack Teagarden (1944), and Muggsy Spanier (1950).

Honeysuckle Rose (music: Fats Waller, lyrics: Andy Razaf, 1929): This beloved jam session tune has been a favorite of jazz musicians since the 1930s. An exemplary riff tune of the Swing Era, the opening phrase has become a common expression in the jazz vocabulary, while the chord progression has provided the framework for many other songs based on the same harmony. The song led to the term "Honeysuckle Bridge," referring to the harmony of the B section of the structure, which also provides the harmony to hundreds of other songs. (For example, "Satin Doll," "Undecided," and "When You're Smiling" all have "Honeysuckle" bridges.)

The story behind "Honeysuckle" seems far-fetched, but then Fats Waller's lifestyle was far-fetched, so it may indeed be true. On the heels of their tremendous success with the show *Hot Chocolates* (1929), Fats and Andy Razaf were engaged to provide the songs for a new show to premier that same year, called *Load of Coal*. The deadline was short. Razaf, knowing how hard it was to even find Waller, let alone pin him down and get him working, invited him for a weekend in Asbury Park at his mother's house. Coincidentally, his mother happened to be a fine cook. Things were going swimmingly, and they had begun sketching out what would become "Honeysuckle Rose," when Fats abruptly excused himself, saying that he needed to return to Harlem. An exasperated Razaf called Waller at his home later that same day, was fortunate enough to reach him, and they completed the song via a long distance telephone call.

Load of Coal turned out to be a tremendous success. It was introduced at the popular Harlem speakeasy "Connie's Inn." Located in Harlem on Seventh Avenue at 131st St., and run by a couple of bootleggers (gangsters, if you will), Connie's featured Black song-and-dance reviews for White audiences. *Load of Coal* starred Louis Armstrong and Dewey Brown (Fats was as yet unknown as a singer and comedian), and the $15 cover charge did not deter the crowds who packed the house.

Surprisingly, it took several years for "Honeysuckle Rose" to catch on. Fletcher Henderson was the first to have a hit with the song in 1934, after which many others had successful recordings. In 1999, Waller's recording of 1934 was inducted into the Grammy Hall of Fame.

Hotter than That (Lillian Hardin Armstrong, 1927): A title that would only be known by jazz aficionados, Louis Armstrong's December 1927 recording caused a sensation at the time, and is considered by many to be one of the best jazz recordings in history. Louis not only plays daringly and beautifully, but lays down a scat chorus that must be heard to be believed. Although Lil's name appears on the copyright, Louis said in a 1951 interview that he had in fact written the song. Considering the improvisational nature of the melody, chock full of phrases that are typical of Louis, his statement seems credible.

On the other hand, Louis achieved such gigantic fame in his life that it is easy to overlook the tremendous part Lil Hardin played in making him who he was. Hardin (1898-1971) grew up in Memphis, Tennessee, became a skillful pianist, and attended Fisk University. At the age of 20 she moved to Chicago and took a job as a sheet music demonstrator, then as a pianist in cabaret orchestras. By 1921 she was playing with King Oliver, one year before Louis joined the band. In August 1922, Louis came on board, and in February 1924 Louis and Lil were married.

Musically, their union was a perfect combination. Lil was classically trained, could read, and knew harmony. Louis had personality, innate musicality, and a gifted ear for improvisation. It is questionable whether he could have prepared his original compositions for publication without her help at that time. What's more, it was Lil who masterminded Louis's career moves and made him take the risks. According to Terry Teachout in *Pops: A Life of Louis Armstrong*, Lil encouraged him to play lead and not second trumpet to Joe Oliver, and when he resisted she handed him the ultimatum: "You can't be married to Joe and to me." He quit, and at first regretted it, asking her "What do you want me to do now?" A short time after that Fletcher Henderson invited Louis to join his orchestra in New York.

Louis caused quite a stir in New York—his name was beginning to have an impact. A year later Lil decided it was time for the next step. She called him back to Chicago, arranged a job for him at the Dreamland Cafe with the band she was leading, and insisted that he be billed as "the world's greatest trumpet player." He balked, but did as he was told. Soon after, in November 1925, Louis went into the studio to make the first of the famed Hot Five recordings. And Lil made it all happen.

In 1962, Lil began writing her autobiography, but stopped when she realized some personal experiences might damage Louis' career. Deeply shaken when he died in 1971, Lil attended his funeral, riding in the family car. Her autobiography remained unfinished at her death, less than two months later, and disappeared from her house.

A Hundred Years from Today (music: Victor Young, lyrics: Ned Washington and Joe Young, 1933): Victor Young (1900-1956) was one of the undisputed masters of American popular song. A child prodigy who was sent to study music in Europe, Victor began to establish himself as a concert violinist as a teenager. He then pursued a career as a theater musician in the United States during the 20s, gradually turning toward popular music. His big break came in 1930. Isham Jones asked him to arrange a ballad version of Hoagy Carmichael's "Stardust," which up until that point had been an up-tempo instrumental number. Young's inventive treatment of the unexpected possibilities of the song inspired Mitchell Parish to add lyrics, allowing it to become one of the great romantic songs of all time. Young went on to pen some of the most beloved songs of the 20th century, including "Stella by Starlight," "My Foolish Heart," "When I Fall in Love," and "Street of Dreams."

Young wrote "A Hundred Years from Today" for the musical *Blackbirds of 1934*. It is about all that survived the flop revue. The song begins with a lilting melody to a common chord progression with a poignant unexpected note occurring in the fourth bar. Similarly, the bridge stays fairly close to conventional patterns until the very end, where a pair of dissonant notes occurs on the phrase "bound to make you feel that way."

"A Hundred Years" has inspired diverse treatments. Ethel Waters had a hit in 1933, and Lee Wiley's 1934 recording is also noteworthy. She re-recorded a wonderful remake of the song in 1957 with trumpeter Billy Butterfield, who was famous for his beautiful tone and lush ballad playing. A 1986 live recording with singer Maxine Sullivan and tenor man Scott Hamilton is also superb. Vocalist Molly Ryan sings a sweet version with guitarist Bucky Pizzarelli on *Swing for your Supper* (2013).

But the musician who "owned" the song was Jack Teagarden (1905-1964), known affectionately as "Big T." Hailed by jazz musicians as "the greatest trombone player in the world" (clarinetist Pee Wee Russell said that) and recognized as one of the most original vocalists of his generation, Jack played, sang, and spoke in a relaxed, easy-going style that is unmistakable. (When asked to name his favorite musician, Louis Armstrong said, "You mean the cat I like to play with the best. Easy. It's Jack Teagarden, Pops."

We can catch Jack performing "A Hundred Years" many times during his long career, but three high points sum up the story. First was his 1933 recording. Jack sings throughout, punctuated by brief solos by himself on trombone and Jimmy Dorsey on clarinet. Then there's his smoothly polished 1941 recording with his own big band, a unit that should have been fabulously famous but wasn't, indicating that the Fates like to create musical heroes and pop icons, but rarely both at the same time. And

"I Ain't Gonna Give Nobody None O' This Jelly Roll," by Spencer Williams and Clarence Williams. Notice the descriptor "Jazz Song," which attempts to cash in on the jazz craze that was then sweeping the nation. (Courtesy Lilly Library, Indiana University, Bloomington, Indiana.)

finally, just five years before he died, a 1959 version for Roulette Records reveals that Jack was still at the top of his game, able to gift us with still another interpretation of the song, singing and playing better than ever.

I Ain't Gonna Give Nobody None of This Jelly Roll (Spencer Williams and Clarence Williams, 1919): (Most often referred to as "I Ain't Gonna Give Nobody None of My Jelly Roll".) By 1919, when he teamed up with publisher Clarence Williams, Spencer was turning out good songs at a steady pace. In 1919, in addition to "Jelly Roll," he wrote "Yama Yama Blues" and "Royal Garden Blues." Although Clarence shared credit on many of Spencer's songs, it is unlikely that he contributed to them. He did, however, promote Spencer's songs tirelessly, using dozens of them on his recording sessions.

The subject matter of the song is "Lil' Willie Green from New Orleans," who refuses to share the cake his mother gave him with his classmates. Of course, in blues parlance, the song's content is open for whatever double entendre suits the listener. The sheet music cover, showing little Willie hoarding his prize while his friends attempt to cajole him, was illustrated by Myron "Grim" Natwick (1890-1990), one of the best in the business. Following his early career of providing sheet music covers for countless songs, Natwick became one of the leading cartoonists in Hollywood, and was the creator of Betty Boop.

"Jelly Roll" fits into the category of tunes that are blues in spirit if not in form. Intended as a fast song ("Tempo d'Jazz" appears in the music), the chord sequence is favorable to jazz improvisation. Clarinetist Wilbur Sweatman (1919) had an early recording of the song

An outstanding July 1944 recording of "I Ain't Gonna Give Nobody" featuring Pee Wee Russell on the clarinet (who topped Benny Goodman in the *Down Beat* poll that year) probably requires a few words of introduction for those unacquainted with his style. (The recording is from Volume 3 of the *Eddie Condon Town Hall Concerts*.) One the most creative jazz soloists ever to play the instrument, Pee Wee's music can come as a shock for those with pre-established opinions about what a clarinet is supposed to sound like. His unpredictable lines, haunting tone, and unexpected squawks, growls, and groans are something of an acquired taste and may take some getting used to. When cornetist Ruby Braff first heard Pee Russell, he is reported to have said, "I thought there was something wrong with my radio. I said 'What is this noise—it's not an instrument.'" Nevertheless, Pee Wee had a huge following, won the *Down Beat* Poll several times as the best clarinetist in jazz, and was loved and respected by his fellow musicians. Pee Wee takes the melody as well as an extended solo on this recording. Incidentally, there is an annual Pee Wee Russell Memorial Stomp sponsored by the New Jersey Jazz Society.

I Can't Believe That You're in Love with Me (music: Jimmy McHugh, lyrics: Clarence Gaskill, 1926): "The simple tune is the great tune," according to McHugh. "You try to limit the range to eight, or at most nine, notes, and to maintain an overall simplicity of theme so it will be easy to sing." "I Can't Believe" follows such a scheme. Moreover, like most of McHugh's tunes, the phrasing is neat, tidy, and orderly, paving the way for the lyricist to complete the song. This symmetry within symmetry, along with antecedent-consequent effect, is so balanced it reminds you of Mozart.

Lyricist Clarence Gaskill (1892-1947) was a professional pianist by the age of 16, began writing songs soon after, and opened his own publishing firm at the age of 21. He was also distinguished by his military service in World War I, as revealed in an article that appeared in the Philadelphia Inquirer on January 5, 1919:

> With the whizzing of bullets and the explosion of shells as an accompaniment, private Clarence Gaskill, of 4023 Girard Avenue, went into the battle of Verdun with unwritten song on his lips. All through the fighting the refrain stayed with him. Unconsciously he sang as he manipulated the big machine gun, until he fell in action, struck by bursting shrapnel. He was taken to the hospital, when, with returning consciousness, the song again recurred to him. Lying on his hospital cot, he put the words and music on paper and sent it to Philadelphia where it was published and has become one of the popular military songs of the day. It is, "As You Were."

Gaskill received a Purple Heart for his heroism and soon resumed his musical activities. Although not a prolific composer, he wrote several hits, including "Doo Wacka Doo" (1924), "Nobody's Business" (1925), and "Prisoner of Love" (1931). He is perhaps best remembered as the lyricist for Cab Calloway's theme song "Minnie the Moocher" ("The Hi-De-Ho Song," 1931).

"I Can't Believe" was McHugh's second big hit, ("When My Sugar Walks down the Street" was the first) and 1926 was when his career began to take off. He had recently broken off with his lyricist Al Dubin ("My trouble with him was that he was always getting drunk and disappearing on me") and was looking for someone who would share his drive and commercial instincts. Gaskill was available and had just supplied the lyrics to Earl Carroll's *Vanities of 1925*. Two years later McHugh would form a steady partnership with Dorothy Fields that would become one the most celebrated songwriting teams in history.

"I Can't Believe" was a sizable hit in its day, but all sizable hits do not become enduring jazz classics. Ultimately, it is the musicians who make the standards by adopting the song in their repertoire and continuing to perform and record it. Louis Armstrong led the way with his 1930 recording, and musicians from Artie Shaw to Charlie Parker to Frank Sinatra have all weighed in with their interpretations.

I Can't Give You Anything but Love (music: Jimmy McHugh, lyrics: Dorothy Fields, 1928): The 20s were the busiest years the Broadway theater ever had. Nowadays, perhaps 40-50 different shows will open per season. In 1928, more than 250 shows opened on Broadway. In the midst of all that activity, if a show ran a few hundred performances, it was considered very successful. *Blackbirds of 1928* ran for 518 performances, making it the longest running all-Black show of its time.

Certainly the popularity of "I Can't Give You" contributed to the success of the show, and vice versa. Surprisingly, the song was not an instant success. According to Fields, sometime before *Blackbirds*, she and McHugh overheard a conversation between a poor couple standing in front of Tiffany's window, with the man saying "Gee, Honey, I can't give you anything but love." She claimed that they rushed home and completed with song within an hour. But they had no use for it just then, so they put it on the shelf. Early in 1928, McHugh convinced impresario Harry Delmar to let them contribute songs to his revue *Delmar's Revels*. Among the songs they contributed was "I Can't Give You Anything but Love." The song was not well received on opening night, and Delmar hated it, supposedly telling them, "Take your song and get it out of the theater." They tried one more time with *Blackbirds* and this time the magic worked. "I Can't Give You" was the major success of the show. It became a runaway hit in 1928 and remains one of the most durable and beloved songs in the American Songbook. It can be heard on *Cheek to Cheek*, the 2014 Grammy Award-winning album by Tony Bennett and Lady Gaga.

I Gotta Right to Sing the Blues (music: Harold Arlen, lyrics: Ted Koehler, 1932) Harold Arlen (1905-1986) never became a household name as did George Gershwin, Cole Porter, and Irving Berlin, but he was known and loved by musicians as soon as his songs began to circulate. It was often noted that of all the White songwriters, Arlen had a gift for capturing the African-American spirit in his songs, and his compositions bear this out: "Come Rain or Come Shine," "Stormy Weather," and "Blues in the Night" are just a few examples. It is not surprising that he was chosen to supply songs for the Cotton Club during its heyday in the early 1930s.

"I Gotta Right" was actually written for a Broadway show: Earl Carroll's *Vanities* (1932). Cab Calloway (1933), Louis Armstrong (1933), and Benny Goodman (1934) all had early hits with the number, but musicians generally associate the tune with Jack Teagarden, who adopted it as his theme song when he formed his big band in 1939. Like Arlen, "Big T" understood this kind of music profoundly, and for that reason is sometimes called "King of the Blues Trombone."

I Never Knew That Roses Grew (music Ted Fiorito, lyrics: Gus Kahn, 1925): Ted Fiorito was a pianist and bandleader who was popular on radio during the 20s and 30s. His recordings sold well: in 1934 Fiorito had two Number 1 hit records, one with Harry Warren's "I'll String Along with You" and one with Johnny Noble's "My

Little Grass Shack in Kealakekua, Hawaii." Fiorito composed more than 100 songs, among them "Toot Toot Tootsie" (1922), "When Lights Are Low" (1923), and "Charley My Boy" (1924).

"I Never Knew" has had staying power. Gene Austin had the first hit in 1926, Sam Donahue revived it for a Number 2 hit in 1947, and the Glenn Brown Trio had a successful recording in 1955. Keely Smith recorded a hard-swinging version with the Billy May Orchestra in 1959. Moreover, "I Never Knew" has remained a favorite jam tune among jazz musicians, both traditional and modern, largely due to the song's alluring chord sequence. It can be heard in the films *Pete Kelly's Blues* (1955) and *I'll See You in My Dreams* (1951), a biopic of lyricist Gus Kahn. Among recent recordings of note are those by Kenny Davern (1988), New Orleans guitarist Larry Scala (*Big Easy Swing*, 2007), and cornetist Ed Polcer with clarinetist Allan Vache (*With Thee I Swing*, 2009).

"I Never Knew," by Tom Pitts, Ray Egan, and Roy Marsh. Beginning around 1920 there was an increasing tendency to include artists' pictures on sheet music covers. By the 1930s illustrated covers all but disappeared. (Courtesy Lilly Library, Indiana University, Bloomington, Indiana.)

I Never Knew I Could Love Anybody like I'm Loving You (Tom Pitts, Ray Egan, Roy K. Marsh, 1920): Paul Whiteman's name appears on the copyright for this song, but it's probable that his only involvement was a promise to plug the number with his band, a common practice of the day. Following his tremendously successful summer engagement in Atlantic City, by late 1920 Whiteman had the hottest band in America. It's hard to fathom just how popular the band was. Three records released in the fall of 1920 became Number 1 hits. He would have 16 top-ten hits in 1921 and 19 top-ten hits in 1922. In October 1921, Whiteman signed an unprecedented two-year contract with the Palais Royal in New York City as the best-paid band in the country.

Whiteman's recording of "I Never Knew" was released in the spring of 1921 and became a Number 7 hit. The tune was a favorite of the Palais Royal crowd, where he played the number every evening. The recording is unique in that it includes a rare feature for Whiteman himself, playing viola in a duet with alto saxophonist Pee Wee Byers. Whiteman's version is, of course, a dance arrangement. Jazz renditions can be heard by Benny Goodman (1946), Jimmy McPartland (1959), and Earl Hines (1973).

I Want Big Butter and Egg Man (Percy Venable, 1926): Initially, "butter and egg man" was simply a term for the deliveryman who brought such items. Later, the term took on the meaning of a rich farmer from the country who came to the city for a good time and eventually, quoting the Oxford English Dictionary: "a wealthy, unsophisticated man who spends freely." The phrase seems to have come in common usage in part because of Texas Guinan.

Mary Louse Cecilia "Texas" Guinan was a saloon keeper and movie actress who ran one of the most elite speakeasies in New York. (George Gershwin used to hang out there and play piano.) She was reported to have referred to her patrons as "butter and egg men." In 1925, George S. Kaufman had a hit comedy on Broadway entitled *The Butter and Egg Man*, about a sly producer who seeks to ensnare wealthy and vulnerable investors. The time was now ripe for a song with that name, and Percy Venable supplied one for Louis Armstrong in 1926. Louis recorded the song in November 1926 with the title of "Big Butter and Egg Man from the West" and his solo is acclaimed as one of the best he ever played. (Muggsy Spanier reproduced the solo verbatim on his recording of the number in 1939).

On Louis' recording, the first vocal chorus is presented by May Alix, who offers a rather stiff version of the melody. But this is exactly what Louis needs to set up his responding chorus, which is sheer fun as he mixes speech, scat, and melody, as only he could do.

A hearty, New Orleans-styled interpretation can be heard by vocalist/trombonist Emily Asher on her 2015 album *Meet Me in the Morning*.

"I Wish I Could Shimmy like My Sister Kate," by Armand Piron, helped to make Clarence Williams one of the leading publishers of his day. (Courtesy Sandy Marrone, Cinnaminson, NJ.)

I Wish I Could Shimmy like My Sister Kate (Armand J. Piron, 1919): Armand Piron (1888-1943) was a Creole violinist and bandleader from New Orleans. In 1915, he teamed up with Clarence Williams, who would later become the most successful African-American music publisher of the 20s, to form the Williams and Piron Publishing Company. The partnership worked splendidly—Williams was a keen businessman and tireless promoter with rudimentary musical skills, while Piron had a thorough music education and fronted a successful band. But when Williams expanded operations to Chicago and then New York, Piron had no interest in relocating. Finally, in 1922, Piron sold Williams his share of the business, which included all of his compositions, published or not. Among these was "I Wish I Could Shimmy," which had been copyrighted by Piron in 1919 and performed by his band, but never published. "I Wish I Could Shimmy" was one of the first publications of the newly formed Clarence Williams Music Publishing Company, and it was a smash hit. More than ten recordings were made in 1922 alone.

Louis Armstrong always claimed that he had written "I Wish I Could Shimmy," not Piron. When asked about this once, Piron said that the song was actually around for a long time before either he or Armstrong played it, performed by various bands in many different ways. Considering the structure of the song, he was probably right: the distinctive but basic chord progression with built-in breaks invites multiple melodic variations, while the concept of the tune suggests many possibilities for the lyrics, undoubtedly many of them risqué.

Here are the published lyrics to the chorus:

> I wish I could shimmy like my sister Kate,
> She shivers like the jelly on a plate.
> My Mammy wanted to know last night,
> Why all the boys treat sister Kate so nice.
> Ev'ry boy in our neighborhood,
> Know that she can shimmy and it's understood.
> I know I'm late, but I'll be up to date,
> When I can shimmy like my sister Kate, I mean,
> Shimmy like my sister Kate.

A "must hear" is the 1939 Muggsy Spanier recording with trombonist George Brunies taking the vocals. The tune has remained popular in New Orleans since it first came out, and can be heard on the 2011 album *Frenchmen Street Parade*, by the New Orleans Moonshiners. This ensemble, founded in 2008 by banjoist/guitarist Chris Edmunds, has become one of the hottest bands in New Orleans. "Sister Kate" was also recorded by Vince Giordano and the Nighthawks for the season 4 finale of the HBO series *Boardwalk Empire*.

I'm Confessin' That I Love You (music: Doc Daugherty and Ellis Reynolds, lyrics Al J. Neiberg, 1930): "Finders keepers" has been a tacit understanding in the music business since Tin Pan Alley days, as crafty publishers snatched up uncopyrighted material and claimed it for their own. The practice seems innocent enough when melodies are "borrowed" from deceased classical composers, but laying claims on a tune that a fellow composer neglected to copyright in a timely fashion might raise an eyebrow or two. The fact is, the melody to "I'm Confessin'" was not written by Daugherty and Reynolds, nor did they so much as contribute a note to it. In December 1929, Fats Waller recorded a tune called "Lookin' for Another Sweetie," which was written by the great African-American songwriter Chris Smith (composer of "Ballin' the Jack," "Cakewalking Babies from Home," and "Down in Honky Tonk Town"). For whatever reason, no copyright was filed for the tune, and sometime the following year Daugherty and Reynolds put their names on it, had Al Neiberg write new words and filed for copyright. Neiberg was a competent lyricist who also wrote "Talk of the Town" and "Under a Blanket of Blue."

Neiberg's rewrite may or may not be an improvement, but Sterling Grant's original lyrics are more than serviceable and somewhat charming, as can be heard on Fats Waller's recording. Fats does not sing on the record (nor does he solo), but instead features Orlando Roberson, a celebrated African-American tenor who was quite popular during the 1930s and 1940s. Nevertheless, "Lookin' for Another Sweetie" did not become popular, while "Confessin'" inspired at least half-a-dozen hits during the following decades. Louis Armstrong's 1930 rendition became the standard in the jazz world, prompting many imitations. For a gently swinging version of recent years, hear Tony Bennett and KD Lang on their 2002 album *A Wonderful World*, which also features traditionally styled saxophonist Scott Hamilton.

The QRS Music Company was the leading producer of piano rolls, capturing the top pianists of the day. Left to right in this ad are Lemuel Fowler, Clarence Williams, J. Lawrence Cook, James P. Johnson, Clarence Johnson, Luckey Roberts and Fats Waller. Sales of piano rolls peaked in the 20s, but QRS is still going strong today as a producer of piano rolls and music software.(Author's personal collection, courtesy of QRS Music Technologies http://www.qrsmusic.com/)

I'm Crazy 'bout My Baby (music: Fats Waller, lyrics: Alexander Hill, 1931): It's hard to picture now, but as of 1931 Fats Waller was virtually unknown as a vocalist, even though he was well established as a composer and pianist. It was publisher Joe Davis who is credited with making Waller a singing sensation. Waller had worked for Davis as a staff writer in 1930, and continued to supply his small publishing firm with songs after that. In February 1931, Davis published Waller's "I'm Crazy," which was recorded by King Oliver that same month. By this time, Oliver's career was in decline, and this instrumental version went nowhere. Davis then came up with the truly brilliant idea of having Fats sing his own song.

He talked to Columbia Records, who suggested that Fats be included on an upcoming session with the Ted Lewis band. This might seem an odd idea. Ted Lewis, though he led a successful organization packed with many of the finest musicians in the country, played arrangements that were somewhat stiff and corny, partial to gimmicks and novelty effects. Fats, on the other hand, came straight out of Harlem, with powerful, hard-swinging jazz pouring out of him. But he and

Davis were not averse to opportunity and they seized the moment. On March 5, Fats recorded "I'm Crazy" and a couple of other vocals with the Lewis band. As might be expected, these recordings did not produce very good results, but what they did do was open the ears of the Columbia executives to the possibilities for Waller as a vocalist. They wasted no time. On March 13, Fats was invited back to the Columbia studios to make his first piano/vocal recordings: "I'm Crazy" and "Draggin' My Heart Around." They would be the first of many to come, and the beginning of his celebrated career as a singer/entertainer.

There is another curious fact associated with this song. Between 1923 and 1931, Fats made 23 piano rolls for the QRS label, the leading company in this field. These rolls were edited by J. Lawrence Cook, an artist and arranger for the QRS company who played piano in a style very similar to Waller's. As Fats' singer career was beginning to heat up, his interest in making piano rolls was waning. He went into the studio in June of 1931 to make what would be his last piano roll for QRS. The tune was "I'm Crazy 'bout My Baby." For whatever reason, the roll could not be completed, and another session was scheduled for the following day. Waller never showed up, and Cook finished the take himself. So Waller's final piano roll is actually a combination of Waller and Cook.

For an outstanding recording of "I'm Crazy" in the Waller tradition, hear pianists Dick Hyman and Ralph Sutton go at it on their album *Just You, Just Me* (1996).

I'm Gonna Sit Right down and Write Myself a Letter (music: Fred Ahlert, lyrics: Joe Young, 1935): Fats Waller had the first big hit with this song, which has become so closely associated with him that many have assumed he wrote it. Fred Ahlert (1892-1953) gets the credit. This tune was actually Ahlert's last big hit, following an impressive list of successes: "I'll Get By," "Mean to Me," "Walking My Baby Back Home," and "I Don't Know Why." The tune was also a culminating effort for Joe Young, who had "In a Shanty in Old Shanty Town," "Lullaby of the Leaves," and "Annie Doesn't Live Here Anymore" to his credit.

Fats' recording is a pleasure to hear—a gem of both simplicity and brilliance. He begins with a four-bar introduction leading to a full chorus of piano. As a pianist, Fats had the ability to work in a lot of pianistic effects and technical brilliance while keeping the texture simple and the melody always in place. Following this is a full vocal chorus with clarinet obbligato—a fairly strict interpretation of the tune with none of the humorous antics that he often included in both live and studio recordings. For the third chorus, trumpet plays the first half and Fats finishes up with a looser interpretation of the melody, ending with a simple tag to complete the tune.

A funny story involving Fats and this tune stems from his 1942 Carnegie Hall Concert. Eddie Condon had been assigned as musical director for the evening, an excellent choice until you consider that both Eddie and Fats were copious whiskey drinkers. Prior to the concert there was a party in Fats' dressing room (was there ever not a party in Fats' dressing room?) and he was 20 minutes late getting on stage. As he sat down at the piano he forgot the scheduled program and went directly into "I'm Gonna Sit Right Down." Remembering that he was supposed to be playing his own compositions, he followed up with "Honeysuckle Rose," and then continued with random songs that came to mind, totally ignoring the prepared song list.

"I'm Gonna Sit Right Down" can be heard on Paul McCartney's 2012 album *Kisses on the Bottom*, which takes its title from the lyrics to the song.

I'm Gonna Stomp Mr. Henry Lee (Eddie Condon, Peck Kelley, George Rubens, and Jack Teagarden, 1929): A rather obscure tune in the Dixieland repertoire, "I'm Gonna Stomp" has a strong blues accent with an unusual chord progression. Trombonist Jack Teagarden co-wrote the song with bandleader Peck Kelley in the early 20s with the title "Stomp It Mr. Kelly," but it was evidently never published.

In the 20s Kelley had a successful band called Peck's Bad Boys, which at various times included jazz musicians such as Jack Teagarden, Pee Wee Russell, Louis Prima, and Wingy Manone. Kelley refused several offers to take the band out of Texas, and no recordings are known to exist. The only known recording of the song under the title of "Stomp It Mr. Kelly" was made by Texas clarinetist Jimmy (Maloney) Joy in 1925.

In 1929, for a recording with Eddie Condon, Teagarden included the song with a new title of "I'm Gonna Stomp Mr. Henry Lee." Whether Henry Lee is a reference to the famous patriot who was father to Robert E. Lee, or was simply a name pulled into the song for a convenient rhyme is unknown. It is likely that the words to the song were added for the 1929 recording by Condon, Teagarden, and Rubens (a friend of Condon's). The playful lyrics contain such nonsense phrases as "When that jazzband they begin, hits me like a quart of gin."

I've Found a New Baby (music: Spencer Williams, lyrics: Jack Palmer, 1925): Williams and Palmer wrote the song as a follow-up to their 1924 hit "Everybody Loves My Baby," and it shows. Both are fast minor key tunes in the key of D minor, with descending riff figures beginning the main chorus. Even the verses are similar. In any case, it worked, with several hit records appearing not only shortly after publication but for decades to come.

There is a curious aspect to the bridge of this tune in that some musicians play the melody two beats ahead of what is printed in the sheet music. It's hard to say when this option first appeared—it works at least as well as the original, and may in fact be an improvement. It is hinted at on Andy Preer's 1927 recording with his Cotton Club Orchestra, and is clearly played with the anticipation on the 1928 recording by Frank Teschemacher and the Chicago Rhythm Kings. Nowadays, both versions are equally common.

A great early recording was made by Joe Venuti's Blue Four, showing off the great technical skills of both Venuti and Jimmy Dorsey, who plays clarinet, alto and baritone saxophone. The song is framed with a very creative and unexpected introduction and ending.

As to the proper title "I've Found" or "I Found," the original sheet music says "I've Found a New Baby," but record labels of the time often read "I Found."

I've Got a Feeling I'm Falling (music: Fats Waller and Harry Link, lyrics: Billy Rose, 1929): Fats Waller and lyricist Andy Razaf had a productive year in 1929: the show *Hot Chocolates* opened on June 20 and became a sensation, introducing a string of great songs, including "Ain't Misbehavin'," which spawned multiple hit records. The show *Load of Coal*, opening in the fall of that year, also produced hit songs including "Honeysuckle Rose." While Waller and Razaf could have become wealthy on the royalties to "Ain't Misbehavin'" alone, about three weeks into the run of the show they foolishly accepted (or were pressured into) a deal to sell all of the *Hot Chocolates* copyrights, along with seven of their other songs, for $500. Before long, they found themselves famous but broke, and were scuffling for money. Both were hustling to write songs for anyone who would buy them.

Fats collaborated with Harry Link (who would later write "These Foolish Things") and Billy Rose (the celebrated lyricist who wrote the words to "Me and My Shadow," "It's Only a Paper Moon," and many others) to write "I've Got a Feeling" as a stand-alone tune. Fortunately, it became a pop hit that summer for Gene Austin, with Fats accompanying at the piano. Fats also recorded a version of the song that year, but as a piano solo—as of 1929 recording executives did not yet know of his talent as a singer.

"Ida, Sweet As Apple Cider," by Eddie Munson and Eddie Leonard, was popularly revived during the 20s. (Courtesy Lilly Library, Indiana University, Bloomington, Indiana.)

Ida, Sweet As Apple Cider (music: Eddie Munson, lyrics: Eddie Leonard, 1903): As the folksy title suggests, this song goes way back. Lyricist Eddie Leonard (1870-1941) was a vaudeville performer and one of the leading minstrels of his day. He published his memoirs in 1934, but strangely does not mention Eddie Munson in the book. Other than "Ida" and one obscure tune published in 1903 called "Go Take a Walk, And Don't Come Back," nothing is known of him.

TUNES OF THE TWENTIES THE SONGS | 101

Munson's lyrics, much in the spirit of the age, express pure innocence and simplicity:

> Ida, sweet as apple cider,
> Sweeter than all I know.
> Come out, in the silv'ry moonlight,
> of love we'll whisper,
> so soft and low.
> Seems though, can't live without you,
> Listen, O Honey, do!
> Ida, I idolize ya,
> Love you Ida, 'deed I do.

"Ida" experienced a revival in the 20s and several hit versions appeared. At some point Eddie Cantor became fond of the song (his wife's name was Ida) and worked it into his routine, singing it on Broadway, in the movies, on radio, and on television throughout his career, providing a tremendous boost to the song's popularity.

Eddie Cantor (1892-1964) was one of most beloved entertainers of his generation. His facial expressions and eye-rolling gestures were his trademark, earning him the nickname "banjo eyes." He was very popular with radio audiences in the 1930s, who loved his personal stories about his wife and five daughters. (See entry on "Margie.") He coined the phrase *March of Dimes* and did extensive work promoting that organization.

Many significant jazz interpretations of "Ida" exist, including those by Red Nichols (a million seller, 1927) and Benny Goodman (1937). One of the finest versions ever recorded can be heard on a 1947 record under Eddie Condon's name. In a simple two-chorus presentation, clarinetist Pee Wee Russell takes the first full chorus, recasting the melody with his fascinating angular contortions, followed by a smooth, lyrical half chorus by trombonist Jack Teagarden and a final, feisty wrap-up by Wild Bill Davison on cornet. It just doesn't get any better than that.

In a Shanty in Old Shanty Town (music: Ira Schuster and Jack Little, lyrics: Joe Young, 1932): The song, which expresses a nostalgic longing for "my tumbled down shack by an old railroad track," was likely inspired by the collections of makeshift dwellings that sprang up during the Depression. In any case, it must have struck a chord with the public, as it inspired several hits: Ted Lewis' 1932 record reached Number 1 and stayed there for ten weeks; Johnny Long revived the song in 1946 and had a million seller; and in 1956, Somethin' Smith and the Redheads had yet another hit with the song.

Ira Schuster (aka John Siras, 1889-1945) was a Tin Pan Alley pianist and songwriter. Jack Little (1899-1956) led a successful society band in the 1930s and recorded prolifically. And Joe Young (1889-1939) was a very successful lyricist, with tunes such as "You're My Everything," "Lullaby of the Leaves," and "I'm Gonna Sit Right down and Write Myself a Letter" to his credit.

The catchy melody and inviting chord progression have made "Shanty" a respectable jam session tune, and several traditional jazz versions can be heard. Recommended are Coleman Hawkins with Teddy Wilson (1944) and Matty Matlock (1958).

"Indiana," by James Hanley and Ballard MacDonald, the "unofficial" state song of Indiana bears a close resemblance to the song that really is the official state song. (Courtesy Lilly Library, Indiana University, Bloomington, Indiana.)

Indiana (music: James F. Hanley, lyrics: Ballard MacDonald, 1917): This song is often entitled by the opening lyric "Back Home Again in Indiana." You might expect it to be the state song of Indiana, but "On the Banks of the Wabash" (Paul Dresser, 1897) holds that honor. "Indiana," however, borrows much of the imagery from "Wabash" and literally quotes the identical melody for the line "When I dream about the moonlight on the Wabash." A comparison of the lyrics to both shows how similar they really are.

Chorus to "On the Banks of the Wabash":

> Oh, the moonlight's fair tonight along the Wabash,
> From the fields there comes the breath of new mown hay.
> Through the sycamores the candle lights are gleaming,
> On the banks of the Wabash, far away.

Chorus to "Indiana":

> Back home again in Indiana,
> And it seems that I can see
> The gleaming candlelight, still burning bright,
> Through the sycamores for me.
> The new-mown hay sends all its fragrance
> Through the fields I used to roam.
> When I dream about the moonlight on the Wabash,
> How I long for my Indiana home.

Official or not, "Indiana" is a signature song for the state. Since 1946, it has been performed during pre-race ceremonies at the Indianapolis 500. For more than 40 years, prior to his retirement in 2014, it was sung by Jim Nabors ("Gomer Pyle" of the *Andy Griffith Show*), backed by the Perdue All-American Marching Band. "Indiana" has also been used as a theme for newscasts and is frequently heard at various state functions. A steam clock plays the song every hour at the Indiana State Museum.

The song has been a ubiquitous jazz standard since its inception, which coincides with the birth of jazz recording. It first appears on the flip side of "Darktown Strutters' Ball" for the Original Dixieland Jazz Band in 1917. Numerous jazz recordings can be found from every decade, and also a number of original compositions that use the same chord progression. Sometimes a certain harmonic structure is so comfortable to improvise on that jazz musicians write new tunes to the same chords. (Chords are not subject to copyright restriction.) Musicologists sometimes call such derivative tunes "contrafacts." One of the most famous jazz tunes based on "Indiana" is Charlie Parker's "Donna Lee."

For many years during the 1950s and 1960s, Louis Armstrong and the All Stars used the song as their opening number in every concert. Barney Bigard, who played clarinet with the All Stars for many years, remembered "He [Louis] knew practically every Dixieland number of any era but every time we opened up he would come with "Back Home Again in Indiana."

Irish Black Bottom (music: Percy Venable, 1926): In 1926, the same year he began his famous Hot Five Recordings, Louis Armstrong was entertaining at the Sunset Cafe in Chicago. And "entertaining" is not too broad a term for what he did there. Ironically, it was Louis's clowning—his scatting, jokes, vocal contortions and just plain messing around, that attracted the attention of the Okeh Record Company and got Louis into the studio. For all of the astonishing jazz improvisation and trumpet virtuosity that can be heard on the Hot Fives, you can also get a good taste for the kind of antics he was pulling nightly at the Sunset.

This brings us to the strange title, "Irish Black Bottom." The song was written by Percy Venable, the choreographer at the Sunset, as a vehicle for Louis to do his stuff. The premise for the title is improbable but simple. In 1926 a new dance called the Black Bottom was all the rage, having surpassed the Charleston in popularity. Like the Charleston, it had a distinctive rhythmic pattern that inspired a certain dance step. For whatever reason, Venable came up with the idea of taking an Irish sounding melody (with a distinctive reference to "Wearing of the Green") and inserting Black Bottom rhythms. The lyrics tell the story of how Ireland has gone "Black Bottom crazy," with lines such as "All the laddies and cooies Laid aside their Irish reels; And I was born in Ireland, So imagine how I feels." The result is sheer fun and games, and Louis doesn't miss a laugh.

Is It True What They Say about Dixie (music: Gerald Marks, lyrics: Irving Caesar and Sammy Lerner, 1936): Gerald Marks once said, "There are probably in the neighborhood of 200 songs written about belles in crinoline and plantation-life dresses and none of the composers had ever been further south than 14th Street in Manhattan." Marks, who was born in Michigan and lived in New York, was probably as guilty as the rest. Nevertheless, there was once a nearly universal appeal for songs about the South and everybody seemed to love them. And 1936, the year Margaret Mitchell published her Pulitzer Prize-winning novel *Gone With the Wind*, was exactly the right time to present this song.

The tune was written for Al Jolson (and it shows), but Jimmy Dorsey had the Number 1 hit with it in 1936 with Bob Eberly on the vocal. Irving Caesar (who also wrote the words to "Swanee," "Tea for Two," and many other hit songs) and Sammy Lerner crafted the lyrics in a series of questions using the standard imagery of the southern stereotype, complete with magnolias, sunshine and possum. Lerner was a successful composer for film but a relatively obscure songwriter. However, one of his songs is particularly well known, even if the author's name is not: Lerner wrote the theme song to *Popeye the Sailor*. Similarly, the name Gerald Marks is not known by many, but his composition "All of Me" has become one of the most enduring standard songs in history.

For my money, the most delightful version of the song ever heard was made by Phil Harris on his 1958 album *That's What I Like about the South*. Harris was a prominent bandleader, singer, songwriter, actor, and comedian, with one of most recognized voices in America. Among his many activities, he was best known to children through his voice work in animation, such as his portrayal of Baloo (the bear) in Disney's *The Jungle Book* (1967).

It All Depends on You (music: Ray Henderson, lyrics: Buddy DeSylva and Lew Brown, 1926): Possibly the best songwriting trio in history, Henderson, DeSylva, and Brown first began their partnership with *George White's Scandals of 1925*. Although nothing memorable came from that show, they realized they were magic together and so did White. He kept them on for the 1926 show, and this time they hit pay dirt. Among the perennial songs that sprang from that show were "Lucky Day," "Black Bottom," and "The Birth of the Blues." They took Broadway by storm, formed their own publishing company, and for the next five years turned out an unstoppable chain of hits. So beloved were their catchy tunes that George Gershwin's mother once asked why her boys didn't write songs like that. The story of the famous trio is told in the 1956 film *The Best Things in Life Are Free*, which showcases many of their songs.

"It All Depends on You" was written for Al Jolson as an interpolation into his hit Broadway show *Big Boy* (1925). Paul Whiteman had a Number 2 hit with the number in 1927, and Ruth Etting, who also scored with a hit record that year, kept the song in her repertoire throughout her career. Pop stars have continued to record the song through the decades. Traditional jazz versions include those by Eddie Lang and Joe Venuti (1927), Eddie Condon (1952) and Pee Wee Russell (1959).

It Don't Mean a Thing If It Ain't Got That Swing (music: Duke Ellington, lyrics: Irving Mills, 1932): It was typical for publisher Irving Mills to add lyrics to Duke's songs after the instrumental version was completed, but this song certainly seems to suggest collaboration. The bluesy melody that opens the tune with the title words is cleverly followed by rhythmically syncopated "doo-ah" syllables, as if to demonstrate the proposition. The origin of the phrase that lends the title is disputed. Some say that it was a favorite saying of trumpeter Bubber Miley, who left Duke shortly before they recorded it and died soon thereafter. Irving Mills said that he himself coined the phrase one night when admonishing Duke's band to play more swing music on a dance gig. And trumpeter Cootie Williams, who replaced Miley, also claimed ownership. In any case, it is one of the first songs to use the word "swing" in the title.

Duke had the first recording in 1932, with Ivy Anderson on the vocals. He again recorded the song in 1945, with a completely different concept and arrangement. As with many of Duke's compositions, the tune immediately became a jazz standard, adopted by both traditionalists and modernists. A fun version was performed by Cleo Laine on *The Muppet Show* (1978). It can also be heard on the 2014 album *Cheek to Cheek* with Tony Bennett and Lady Gaga. Their driving big-band arrangement is marvelous, and their vocal interplay is splendid, but the real highlight of the cut is a dazzling swing-styled trumpet solo by George Rabbai.

Ja-Da (Bob Carleton, 1918): Pianist/composer Bob Carleton (1896-1956) published hundreds of songs that were popular in their day, but "Ja-Da" is the one that has thrived as a popular standard. It's hard to say what the public found so attractive in t he short (16-bar) song with a simple melody and nonsense lyrics:

> It goes Ja Da, Ja Da, Ja Da Ja Da, Jing Jing Jing
> Ja Da, Ja Da, Ja Da Ja Da, Jing Jing Jing
> That's a funny little bit of melody
> It's so soothing and appealing to me
> It goes Ja Da, Ja Da, Ja Da Ja Da, Jing Jing Jing!

Serious jazz musicians have shied away from some novelty songs, but not this one—it became a jazz standard from the beginning. Perhaps one reason is the compelling harmonic sequence. "Ja-Da" appears to be the first well-known song to use what has become a common chord progression. For example, the 1924 song "How Come You Do Me Like You Do" uses nearly the exact same chords. Even the modernists found the progression irresistible: Sonny Rollins uses a similar structure for his "Doxy," (1954), as does Horace Silver for his "The Preacher" (1955). (Ironically, "The Preacher" has since worked its way into the traditional jazz repertoire.)

Among the many traditional jazz recordings of "Ja-Da" are those by Bobby Hackett (1938), Bunk Johnson (1945), and Muggsy Spanier (1947).

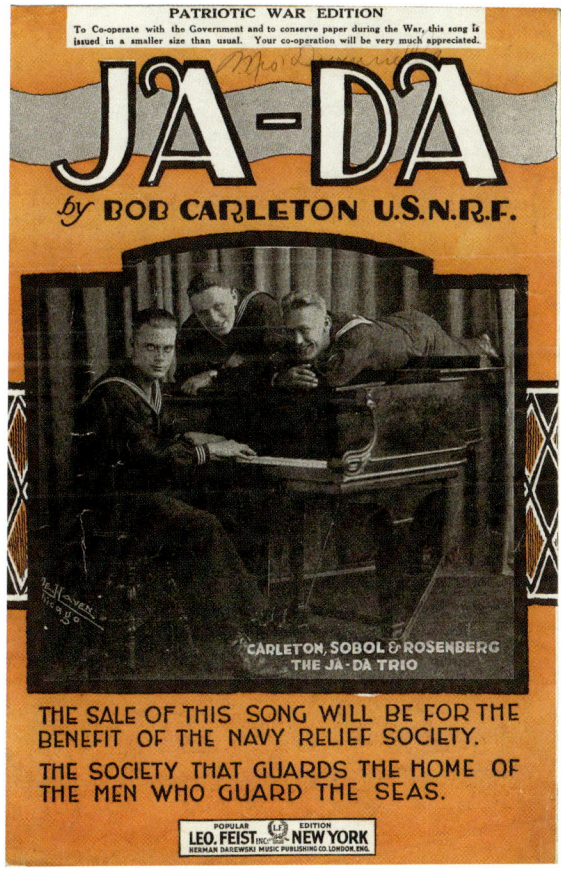

"Ja-Da," By Bob Carleton, in a Patriotic War Edition. The insert reads "To Co-operate with the Government and to conserve paper during the War, this song is issued in a smaller size than usual. Your co-operation will be very much appreciated. (Author's personal collection.)

"Japanese Sandman," by Richard Whiting and Raymond Egan, was on the flip side of "Whispering," the record that catapulted the Paul Whiteman Orchestra into fame and fortune. (Courtesy Lilly Library, Indiana University, Bloomington, Indiana.)

The Japanese Sandman (music: Richard A. Whiting, lyrics: Raymond B. Egan, 1920):

In the spring of 1920, Paul Whiteman's relatively unknown band, based in Los Angeles, landed a summer job at the Ambassador Hotel in Atlantic City. At first business was dismal, but a stroke or two of good fortune came his way. A female patron, who was never identified, loved his music so much that she kept returning, bringing with her an ever-increasing group of enthusiastic friends. As the room filled to near capacity another lucky break occurred: The Victor Phonograph Company was having its annual convention in Atlantic City, and a number of their salesmen heard the ensemble. They were impressed with the energy Whiteman's boys created and convinced their bosses to sign the band. In August, the Whiteman band went into Victor's Camden studio and made several recordings. Pressings of "Whispering" with "The Japanese Sandman" on the reverse side began to be shipped in September. Both songs became giant hits, the record sold over two million copies, and the Paul Whiteman Orchestra soon became the premiere dance band of the 20s.

The tune is a bit more than the typical novelty tune about far-away places. Richard Whiting's melody really does evoke the indigenous music of Japan, while Egan's lyrics reach beyond the typical silliness to offer something bordering on spiritual: "He'll buy your old day from you, he will take every sorrow of the day that is through, and he'll give you tomorrow just to start a life anew." Noteworthy recordings include those by Bix (1928), Django Reinhardt (1937), Dicky Wells (1937), and (of historic interest) Whiteman's recreation of 1954. Vince Giordano and the Nighthawks recorded a high-fidelity version of Whiteman's original arrangement in 2010 for the *Boardwalk Empire* HBO Series.

Jazz Me Blues (music and lyrics: Tom Delaney, 1921): Delaney (1889-1963) was quite successful in the 20s as a blues composer and pianist. He served as accompanist/manager for Ethel Waters and wrote her first hit song, "Down Home Blues" (1921). His songs, recorded by the leading blues singers of the era, include "South Bound Blues" (Ma Rainey), "Troublesome Blues" (Clara Smith), "Log Cabin Blues" (Trixie Smith), and "Follow The Deal on Down" (Bessie Smith).

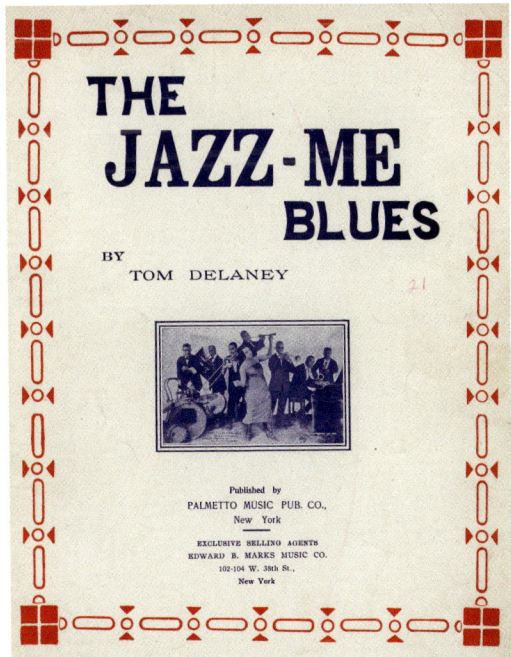

"Jazz Me Blues," by Dom Delaney, became a staple of the traditional jazz repertoire after the famous recording by the Original Dixieland Jazz Band. (Courtesy Lilly Library, Indiana University, Bloomington, Indiana.)

Today, "Jazz Me Blues" is recognized as one of the solid war horses of traditional jazz, and the 1921 recording by the Original Dixieland Jazz Band is famous. But prior to its publication date, it was recorded by blues singer Lucille Hegamin in November 1920. Listening to the recording of the well-known jazz tune is a clear indicator that jazz and blues were not quite the same thing in the early 20s, even though they shared much of the same repertoire. The four-square rhythm behind Hegamin's singing is much closer to Ragtime than to jazz.

In any case, it was the ODJB who had the hit on "Jazz Me Blues" with their May 1921 recording. As with all of their records, it was scrutinized and imitated by early jazz musicians. It made such an impact on Bix Beiderbecke that he chose it for his very first recording session, and it became his first record to be released (with "Fidgety Feet" on the flip side).

"Jazz Me Blues" became and remained a core number that jazz bands were expected to play frequently. Musicians could sometimes become weary of playing the same numbers night after night, and efforts to ward off the boredom sometimes failed. A 1950 recording session featuring Sidney Bechet and Wild Bill Davison resulted in a disagreeable incident. Pianist Joe Sullivan tended to become nasty when he drank, and he'd been drinking heavily during the recording session. When Bechet called "Jazz Me Blues," Sullivan let out a sarcastic groan. Bechet, who may or may not have been drinking, was known for his volatile temper, and he demonstrated it on this occasion. He pulled a knife and approached Sullivan's throat, threatening, "One more crack and I'll cut your head off." Sullivan picked up the piano stool as a weapon and the recording session ended there and then. A week later they resumed, with Ralph Sutton on the piano.

For a recent version of "Jazz Me," listen to the Barbone Street Jazz Band's 2003 album *To Mac with Love*. To the best of my knowledge, all musicians played the song willingly and no knives were pulled.

"Jelly Roll Blues," was the first published composition by Jelly Roll Morton, an iconic figure of early jazz. (Courtesy Lilly Library, Indiana University, Bloomington, Indiana.)

Jelly Roll Blues (Jelly Roll Morton, 1915): Jelly Roll claimed to have written the song in 1905, ten years before the publication date. "Jelly Roll Blues" was most likely the song referred to in "Darktown Strutters' Ball" in the lyric "when they play the Jelly Roll Blues." It was not only the first published composition of Jelly Roll Morton, but also the first bona fide jazz piece to be written down. Up until this point, there were many published rags and a number of published blues songs, but jazz had been improvised and played without music. Jelly Roll's compositions as well as his playing affirm his position as a transitional figure between Ragtime and jazz. Another historic aspect of this composition is the use of the habanera rhythm, typical of the earliest jazz and blues ("St. Louis Blues" also incorporates this rhythm). Jelly Roll considered Spanish rhythms essential to jazz: "If you can't manage to put tinges of Spanish in your tunes, you will never be able to get the right seasoning." Finally,

Jelly Roll's first composition conforms to his belief that "breaks are one of the most essential things that you can ever do in jazz ... without beautiful ideas in breaks, you don't need to even think about doin' anything else."

Jelly Roll recorded the number in 1924 as a piano solo, and then again in 1926 with his famous Red Hot Peppers. The song has more often been recorded as a piano solo, but instrumental versions can be heard: Yank Lawson/Bob Haggart (1952), Louis Armstrong (1959), and James Dapogny (1993).

Jitterbug Waltz (Fats Waller, 1942): The composition of this number was witnessed by Waller's son Maurice, as reported by Nat Shapiro and Nat Hentoff: "There was a Sunday morning I especially remember. When my father got up that day, he went downstairs to the Hammond organ we had in the house, and then called me down—I was about thirteen—to listen to a new idea he had. He'd awakened with the tune on his mind. In about ten minutes flat, the tune was finished and it was *Jitterbug Waltz*."

Written just a year before his untimely death, Fats intended this instrumental number to be a clever response to the jitterbug dance craze. (The joke is that the jitterbug was a dance to be performed to a hot swing number in 4/4 time, not 3/4!) His 1942 recording received little immediate attention, but is significant for two reasons. For one, Fats played the Hammond organ, an instrument that would soon become very important in jazz. More significantly, the tune is one of the first jazz waltzes ever written. True, the great songwriters often wrote waltzes, but they were not performed as swing or jazz numbers. Dancers must have been perplexed by the syncopated triple meter of the "Jitterbug Waltz."

It was actually the progressive jazz musicians of the 1950s that brought the waltz to jazz music. Sonny Rollins' "Valse Hot" (1956) seems to have opened the door, and in 1957 Max Roach dedicated an entire album to triple meter, *Jazz in ¾ Time*. This movement ultimately led to the rediscovery of the "Jitterbug Waltz" by both traditional and modern jazz musicians. The tune is now a jazz standard and can be heard on recordings by Al Hirt (1959), Bobby Hackett (1970), and Tim Laughlin (1994).

One final note on "Jitterbug:" Composers have a tendency, if not an obligation, to listen to what has come before receive inspiration from it. Jazz music in particular is part of a continuum that begins at the turn of the 20th century and continues to the present. Sometimes musicians are influenced by something that came before without even knowing it. Jazz pianist Vince Guaraldi was certainly familiar with Fats Waller's music. The melodic similarity between "Jitterbug" and Guaraldi's "Skating" from *A Charlie Brown Christmas* (1965), to my mind, is too close to be coincidental.

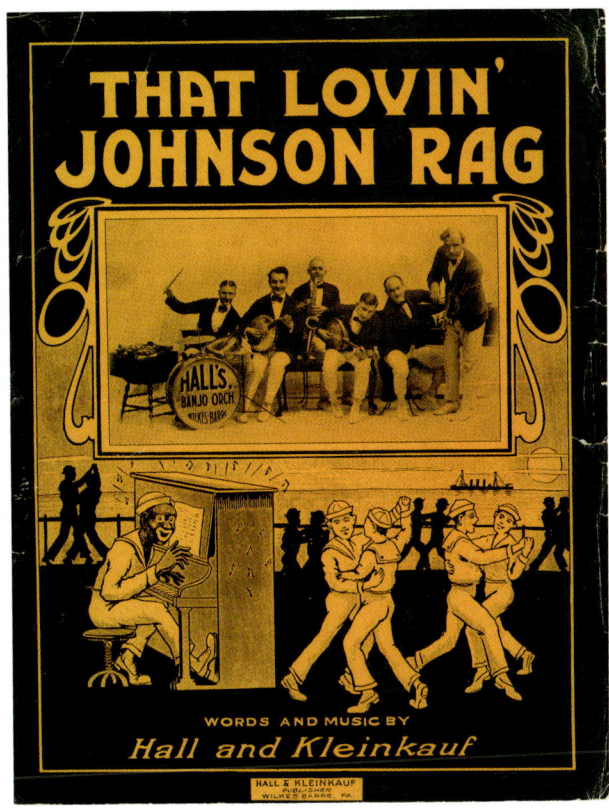

"Johnson Rag," by Guy Hall, Henry Kleinkauf and Jack Lawrence, would have been lost to obscurity had not Glenn Miller revived it during the Big Band Era. (Courtesy Lilly Library, Indiana University, Bloomington, Indiana.)

Johnson Rag (music: Guy Hall and Henry Kleinkauf, lyrics: Jack Lawrence (1917, 1940): This number has an unusual history. It seems that in 1917 a couple of local musicians from around Wilkes-Barre, Pennsylvania wrote and self-published the song. Little is known about them, and their one successful song would also have been forgotten had it not been discovered by Glenn Miller in the late 1930s. Miller's attraction to the song is understandable—it has a repeating riff structure that seems more in step with the Swing Era than the Ragtime Era. (Note the similarity to Benny Goodman's "Stompin' at the Savoy.") Miller's recording of the song didn't reach the charts, but in 1939 Larry Clinton's did.

Around this time Miller got the idea of turning the number into a full-fledged popular song with lyrics, and invited composer Jack Lawrence to do just that.

(Lawrence wrote "All or Nothing at All," Frank Sinatra's first hit record, that same year.) Lawrence supplied a middle section to complete the standard 32-bar format, added lyrics, and a verse (seldom played). In his own words, "When I wrote this in 1940 there were a lot of silly lyric ditties that were popular, like "Mairzy Doats," etc. So I wrote my lyric as a series of funny sounds: Hep hep, juke juke, zoom zoom, etc."

While many recordings were made, a hit record on Lawrence's rewrite of the song didn't come along until 1949 (the Jack Teter Trio), with three more in 1950 (Russ Morgan, Jimmy Dorsey, and Claude Thornhill). Then in 1951, the song was used in the film *Royal Wedding*, starring Fred Astaire and Jane Powell. It was most likely Jimmy Dorsey's version that planted the song squarely in the Dixieland repertoire—his small band version featuring Charlie Teagarden on trumpet, Cutty Cutshall on trombone, and Ray Bauduc on drums swings like mad.

Jubilee (music: Hoagy Carmichael, lyrics: Stanley Adams, 1937): Not a very well-known number, "Jubilee" is a clever composition with a spirited melody and an unusual chord progression that provides a challenging but stimulating vehicle for jazz improvisation. The lyrical content is just what you'd expect, inviting the listener to "Have a lot of fun singin' in the sun." The harmonic structure of the song is unique. The first eight bars seem routine enough, but the second eight shift upward by an unexpected interval. The bridge follows a rather common chord sequence, but the last section, 12 bars long, literally repeats a two-bar phrase three times, providing an effectively jubilant climax to the chorus.

The number was introduced Louis Armstrong (playing himself) in the comic film *Every Day's A Holiday* (1937), starring Mae West. The street scene presenting the song is subtitled *A Jubilee of Music and Laughter with Louis Armstrong Blowin' Sweet and Sassy*. Louis is seen leading a parade band, playing trumpet, singing, and hamming it up like only he could.

Louis' performance of "Jubilee" for the movie was fine, but the remake of the tune that he did for Decca Records in January 1938 is simply breathtaking, and ranks among the best records he ever made. The recording opens with a drum roll played by New Orleans drummer Paul Barbarin, whom Louis greatly admired from his early days. Louis sings the first chorus, staying closer to Hoagy's melody than he does in the film version. Following another drum roll, Louis takes a chorus on the trumpet, playing the melody, but making it hot. Barbarin is again heard from on the drums, leading to the final "shout" chorus. For this one the band begins with the melody with Louis's trumpet riding over top. He then takes over the melody for the final half-chorus, ending on a spectacular high note. When someone played the record for Louis again, more that 20 years after he made it, he had nothing to say about his own playing, but remarked, "That's that old Barbarin, you know, with that street parade jive."

There haven't been a lot of recordings of "Jubilee" over the decades, but in recent years the song has been getting more attention. Guitarists Marty Grosz and Mike Peters recorded a brilliant interpretation of the number on their 2008 album *Acoustic Heat*.

June Night (music: Abel Baer, lyrics: Cliff Friend, 1924): Abel Baer may be a forgotten name today, but he was a very successful songwriter of the 20s. Abandoning his dental practice in 1920, Baer became one of the most popular songwriters on Tin Pan Alley, turning out many hits, including "There Are Such Things," "My Mother's Eyes," "Gee But You're Swell," and many others. After 1929 he moved to Hollywood and wrote for the movies. "June Night" dates from 1924, and that same year became a hit for both Ted Lewis and Fred Waring. The song is heard in the 1952 film *Somebody Loves Me*, starring Betty Hutton, and saw a significant revival in the 1950s.

There is a fascinating story involved with the tune's most successful recording. In late 1956, Jimmy Dorsey recorded "So Rare," which became an incredible hit for him, charting throughout most of 1957 and peaking at Number 2. It was the greatest big-band hit of the 1950s and one of the last big-band records to reach the charts. Dorsey's recording label decided the time was right to do an entire album around the single. Unfortunately, Jimmy had throat cancer and died on June 11, 1957. ("So Rare" was in the Number 4 position when he died.) The album was to include "June Night" with a saxophone solo, which Jimmy decided should be played by his sax man Dick Stabile, who sounded just like him. The band went into the studio just days after Jimmy died, with Stabile playing Jimmy's solo, as planned, under the direction of Jimmy's trumpet player Lee Castle. (Lee, whose real name was Aniello Castaldo, was still leading the band when I was with them in the 1970s.) Since "June Night" claimed to feature the Jimmy Dorsey Orchestra, which it did, the public was never informed that it was Stabile, and not Jimmy Dorsey, who played the solo. In August, while "So Rare," was still high up in the charts, "June Night" also became a hit, reaching Number 21 and remaining on the charts for some three months.

Having given it that build up, I can't exactly recommend this recording, except out of historic interest. The band is tight, and the saxophone playing is great, but the imitative rock-and-roll feel coupled with an overbearing pop choir (with plenty of "doo-wah" interjections) is not very appealing, and it's the furthest thing imaginable from a 20s feel. On the other hand, it provides a great example of how a good song can hold up in many contexts. To take this even further, the "King of Polka" Frankie Yankovic recorded "June Night" on his 1968 album *Polka Time*, and it sounds great! And then there's a smoking hot big-band version by famous blues shouter Jimmy Rushing from his 1960 album *Rushing Lullabies* (ouch!), and that works too. Okay, and how about the version recorded by Miles Davis on the album *Stockholm 1960 Complete*. Actually, Miles doesn't play on the tune, but his rhythm section does, and pianist Wynton Kelly makes the song sound like it was written for him. But for recent recordings with a traditional jazz feel listen to those by Norbert Susemihl with Papa Tom's Lamentation Jazzband (1984), Ed Polcer (*Coast to Coast*, 1991), and the Atlantic City Jazz Band (*Makin' Waves*, 2010).

Just a Closer Walk with Thee (traditional): One of the most popular of African-American spirituals, this song most likely dates from before the Civil War. It is frequently performed by jazz bands and at New Orleans funerals. Despite the hymn's deep historical roots, it was relatively unknown nationally prior to the 1930s. At that time, African-American churches began to hold national conferences and conventions, which featured the performance of gospel music. Possibly at one of these gatherings, or perhaps elsewhere (there are conflicting stories), gospel composer Kenneth Morris (1917-1988) discovered the song, wrote additional lyrics, and published a choral arrangement of it. While Morris cannot be said to have composed the song, he presented the version that we know today, and is in large part responsible for its revival and popularity. From the early 1940s through the present day, hundreds of recordings have been made of the song, and several of them became hits. Mahalia Jackson frequently sang the song during the 1960s.

"Just a Closer Walk" is as signature tune of the great clarinetist Pete Fountain (born 1930). A native of New Orleans, Fountain began playing the clarinet as a child as a recommendation from a doctor to address a serious lung condition. In time it not only cured his condition, it made him world famous. Fountain began gigging around New Orleans in the early 1950s before landing a job with the Lawrence Welk Orchestra in 1957. That lasted for two years, until the leader's insistence on straight dance music began to clash with Fountain's predilection for jazz, or as he later put it, "Champaign and bourbon don't mix." Returning to New Orleans, he then joined the Dukes of Dixieland for a while, but left to start his own band as well as open his own jazz club on Bourbon Street in 1960. His club was highly successful and some of the biggest stars in the country sometimes dropped in. Supposedly, when Benny Goodman visited he didn't bring his clarinet. Fountain's 1959 recording of "Just a

Closer Walk" was a resounding hit for him, and the song forever became associated with him. When asked if it was one of his favorite tunes, he replied, "I have to play it every night, whether it's my favorite or not!"

"A Closer Walk" is frequently played at jazz funerals. This ceremony is best described by someone who was there in the early years of the 20th century—the New Orleans bassist Pops Foster, who remembers in his autobiography:

> A whole lot has been written about colored funerals in New Orleans.... No matter how much of a bum a guy was, his friends would pass a cup to get money for a funeral when he quit the scene. If there was any money after paying for the funeral the widow would get it. The guys would rent a set of tails for the grand marshal, hire a brass band, and buy some flowers. Going out to the cemetery the band would play hymns like "Nearer My God to Thee" and "When the Saints Go Marching In" very slow. These are hymns and you never played them fast or jazzed them up.... A soon as they put the guy in the ground, the trumpeter would hit a couple of high notes. When the trumpet hit the last note the bass drum would start off boom-boom-boom-boom, boom-boom-boom-boom, and then everybody would take off on something like "Didn't He Ramble." We'd play jazz music all the way back.

Kansas City Stomps (Jelly Roll Morton, 1925): As he approached 30 years of age, after years of traveling and several changes of location, Jelly Roll settled down in Los Angeles, putting together a band and working various locations in southern California. This was probably not a wise choice at the onset of the 20s, because things were just starting to get hot in Chicago, where his music would presumably have been very much in demand. Nevertheless, he seemed to like California, was getting enough work, and his life was about as orderly as it was ever going to get.

One of the venues where Jelly Roll found work was a Black-owned establishment in Tijuana called the Kansas City Bar. Prohibition began in January of 1920, so California residents gleefully crossed the border into Mexico where alcohol was legal. Jelly Roll liked the place and named a composition after it. He sure seems to be in good spirits from the nature of the tune. "Kansas City Stomp" is a cheerful number that mixes the good-time feel of Ragtime with the swing rhythm and more adventurous harmonies of early jazz. He recorded the number as a piano solo in 1923 and then with his Red Hot Peppers in 1928.

Keepin' Out of Mischief Now (music: Fats Waller; lyrics: Andy Razaf, 1932): In 1930, Waller and Razaf went their separate ways, breaking up the songwriting team that had turned out so many hits. But they briefly reunited in 1932. In terms of sentiment, "Mischief" is pretty much a reworking of "Ain't Misbehavin'," a promise to quit partying and running around, which obviously did not apply to Waller at all. Musically, the tunes are quite different. "Misbehavin'" is in standard 32-bar form, while "Mischief" has the unusual structure of 20 bars (16 + 4).

While the tune invites a slower treatment, and is sometimes done as a ballad, early recordings do not reflect this. Both Louis Armstrong and Coon-Sanders had sizable hits with the song in 1932, and both recordings move along at a sprightly dance tempo. By contrast, Waller's own recording (1937) and Armstrong's 1955 version both incorporate a more relaxed tempo, bringing out more of what the tune has to offer. An excellent rendition can be heard by pianist Jeff Barnhart on his 2012 album *Reflections of Fats*.

King Porter Stomp (Jelly Roll Morton, 1924): Jelly Roll published most of his songs in the 20s, but in most cases he had composed them many years earlier. "King Porter" dates from around 1905. It is named after a Florida pianist called Porter King. Jelly Roll made a piano recording of the song in 1923 and another in 1939, but it was a big-band arrangement of the song that made it historic. Fletcher Henderson wrote a couple of arrangements of the number for his band, and then did one for the Benny Goodman band after he dissolved his own group in 1934.

Benny Goodman (1909-1986), today known as the "King of Swing," was born into a poor family in Chicago. He became proficient on the clarinet at an early age and was working professionally while still a teenager. After four years with Ben Pollack, who led one of the most successful White bands of the late 20s, Benny struck out on his own and became a top-notch free-lance musician in New York City. In 1934 he started his own band, and was determined to find a market for the hard-swinging jazz music he loved, instead of the softer dance arrangements that most of the White bands played.

According to Benny Goodman, it was "King Porter Stomp" that saved his band near the end of a discouraging tour to the West Coast in 1935. It seems that audiences were not responding to his swing music, forcing him against his wishes to play the more traditional dance music. On the night of August 21, 1935, at the Palomar Ballroom in Los Angeles, Goodman was playing it safe, calling the numbers he thought the crowd wanted to hear, but it wasn't working. Figuring he had nothing to lose, he called one of his hot swing numbers, "King Porter Stomp," and the audience went wild. It was exactly what they wanted to hear, the turning point in Benny Goodman's career, and the birth of the Big Band Era.

"King Porter Stomp" became famous as a big-band swing number, but traditional jazz bands adopted the tune as a staple. One of my favorite versions is a hard-driving arrangement by Jack Teagarden (1954). For a rendition that maintains Jelly Roll's original conception of the number, hear Duke Heitger (2007). Heitger is one of most compelling Armstrong-inspired trumpet players active today.

Lazy River (Hoagy Carmichael and Sidney Arodin, 1930): A diehard jazz enthusiast from the beginning, one night Hoagy went to a club in New York City to hear New Orleans clarinetist Sidney Arodin. An original composition of Arodin's caught his attention, and Hoagy suggested that they might make a tune out of it. Arodin agreed, and one afternoon they worked out a verse, made slight modifications to the melody, and added lyrics. While Hoagy became known primarily as a composer in later years, he was a fine lyricist in his own right, writing the words to several of his early songs, including "Rockin' Chair" and "New Orleans." Although both men shared credit for the tune, it is likely that Hoagy was responsible for the words, as they are completely in character for him.

The river referred to must have been a long and winding one if the melody is any indication, which sweeps across arpeggios in the manner of a jazz improvisation. Indeed many singers to this day leave out most of the contours of the original tune, reducing it to something more manageable for the voice. Louis Armstrong started this convention with his 1931 recording, which pretty much ignores the melody, following the words and harmony only—something like a trumpet solo for the voice. Hoagy's own hit recording (1930) as well as that of the Mills Brothers (1952) both present the melody in its original form. Of particular interest on Hoagy's recording are excellent solos by Jimmy Dorsey, Tommy Dorsey, and Joe Venuti. The exchange between Tommy Dorsey and Venuti during the final chorus is fascinating—Venuti, who could display violin technique by the bucketful when he felt like it, runs up and down rapid scale figures like an acrobat, while Dorsey provides a lyrical melodic contrast as only he could.

Lazybones (music: Hoagy Carmichael, lyrics: Johnny Mercer, 1933): The song was Mercer's idea. He had just begun collaborating with Hoagy, but nothing had clicked for them yet. One day Mercer walked into Hoagy's New York City apartment and announced that he'd like to write a tune called "Lazybones." He had a concept and the first line in his head, but nothing more. Hoagy's inspiration for the melody came from a solo piano interlude he had played on "Washboard Blues" some years before. Mercer, who was only 23 at the time, struggled for months to come up with a lyric, but eventually he did. It proved to be a superb example of his mastery of dialect resulting from his Savannah upbringing.

Returning from a European tour in the summer of 1933, Hoagy was astonished to learn that his song had become not only a hit but a cultural sensation. The name "Lazybones" was being used as a marketing ploy for everything from shoes to lawn furniture to nightgowns. Cartoonists were mocking politicians with the term. For an ironic boost in publicity, Hitler's new Nazi regime banned the song in Germany for encouraging idleness. Within three months the song had sold 350,000 copies of sheet music. Ted Lewis had a Number 1 hit with it, while Don Redman and Mildred Bailey were not far behind. Unfortunately, what appeared to be the start of one of the greatest songwriting teams in history did not last long. For no obvious reason, the two went their separate ways and drifted apart. As Hoagy said in later years, "Johnny and I could have flooded the market with hit songs. We were atune [sic] and I knew he 'knew' and he knew I 'knew.' But the chips didn't fall right."

Life Is Just a Bowl of Cherries (music: Ray Henderson, lyrics: Buddy DeSylva and Lew Brown, 1931): You might guess from the title that this is a typical song by Henderson, DeSylva, and Brown and you'd be mostly right, but not quite. The truth is, after many successful years together, the team was finally breaking up. "Cherries" was written for *George White's Scandals of 1931*, and although the team shared the copyright (listed as DeSylva, Brown and Henderson, Inc.), the playbill for the show clearly states that the music is by Ray Henderson and the lyrics by Lew Brown. DeSylva had already left for Hollywood. This discrepancy has resulted in conflicting information in references to the song. Aside from the trivia, the tune fits right in the pocket as totally characteristic of the style of the famous trio.

It appears that the song "Life Is Just a Bowl of Cherries" is actually the first usage of the idiom in history. Ironically, the lyrics were are not meant to imply that everything is going swimmingly, but rather just the opposite: "Don't make it serious, life's too mysterious." The message is that you work hard for your money, but you might lose it all, and you can't take it with you when you die, so just enjoy yourself while you can. No wonder the song caught on so well just as the country was sinking into the worst depression in its history. Ethel Merman sang it in *Scandals*, but Rudy Vallee, who was also in the cast, had the hit record. (President Herbert Hoover once told Rudy Vallee, "If you can sing a song that would make people forget their troubles

... I'll give you a medal." You'd think that this tune would fit the bill, but the medal never came.) A more spirited, jazzier version can be heard by Jack Hylton (1931). Hylton was a British bandleader with an ensemble that sounded a lot like Paul Whiteman's unit. His cornet soloist is featured on this record and clearly reminds you of Bix Beiderbecke.

"Limehouse Blues," by Philip Braham and Douglas Furber, derives its name from a district in London. (Courtesy Lilly Library, Indiana University, Bloomington, Indiana.)

Limehouse Blues (music: Philip Braham, lyrics: Douglas Furber, 1922): This is a title that demands an explanation. The Limehouse district of London is the location of a famous port on the north side of the Thames that dates back to medieval times. In Old English the name actually referred to the kilns, "lime oasts," but the phrase eventually evolved into "lime house." During the late 19th century, Limehouse became London's Chinatown.

The song was written as an instrumental, and is usually performed that way, but words were added for its appearance in the show *Andre Charlot's Revue of 1924*. The lyrics tell of the wretched life of a child growing up in the area, which probably explains the use of the word "blues" in the title. Melodically, the "blue" notes in the song result not from inflection but from the strange chord progression. The verse to the song is also highly unusual, wandering through unexpected keys until an abrupt turnaround sets up the chorus.

"Limehouse" is a unique composition and has inspired a variety of treatments over the years. Paul Whiteman (1924) and Duke Ellington (1931) each had hits with moderate-tempo versions of the song, but more frequently it is played at a rapid (Django Reinhardt, 1936) if not frenetic speed (Cliff Jackson, stride piano, 1944).

Linger Awhile (music: Vincent Rose, lyrics: Harry Owens, 1923): A member of the Songwriters' Hall of Fame, Vincent Rose (1880-1944) wrote hundreds of songs, including "Whispering," "Avalon," and "Blueberry Hill." Born and musically trained in Palermo, Sicily, he prospered in America and had a long and successful career as an orchestra leader. Harry Owens (1902-1986) was a composer, bandleader and songwriter best known for his collaboration with Bing Crosby and promotion of Hawaiian music and culture. He is the composer of "Sweet Leilani."

"Linger Awhile" has an unpretentious melody that lives up to its name. It is a well-constructed tune that has endured in the repertoire of traditional and modern jazz musicians alike. Paul Whiteman had a 1924 Number 1 recording that sold two million copies. It was Whiteman's third million-selling record, and reveals something about popular taste of the day. The subtitle to the sheet music of "Linger Awhile" reads "A Dancing Song," and there is no vocal chorus to the arrangement—it is entirely instrumental. That was also true of Paul's earlier million sellers, "Whispering" (1920) and "Three O'clock in the Morning" (1922). What these recordings do contain, however, are unusual instruments. Both "Whispering" and "Linger Awhile" feature a chorus of slide whistle, and "Three O'clock in the Morning," not entirely unexpectedly, opens and closes with chimes. "Linger Awhile" eventually became an up-tempo feature for Whiteman's banjo player, Mike Pingatore, who worked with Whiteman for 25 years. He can be heard and seen performing this number in Paul Whiteman's 1930 film *King of Jazz*.

"Linger Awhile" is also well adapted to swing settings as can be heard on performances by Lester Young (1943), Ben Webster (1944), Ruby Braff (1954), Earl Hines (1964), and Zoot Sims (1974).

Fine as all of these recordings are, my favorite is a stride piano version, not only because it's so good, but also because it's so rare. Let me explain. As everybody thinks they know now, and thought they knew then, there were three giants of stride piano who emerged in the 1920s and reigned supreme for years to come: James P. Johnson, Willie "The Lion" Smith, and Fats Waller, with Art Tatum joining the ranks in the 1930s. Other great pianists would come along, but they played "modern" style, and if you wanted to hear the brilliant left-hand stride work, these were the champions, because nobody else could cut it. Or so they thought.

As it turned out, there was a hidden genius by the name of Donald Lambert (1904-1962), who had no desire to be rich, famous, or widely known. He had a steady job at a neighborhood tavern in Orange, New Jersey, where he played regularly, honing incredible skills that hardly anyone knew about, and watching the world go by. He seldom saw a need to interrupt his hobbit-like schedule, and made only a handful of recordings during the 40s and 50s. But Lambert, uncharacteristically, appeared at the 1960 Newport Jazz Festival, along with Eubie Blake and Willie The Lion. Lambert went on first, and his performance stunned everyone present. Eubie asked, "How do we follow that?" to which Willie The Lion replied "I don't know about you, but I plan to do a lot of talking."

Fortunately, a year later, Lambert was persuaded once again to leave his hobbit-hole to record an album, which included the song "Linger Awhile." His approach to the song begins quietly, with an opening rubato chorus that soon gives way to a romping display reminiscent of a Harlem rent party. At a time when pop music was reverting to simple harmonies, and free jazz was dispensing with chords altogether, who knows what the public thought of this. But chances are no one on the planet was capable of matching what Lambert produced on this session.

"Livery Stable Blues," by Ray Lopez and Alcide Nunez, was published as "Barnyard Blues" by members of the Original Dixieland Jazz Band, who contested its authorship. (Courtesy Sandy Marrone, Cinnaminson, NJ.)

Livery Stable Blues aka "Barnyard Blues" (Ray Lopez and Alcide Nunez, 1917): This was the tune that started it all. On February 26, 1917, the Original Dixieland "Jass" Band went into the Victor studios and recorded "Barnyard Blues" and "Dixie Jass Band One-Step." The record was a hit, qualifying as the first commercially released recording of a jazz band, and possibly the first popular song to sell a million records. Within a few short years the band had other best-selling records and the Jazz Age was launched.

The composers of the song, Lopez and Nunez, were New Orleans musicians who had played with ODJB members, but were not in the band when they began recording. (Clarinetist Nunez had left the band only a few months before.) When members of the ODJB published the tune as "Barnyard Blues" they discovered that Lopez and Nunez had already copyrighted the tune as "Livery Stable Blues."

A law suit resulted, with the judge declaring the work "public domain," effectively allowing separate publishing houses to sell the same song under different names.

Both names for the tune refer to the chorus where the instruments imitate animal sounds— the clarinet a rooster, the cornet a horse, and the trombone a cow. Despite the novelty aspect of the song, it is a real jazz song played by a real jazz band, and holds a venerated place in jazz history. In homage to the birth of jazz recording, Paul Whiteman opened his 1924 concert *An Experiment in Modern Music* (in which *Rhapsody in Blue* was premiered) with "Livery Stable Blues."

Lonesome Road (music: Nathaniel Shilkret, lyrics: Gene Austin, 1927): The song is believed to be an adaptation of a Negro spiritual, but there seems to be no written record of any such hymn prior to the publication date. In any case, it sure sounds like a spiritual, and was put together by two of the most important figures in 20th century popular music. Gene Austin is known as one of the first crooners, and sold some 80 million records for Victor in the late 20s and early 1930s, a feat not matched again for another 40 years. Considering the much smaller market of his day, a case could be made that Austin was the biggest selling artist in recording history.

Shilkret was an amazing musician—a child prodigy on the clarinet who held jobs with major symphonies at a very young age, he worked for the leading conductors of the day including Gustav Mahler, and soon became a conductor himself. He took a position as manager for Victor Records, and presided over their most prestigious recordings. He was also very active as a conductor, and virtually all of the top musicians of the day worked under his baton. He was a composer of both popular and classical works and wrote film scores for RKO Pictures and MGM studios.

For all of the powerful credentials of the authors, "Lonesome Road" is a model of simplicity and straightforward sentiment. It has been successfully adapted to traditional jazz, modern jazz, gospel, blues, big-band and adult-pop venues and has endured remarkably well over the decades. An interesting aside, and somewhat of a head-scratcher, is that for the 1929 film version of *Showboat*, "Lonesome Road" was used in place of "Old Man River" as the finale!

Louisiana (music: J.C. Johnson, lyrics: Andy Razaf, 1928): Although Razaf was writing with Fats Waller by the mid 20s, his first real hit was in 1926 with a song called "My Special Friend Is Back in Town," which he wrote with composer J.C. Johnson (not to be confused with the famous Harlem Stride pianist James P. Johnson). In 1928 the Johnson/Razaf team hit pay dirt again, producing three hits: "Louisiana," "Dusky Stevedore," and "Guess Who's in Town?" While "Dusky Stevedore" had two successful recordings (Nat Shilkret's and Frankie Trumbauer's), and the lyrics to "Guess Who's in Town" contain some masterful word play, it was "Louisiana" that stood the test of time. Paul Whiteman had the hit, featuring the Rhythm Boys with Bing Crosby on lead and a cornet solo by Bix Beiderbecke. Bix liked the tune so much that he recorded it with his own band later that same year.

Jazz musicians have always been particularly fond of the tune, which in truth has a harmonic progression that is more interesting than the melody itself. Of the many splendid versions of the tune, one that stands out is from the 1951 album *The Dixie Style of Pete Kelly's Big 7*. This requires some explanation, since there was no Pete Kelly. Following up on the successful radio drama series *Pete Kelly's Blues*, starring Jack Webb, the band from the show was assembled in the studio to make an album. Twenty-four-year-old Dick Cathcart plays cornet and does an astonishing job of playing in the style of Bix.

A tasteful swing version of "Louisiana" can be heard by guitarist Larry Scala on the 2007 album *Big Easy Swing*.

Love Is Just Around the Corner (music: Lewis Gensler, lyrics: Leo Robin, 1934): We can thank Herbert Hoover for the title, for it is almost certainly mocking his muchmaligned prediction of 1932, the darkest year of the Depression, that "prosperity is just around the corner." And levity is the goal of Robin's lyric, with the absurdly irresistible lyrics referring to Venus de Milo: "you are cuter than Venus, And what's more you've got arms."

Following the decade when many popular songs came from Broadway shows, the 1930s introduced many new songs that came from film. This one was called *Here Is My Heart*, starring Bing Crosby and Kitty Carlisle. The plot is about a famous singer who pretends to be destitute in order to win the affection of the woman he loves, who happens to be a European Princess. (Even if you never saw the movie, you can picture Bing playing this role in a heartbeat.) The movie produced two other hits as well, "June in January" and "With Every Breath I Take," both by the famous duo of Ralph Rainger and Leo Robin. But for "Love is Just Around the Corner," Robin teamed up with his original partner, Lewis Gensler, and this classic song is the result.

"The Love Nest," by Louis A. Hirsch and Otto Harbach, was the well-known theme song of Burns and Allen. (Courtesy Lilly Library, Indiana University, Bloomington, Indiana.)

Love Nest (music: Louis A. Hirsch, lyrics: Otto Harbach, 1920): The famous comedy team of George Burns and Gracie Allen adopted this number as their theme song when they first appeared in vaudeville in the 20s and never changed it. It could be heard during their radio days of the 1930s and 40s, in their movies, and in their television years of the 1950s. (When I performed in the orchestra for George Burns' stage shows in the 1990s, he still opened and closed each performance with "Love Nest." This has to be the longest running theme song in history!)

Some people don't realize that the song has words, but it certainly does: "Just a love nest cozy with charm, like a dove nest down on the farm." In fact, considering the subject matter and the use of unexpected words such as "veranda" and "Jack and Jill" in the lyrics, one wonders if Oscar Hammerstein received his inspiration for "The Folks Who Live on the Hill" from this song.

It was a hit in its day—in fact a big hit: Number 1 for both Art Hickman and John Steel, and Number 6 for Joseph Smith's Orchestra. Composer Louis Hirsch (1887-1924) was quite successful in the theatre during the first decades of the 20th century, and would have achieved even greater success had he not died of pneumonia at the age of 36. Otto Harbach (1873-1963) was a highly respected lyricist who is also noted for being Oscar Hammerstein's mentor. He served as lyricist and librettist to some 50 musical comedies.

Among jazz versions of the "Love Nest" from the 20s are two recordings by Bix Beiderbecke from 1928. The first, with the Paul Whiteman Orchestra, features him on a short but spirited solo toward the end. Later that year, he has the opportunity to stretch out a bit more on a more relaxed version by the Frankie Trumbauer Orchestra.

A hard-driving, Chicago-style rendition of the song can be heard by Eddie Condon (1944) on one of the Town Hall concerts. I cite this group of recordings frequently because they were pivotal in the revival of traditional jazz, and because they capture the musicians from the 20s still performing as they did some two decades before. As the Blue Network, which broadcast the concerts, aptly announced, these performances offered "the only unrehearsed, free-wheeling, completely barefoot music on the air." Later, in the 1950s, when these musicians went into the studio to record high-fidelity LPs, the sound, spirit, and feel were completely different. Fortunately, the Town Hall broadcasts were recorded and can be heard today on a set of 23 CDs issued by New Orleans-based Jazzology Records.

Recordings of "Love Nest" from the past several decades are likely to be anything other than traditional jazz. (Even the Tijuana Brass recorded the tune in 1968.) For a solid jazz rendition, listen to bassist *Ed Wise and His New Orleans Jazz Band* (2008).

"Mahogany Hall Stomp," by Spencer Williams, is named after a luxurious brothel on Basin Street. The structure appears on the far right in this postcard.(Basin Street "up the line," photographer unknown, public domain, via Wikimedia Commons.)

Mahogany Hall Stomp (Spencer Williams, 1929): The most celebrated brothel in America, Mahogany Hall, 235 Basin Street, was run by the "octoroon queen" Lulu White. The souvenir booklet (!) states: "The house is built of marble and is four story; containing five parlors, all handsomely furnished, and fifteen bedrooms." It also boasts of the madam's credentials: "As an entertainer Miss Lulu stands foremost, having made a life-long study of music and literature. She is well read and one that can interest anybody and make a visit to her place a continued round of pleasure."

If anyone had the right to compose a song about the establishment it was Spencer Williams (1889-1965). (Not to be confused with the actor Spencer Williams [1893-1969], best known for playing Andy in the *Amos 'n Andy* television show). Williams was Lulu's nephew, adopted by her after his mother's death, and literally grew up in Mahogany Hall. With practically free rein of the house and neighborhood,

Williams listened to all the music he could. By his mid-teens he was a passable pianist himself, and with his ears full of the best Ragtime of the day he began to write his own songs. He moved to Chicago and later New York, and soon began to produce hits.

By 1929 Williams' career was in full stride—he was publishing songs regularly and they were being recorded by the leading artists, such as Louis Armstrong ("Fireworks," "Skip the Gutter," and "Basin Street Blues"), Bessie Smith ("I'm Wild About That Thing" and "You've Got to Give Me Some"), and Duke Ellington ("Tishomingo Blues"). In May of 1929, Louis Armstrong recorded a historic version of "Mahogany Hall Stomp." In addition to his superb playing, it features Lonnie Johnson performing what is possibly the first recorded jazz guitar solo. New Orleans-born Johnson (1899-1970) was a pioneering blues singer and jazz guitarist, credited as being one of the first guitarists to take solos by picking individual notes.

Unfortunately, the Depression, as well as the rise of sound pictures, were not good for Williams' fortunes. The recording industry was devastated and publishing houses were being bought up by the big movie studios. True, Hollywood was also hiring songwriters for their films, but African-American musicians were not welcome in these circles. Williams soon left for Europe and spent nearly the rest of his life there.

Few musicians wished to invite comparison with Louis on "Mahogany Hall Stomp," but Bunny Berigan was up to the challenge. One of the most powerful trumpet players of the Big Band Era, Berigan (who died tragically in 1942) and his big band recorded the number in 1937 with spectacular results. Bunny demonstrates that he knew Louis' recording inside out, but he was no copycat, and his playing incorporates his own musical ideas and style (such as his smooth legato phrasing.) Exactly ten years later, Louis repeated his dazzling interpretation of "Mahogany" on a live performance from Symphony Hall in Boston (1947), proving that he hadn't lost his fire.

"Mahogany Hall Stomp" has seen an active revival over the past few years. Wynton Marsalis can be heard and seen performing the number on the 1996 television broadcast *A Celebration of American Music*. Notable recordings of recent years include those by Allan Vache (*Oh Yeah! 2008*), Duke Heitger (*Celebrating Satchmo, 2010*), and an energy-packed version by trumpeter Ben Polcer with the Orleans Six, recorded live in 2013 at the Spotted Cat Music Club in New Orleans.

Makin' Whoopee (music: Walter Donaldson lyrics: Gus Kahn, 1928): The song is from the show *Whoopee* and was sung by Eddie Cantor, who had the hit recording. He also sang it in the film version of 1930. It was Cantor's first film and essentially opened the door to Hollywood for him. Unfortunately, the making of the movie was not such a pleasant experience for Florenz Ziegfeld, who had produced *Whoopee* on Broadway. Ziegfeld was virtually wiped out in the stock market crash of 1929. Although he had a hit show running, he lacked the capital to continue his operations. Subsequently, he was forced to close the show in November of 1929, selling the movie rights to Samuel Goldwyn. To make matters worse, Ziegfeld hated movies, and though he was present for the making of the film in April of 1930, he was afforded virtually no say in the production, forcing him to watch in horror while his brilliant stage effects were dismantled.

The term "makin' whoopee" seems to have been introduced by gossip columnist Walter Winchell. Some say that he took the term from speakeasy proprietress Texas Guinan (see the entry on "Butter and Egg Man"). In any case, the song and the show made the phrase popular, and its meaning needs no explanation. The tune offers a bouncy melody, lighthearted lyrics, and a bridge that is somewhat off the beaten harmonic path. It tells story of courtship leading to marriage and initial bliss, followed by the chores and responsibilities that soon follow, and then the inevitable marital difficulties.

Besides Cantor, Paul Whiteman and Ben Bernie also had early hits with the number. Bernie's recording begins with a snippet of Wagner's Bridal Chorus, but Rudy Vallee's recording of 1928 goes one step further with an extended quotation from Mendelssohn's Wedding March as the introduction, and prominent organ accompaniment behind the opening vocal chorus. "Makin' Whoopee" has proven to be quite attractive to modern jazz musicians and pop stars. Gerry Mulligan and Chet Baker recorded an astounding creative version of the tune in 1953, eliciting musical possibilities that Donaldson could not have dreamed of. Cyndi Lauper performed the song as a duet with Tony Bennett on her 2003 album *At Last*. Rod Stewart did a duet with Elton John on Stewart's CD *The Great American Songbook*. And Cookie Monster did a parody of the song called "Eatin' Cookie" on *Sesame Street*.

"Mandy," by Irving Berlin, was composed for a show that Berlin wrote while in the army. (Courtesy Lilly Library, Indiana University, Bloomington, Indiana.)

Mandy (music and words: Irving Berlin, 1918): The song dates from Berlin's army days. In early 1918, at the age of 29, he was drafted into the army and sent to Camp Upton in Yaphank, Long Island. A lifelong insomniac with nocturnal work habits, the army schedule did not suit Berlin. By this time, Berlin was a well-known songwriter on Broadway, and he found a way to use his influence: He talked the camp commander into letting him write a show as a fundraiser, with all proceeds going to the army. Additionally, he was allowed to work on his own schedule, sleeping well past reveille. The show, called *Yip Yip Yaphank*, was enthusiastically received, and after opening in the camp's own theater was soon moved to Broadway. Berlin appeared in the show himself, singing his number "Oh How I Hate to Get Up in the Morning." Berlin also composed "God Bless America" for the show, but, astonishingly, he decided not to use it and shelved it for 20 years, only to revive it in 1938, when war clouds were stirring and all eyes were on Europe.

The song "Mandy" was performed in the show as a minstrel number (complete with blackface) and was set as a Cakewalk. It is a short but straightforward song (18 measures with a tag), and opens with the catchy alliteration/rhyme "Mandy, there's a minister handy." The tune appeared in the *Ziegfeld Follies* the following year, and was revived for *This Is the Army* (1942). It can also be heard in the films *Kid Millions* (1934), *This Is The Army* (1943), *Blue Skies* (1946) and *White Christmas* (1954). There are relatively few jazz recordings of "Mandy," but Fats Waller sang a romping version in 1934 and, trombonist Turk Murphy included the number in one of his last performances (1986).

On his 1924 recording of "Mandy Make Up Your Mind," Sidney Bechet unexpectedly played a solo on the sarrusophone, a rare instrument that was already practically obsolete at the time. (Courtesy Matthias Kabel, licensed under CC BY-SA 3.0 via Wikimedia Commons.)

Mandy Make Up Your Mind (music: George W. Meyer and Arthur Johnston, lyrics: Roy Turk and Grant Clarke, 1924): The song comes from a show called *Dixie to Broadway*, which with a run of just over two months was considered a success for its day, a time when a flurry of new shows opened and closed on a regular basis.

Meyer, Johnston, Turk, and Clarke, among the foremost songwriters of the 20s, all contributed to the show, but there is no way to know if they actually co-wrote it or not. (Copyright information does not necessarily pinpoint the origin or authorship of a song.)

The show was the brainchild of Lew Leslie, a famous impresario who was among the first to present African Americans on stage. He would later go on to produce the famous *Blackbird* and Cotton Club reviews. *Dixie to Broadway* was possibly the first all-Black show to have a mainstream Broadway production. (The immensely successful *Shuffle Along* of 1921 had actually travelled on the road for a year before coming to Broadway.) It did much to further the career of Florence Mills, who would go on to become one of the most famous Black performers in America prior to her untimely death at the age of 32.

The tune is instantly likeable and was adopted by jazz musicians early on. It has a built-in Charleston rhythm accentuating a unique harmonic shift in the first two bars. The lyrical content is similar to Irving Berlin's similarly named tune, with "Wedding bells are dandy" and "Preacher man is handy" recalling "Mandy, there's a minister handy." Evidently Berlin had not exhausted all the good rhymes implicit in the name. Among the many fine recordings are those by Muggsy Spanier (1939, one of the "Great Sixteen"), Eddie Condon (1944, *Town Hall Concerts*), Wild Bill Davison (1952, with Condon), and, more recently Ed Polcer, on the 1993 album A Salute to Eddie Condon *(Complete Concert)*. Among the fine musicians featured on this album is trombonist Bob Havens, known to many as a permanent member of the Lawrence Welk orchestra for more than 20 years.

A 1924 session by Clarence Williams' Blue Five featuring Louis Armstrong and Sidney Bechet produced one of the most bizarre recordings in all of jazz history. Armstrong and Bechet were the leading soloists of their day, but only recorded together a handful of times. (See entry on "Cakewalkin' Babies from Home.") But the big surprise on their version of "Mandy Make Up Your Mind" is a stunning solo taken by Bechet on the bass sarrusophone, a rare instrument that most people have never seen or heard. The sarrusophone family of instruments was developed in the mid-1800s for use in wind bands as a replacement for the oboe and bassoon, which lacked the carrying power to be used outdoors. Soon after the turn of the 20th century, the sarrusophone became obsolete and today is considered a historic relic or novelty instrument. Bechet handles the instrument with confidence and agility, producing a brilliant solo, punctuated by Armstrong's inventive obbligato interjections. Versatile reedman Scott Robinson offers a remake of this historic moment on his 1997 album *Thinking Big*, complete with a bass sarrusophone solo!

"Maple Leaf Rag," by Scott Joplin might never have been published were it not for the supplications of a little boy. (Courtesy Lilly Library, Indiana University, Bloomington, Indiana.)

Maple Leaf Rag (Scott Joplin, 1899): This was the composition that changed the face of American music. It was the first rag to become nationally popular, eventually selling over one million copies of sheet music. "Maple Leaf" embodied the Ragtime spirit that soon overtook popular culture—not just a thirst for the infectious rhythmic syncopation of the music, but the quest for humor, fun and enjoyment that seemed to be stifled by the previous generation. Nearly 2000 rags were published during the first decade of the 20th century, not to mention the thousands of popular tunes that either sounded like rags, used the word "Ragtime" in the title, or both (such as "Alexander's Ragtime Band"). Ragtime was not just the popular music of one particular time period—it was the music associated with the first flowering of urban popular culture in America, and it was everywhere.

Thirty-year-old Scott Joplin was struggling to earn a living at music in Sedalia, Missouri when he walked into the publishing house of John Stark and Son, attempting to interest the firm in a composition of his. The "Son" of John Stark and Son was Will Stark, who was in the shop with his father and little boy that day. As Joplin sat down to demonstrate the piece, things did not go so well at first. Stark liked the number, but considered it too hard for amateurs to play. The little boy, however, began to dance enthusiastically, urging his father to buy the music. Will was persuaded, and soon the grandfather was as well. Stark soon became a dedicated advocate for Ragtime. Sales were slow at first, and it took nearly a year to sell the 400 copies from the first printing, but Stark was determined. When his printer put him on a waiting list for a second printing, Stark moved his operations to St. Louis and later to New York. He would remain a champion of Ragtime for the rest of his life.

Not surprisingly, early jazz bands routinely included the rags of Joplin and others in their repertoire. In fact, there was collection of rags nicknamed the Red Back Book (after the color of the cover) that became a staple for many jazz bands. In this collection of 15 rags (published by Stark), six were written by Joplin. "Maple Leaf Rag" was one of the rags that entered the jazz repertoire at the very beginning and never left.

An irksome addendum to the story of "Maple Leaf Rag" demonstrates how cutthroat the publishing industry was (and continues to be). When the time came to renew the copyright on the "Maple Leaf Rag," January 12, 1926, the Starks neglected to file promptly. Melrose Brothers Publishing (the outfit that swindled Jelly Roll Morton out of thousands of dollars) saw their chance, snatched it up in a heartbeat, and claimed it as their own, robbing Stark & Sons of the biggest hit they ever had.

"Margie, by J. Russel Robinson and Con Conrad, was named for the young daughter of singer Eddie Cantor. (Courtesy Lilly Library, Indiana University, Bloomington, Indiana.)

Margie (music: J. Russel Robinson and Con Conrad, lyrics: Benny Davis, 1920): In case you've ever wondered, "Margie" was named after the five-year-old daughter of Eddie Cantor. He first performed the song at the Winter Garden Theater and then used it in the 1921 show *The Midnight Rounders*. His recording was a Number 1 hit, and many other artists had successful renditions of the tune.

J. Russell Robinson (1892-1963) was a jazz pianist and member of the Original Dixieland Jazz Band. He composed many of the standard tunes of the traditional jazz repertoire, including "Eccentric," "Singin' the Blues," and "Aggravatin' Papa." Con Conrad (1891-1938) was responsible for such standards as "Ma, He's Making

Eyes at Me" and "Palesteena." He received the first Academy Award for Best Song for "The Continental" in 1934. Benny Davis (1895-1979) was a vaudeville performer and lyricist perhaps best remembered for his classic "Baby Face."

"Margie" is an unassuming tune that has held up well over the years. In addition to countless recordings, it has been used in several films, including *Margie* (1946) starring Jeanne Crain, and *The Eddie Cantor Story* (1953) in which the song is sung by Cantor himself.

Mean to Me (music: Fred E. Ahlert, lyrics: Roy Turk, 1929): Ruth Etting had a million-seller with this number on a disc with "Button Up Your Overcoat" on the flip side. "Mean to Me" rose to Number 3 in the charts. In spite of such an auspicious beginning, the tune seems to have drifted from popularity in the years that followed, possibly because of the deepening depression and demand for more upbeat songs. (Actually, "Mean to Me" is somewhat of a hybrid, having a melody that invites a bouncy rendition, but lyrics that are somewhat dark and sullen.)

The song might have fallen into oblivion (as many hit songs did) except that Teddy Wilson included it on a recording session with Billie Holiday in May of 1937. Billie's career had taken off two years before, when she was only 20 years old; by 1937 she had a string of hits behind her and was recording with the best jazz musicians in the world. The lineup on this session, typical of many for her, was simply astounding: Teddy Wilson, piano; Lester Young, tenor saxophone; Buck Clayton, trumpet; Buster Bailey, alto saxophone; Freddie Green, guitar; Walter Page, bass; Jo Jones, drums. It was a band made in heaven, and it sounded like it. What's more, the recording was a hit, rising to Number 7 in the charts, reintroducing the tune to the public, and endearing it to the hearts of jazz musicians, who idolized Billie and Lester especially, from that time till the present.

If you listen to this recording (and you must), you'll notice that Billie doesn't sing the melody. She adheres to the harmony, sings the bridge pretty much the way it's written, but mostly makes up her own notes. What's going on here? Was Fred Ahlert's melody not jazzy enough so that it had to be changed? A better interpretation is that everyone knew the melody, and Billie's improvisations were meant to be heard against the backdrop of the original version. It's hard for us to imagine now but back then the song was what became popular, not just a particular version of it; everybody knew the tune because everybody was performing it, recording it, humming it, or whistling it. So, in the same sense that a jazz musician plays the melody once and then improvises on it, Billie just assumes "Well, you know how this goes, so let's just get to it."

Memories of You (music: Eubie Blake, lyrics: Andy Razaf, 1930): James Hubert "Eubie" Blake (1887-1983) was an African-American pianist, composer, and lyricist of tremendous importance in the history of both jazz and American musical theater. Roughly the same age as Jelly Roll Morton, Eubie was also a transitional player in the movement from Ragtime to jazz. But Eubie was from Baltimore, developing his style on piano jobs in Baltimore and Atlantic City, calling into question the common belief that jazz developed in New Orleans and then spread to the rest of the country.

In the mid-teens, Eubie teamed up with singer/lyricist Noble Sissle to form one of the most celebrated songwriting teams of the era. Shortly after the war, they became a stage act, the "Dixie Duo," becoming among the first African Americans to perform in the White vaudeville circuit. They also provided the music to several Broadway shows, including *Shuffle Along* (1920), the most significant achievement in Black musical theater of its time. Sissle and Blake parted ways in 1927 but remained lifelong friends. Blake lived to be nearly 100 years old, and was fortunate enough to witness the Broadway musical *Eubie* (1978), which celebrated his music.

Producer Lew Leslie, who had had great success with presenting African-American performers on the Broadway stage, had used primarily White songwriters (such as Jimmy McHugh and Dorothy Fields for *Blackbirds of 1928*). For the 1930 edition of *Blackbirds*, however, he decided to entrust the entire score to Black songwriters. He approached Eubie Blake, asking if he would write the score for his new revue with Andy Razaf as lyricist. Blake was eager to write for the stage again and accepted Leslie's offer.

Razaf had collaborated with Fats Waller on two successful shows in 1929, writing a number of fabulous songs, including "Honeysuckle Rose," "Black and Blue," and "Ain't Misbehavin'." But Razaf and Waller were drifting apart as well. The more disciplined Razaf was having a little trouble working with Fats, who was very much a free spirit and about to embark on a new career as a pianist/singer/entertainer. Blake and Razaf worked well together. They would eventually collaborate on some 80 songs, but none would be more highly acclaimed than their enduring ballad "Memories of You."

Blake said that his inspiration for the song came from Edward MacDowell's piano sketch "To a Wild Rose," and the similarity is apparent. Blake's tune is quite expansive, covering a range of an octave and a half in just the first few bars. In fact, "Memories of You" was written for Minto Cato, a singer in the show who was known for her extremely wide vocal range. Perhaps for this reason, the tune is favored more by instrumentalists than vocalists. Clarinetists, perhaps because of the expansive range of the instrument, are particularly partial to the tune. Benny Goodman loved the number and recorded it some two dozen times. The first hit recording of the song, by Louis Armstrong and Lionel Hampton (1930), is of historical significance for another reason: it documents the first use of vibraphone on a jazz recording. Eubie himself recorded the song one last time in 1973, at the age of 86, with as much style and energy as ever.

Just about every clarinetist includes "Memories of You" in their repertoire. A very introspective interpretation can be heard by Atlantic City-based Joe Barrett on his album *Memories of You* (2012) with the George Mesterhazy Trio.

"The Memphis Blues" brought W.C. Handy fame, but fortune would have to wait for future compositions. (Courtesy Lilly Library, Indiana University, Bloomington, Indiana.)

Memphis Blues (W.C. Handy, 1912): Known as the "Father of the Blues," W.C. Handy (1873-1958) was one of the most influential songwriters in history. He was not the first to perform or publish a blues song, but he championed the music tirelessly, and due to his influence the blues became one of the dominant forces in American music.

During his early years, Handy scuffled to make a living as a musician. Cornet was his primary instrument, but he played several other instruments passably, wrote arrangements, led bands, and did whatever he could to earn money, sometimes having to work as a day laborer. In 1903 he took a job leading a band in Clarkesville, Mississippi, in the heart of what we would now call Delta blues territory. As his band travelled throughout the region, Handy paid attention to the music that he heard, liked it, and tried to work it into his own band arrangements. In 1908, when his reputation as a leader had begun to attract attention, he decided to move to Memphis to seek further opportunities.

Such an opportunity came shortly. In 1909 a politician named Edward Hull Crump was running for mayor and sought a campaign song to stir up the Black vote. It was suggested to him that he seek out Handy, which he did, and the result was Handy's first blues, which he entitled "Mr. Crump." Crump won his election, but, more importantly, his song was a sensation and locals continued to ask for it long after the campaign was over. Handy decided to change the name to "Memphis Blues" and get it published.

For three years, Handy peddled his song to various publishing houses with no success. More than one publisher pointed out that the song had an incorrect number of measures. Most blues songs have 12 bar strains, as opposed to most popular songs that are based on multiples of eight, but at the time few people knew this. Finally, Handy decided to publish the song himself. He sought the help of two White men—a department store clerk who agreed to arrange for the printing and a publisher who agreed to act as a sales agent. Unfortunately, they were setting him up for a scam. A week after the song went on the market, he was informed that hardly any copies were sold, and was offered $50 cash for the copyright. He took the offer, not knowing that the first 1000 copies printed had sold out in a few days. The song soon became a national sensation; sheet music sales soared, several recordings appeared, and the celebrated dance team of Vernon and Irene Castle were using the tune as the accompaniment for their new dance, the foxtrot. For decades to come, the song remained popular, and Handy never received a dime for it.

Midnight in Moscow (music: Vasily Solovyov-Sedoi, lyrics: Mikhail Matusovsky, 1955): The song has a convoluted pedigree. Classical composer Solovyov-Sedoi and poet Matusovsky teamed up to write a song which they called "Leningrad Nights."

Of course, Leningrad was the name for St. Petersburg during the Soviet Era, and Solovyov-Sedoi lived there his entire life. At the request of the Soviet Ministry of Culture, however, the name was changed to *Moscow Nights*. In 1957, the song was used as an anthem for the International Youth Festival in Moscow where it attracted the attention of both Soviets and foreigners. Within a few years, the song became popular throughout the world.

In 1961, the British traditional jazz band Kenny Ball and his Jazzmen recorded the song under the name of *Midnight in Moscow* and it became a hit in the United States the following year, reaching Number 1 on the Easy Listening Chart. That same year, the sheet music was published in the United States under the name of *Moscow Nights*, with English lyrics credited to Hal Saunders, Robert Iredale and Franz Conde.

The tune is a simple 16-bar folk song with a tag, and it's hard to believe its history could be so complicated. The tag is actually quite unusual—a literal repeat of the last eight bars or second half of the tune. In fact, many an unwary musician has been confused by the form when playing it for the first time. Among the noteworthy jazz versions is Eddie Condon's 1962 recording from the album entitled *Midnight in Moscow*, featuring Bobby Hackett on cornet, Peanuts Hucko on clarinet, and Lou McGarity on trombone.

Minor Drag (Fats Waller, 1929): The tune comes from the famous session that also produced "Numb Fumblin" and "Handful of Keys," two Fats Waller piano solos that cemented his stature as one of the most acclaimed masters of Harlem Stride. In particular, "Handful of Keys" became his signature tour de force, as "Caroline Shout" did for James P. Johnson and "Finger Buster" for Willie The Lion Smith.

As Eddie Condon relates in his 1947 memoir *We Called It Music*, he had been hired by a Mr. Adams from the Southern Music Company to find Fats Waller and ensure that he arrived in time for the recording session, prepared and in condition to play. Fats was well known for his carousing and partying and the producers were worried. Condon took his charge seriously, following Fats around for several days, with the inevitable result that he soon became Waller's drinking buddy rather that his chaperone. According to Condon, the morning of the session they woke up under the tables at Connie's Inn, made some quick phone calls to assemble the band, got into a taxi and picked up the other band members on the way. Fats made up a couple of tunes in the cab and taught them to the other musicians en route.

The two band numbers were "Minor Drag" and "Harlem Fuss." (Fats made up the names in the studio, though the executives believed that everything had been planned and rehearsed.) The results were spectacular. Mr. Adams was so pleased that he promised more studio dates, commending the musicians for their "planning and preparation." Condon adds, "After that the Southern Music Company, with careful planning and preparation, brought out the record on a Victor Label with the titles reversed: 'Harlem Fuss' was called 'The Minor Drag' and 'The Minor Drag' was called 'Harlem Fuss.' I got my seventy-five dollars."

There haven't been many recordings of "Minor Drag" since Waller's. Reedman Jim Galloway recorded the song in 1973 with Dick Wellstood laying down some great stride piano. More recently, the New Orleans-based band Tuba Skinny included the number on their 2011 album *Garbage Man*. And pianist Jim Hession, protégé of the great Eubie Blake, recorded the number on his 2008 album *Giants of Stride*.

Mississippi Mud (Harry Barris, 1927): By the mid 20s, Paul Whiteman was in a position to hire practically any act or musician that appealed to him. In late 1926, while on the West Coast, he heard the duo of Bing Crosby and Al Rinker, liked them, and recruited them into his band. Unfortunately, they were not successful with Whiteman's audiences, and it appeared that they might be canned.

Ironically, it was Paul Whiteman's father who saved the day. Professor Wilberforce Whiteman was superintendent of music education for the Denver school system, a prominent citizen, and successful music teacher. Among his accomplished students were the famous bandleaders Jimmie Lunceford and Andy Kirk. The professor never really liked Paul's music, but he was proud of his son and always ready to help. When a very talented musician named Harry Barris passed through his system, he sent him to New York to audition for his son.

Whiteman was impressed by Barris, added him to Crosby and Rinker's act, and named the trio the Rhythm Boys. It was a good move. They were a very popular attraction for Whiteman over the next three years and recorded a series of numbers with the orchestra. In spite of their popularity, they were infamous for their drinking and mischievous conduct, causing Whiteman much grief. In 1930 he had finally had enough and fired all three of them. After leaving Whiteman, they continued to perform together until 1931, when Bing left to begin his solo career. Even their breakup was somewhat of a scandal—they walked out on their contract with the Cocoanut Grove in LA and were subsequently banned by the musicians' union. By this time Bing had a solo hit with "I Surrender Dear" (also written by Barris) and really didn't care.

"Mississippi Mud" was one of the first tunes Barris wrote for the Rhythm Boys. They first recorded the number in June of 1927, accompanied by Barris on the piano. This version is fun to listen to, revealing how tight they were as a trio, as well as their penchant for clowning around. Paul Whiteman's February 1928 recording was the big hit, featuring Irene Taylor on vocals in addition to the Rhythm Boys and Bix Beiderbecke on cornet. Frankie Trumbauer's January 1928 recording also became a hit, also featuring the Rhythm Boys and Bix, and is probably the most musically rewarding of these early versions. the Rhythm Boys can be seen and heard performing "Mississippi Mud" in Whiteman's film *King of Jazz* (1930).

Muskrat Ramble (music: Kid Ory, lyrics: Ray Gilbert, 1926): The song was first recorded as the third of the famous Hot Five recordings on February 26, 1926. In later years, Ory claimed that he had written the number in 1921 while living in California, basing the melody on a figure from an exercise book, and that Lil Armstrong supplied the name for the recording session. Louis Armstrong, however, claimed that he wrote the song and Ory supplied the name. Sidney Bechet said that neither of them wrote it—that it was based on an old folksong that jazz musicians used to play in New Orleans back in the Buddy Bolden days. Considering that the tune has three sections with distinct melodies, it is likely that all three men were partially right. Ray Gilbert played no part in the tune's creation—only adding the lyrics many years later in 1950.

"Muskrat Ramble" has become a reliable war horse in the Dixieland repertoire and for good reason. Its opening refrain recalls the Ragtime tradition, and the contrasting sections mesh well, with plenty of syncopation and harmonic contrast. Whether he wrote it or not, Ory obviously had strong command of the number, which really accentuates his tailgate style. His trombone tag at the very end has become practically a requirement for any performance.

Recommended is a recent recording by German-born New Orleans-style trumpeter Norbert Susemihl from the album *Live at Maribo Jazz Festival* (2007).

My Baby Just Cares for Me (music: Walter Donaldson, lyrics: Gus Kahn, 1930): By 1930, Donaldson's career was flourishing. After many years as a successful Tin Pan Alley composer with interpolations of individual songs in shows here and there, he wrote the full stage score for the Ziegfeld hit *Whoopee* in 1928, starring Eddie Cantor, which included "Makin' Whoopee" and "Love Me or Leave Me." Capitalizing on his growing success, about this time he resigned from Irving Berlin's publishing company to start his own. In 1930, Donaldson was asked to do the film version of *Whoopee* to which he added "My Baby Just Cares for Me"—another hit.

By this time, he had moved to California to write exclusively for the movies and never looked back. *Whoopee* was to be the only full Broadway score he ever wrote.

Eddie Cantor sang "My Baby" in *Whoopee*, the movie that launched his long and successful film career. He subsequently adopted "My Baby" as his signature song. But it was Ted Weems, with vocals by Art Jarrett, who had the hit record, charting at Number 4. The tune has a somewhat repetitive opening phrase, which complements the lyric, but makes the tune more of a vocal than an instrumental number. For this reason, it was not played much by jazz bands until it was rediscovered by pop stars in the 1950s. Among these recordings, one was to have an exceedingly long-range impact: Nina Simone included the song in her 1958 debut album *Little Girl Blue*. The recording received little attention at the time, but in the late 1980s the Chanel No. 5 perfume company decided to use the cut in their British commercials. The track was soon released as a single and became a hit, her biggest in many years. A charming clay animation video set to Nina's recording was made in 1987.

My Blue Heaven (music: Walter Donaldson, lyrics: George Whiting, 1924): The tune got off to a slow start but eventually made up for it, becoming one of the giant hits of the 20th century. In 1924, Donaldson teamed up with vaudeville singer George Whiting (not to be confused with Richard Whiting), who contributed the words and put the song into his act. No one paid much attention for a few years, until a few people started to realize the song's potential. Ziegfeld interpolated the song into his *Follies of 1927* for Eddie Cantor to sing. Radio personality Tommy Lyman (see entry on "My Melancholy Baby") liked the song so much that he made it his theme song. And in July of 1927 Paul Whiteman recorded the number, which eventually became a Number 1 hit for him. But it was Gene Austin's recording that made the history books, and it almost didn't happen.

Austin had been unhappy with Victor Records for some time, feeling that they weren't allowing him to record the best songs. For a September 1927 recording session, he asked to record a couple of numbers of his own choice, including "My Blue Heaven." The executives agreed, but scheduled them last on the session. When all the songs except Austin's requests had been recorded, the musicians began to pack up and go home. Austin was told that they had other engagements, but he would not be dissuaded. He desperately begged any musician who could to stay and help him out. He ended up with a piano player, a cello player and a stagehand who could do bird calls (suitable for the opening line of the song "When whippoorwills call"). Going ahead with this unlikely combination they recorded "My Blue Heaven." The strange mix of sounds worked magic with the public. According to Austin, that record sold eight million copies, an unheard-of number at that time. He would go on to record the song several times, amassing a total of some 13 million copies sold.

A sad footnote to the story: The subject of the song is a happy husband returning home to his wife and baby, his idea of heaven. A short time after the recording, ready to leave for home to be united with his family after a long period of absence, Austin received news of the death of his newborn son.

"My Buddy" was the first effort of the celebrated songwriting team of Walter Donaldson and Gus Kahn. (Courtesy Lilly Library, Indiana University, Bloomington, Indiana.)

My Buddy (music: Walter Donaldson; lyrics: Gus Kahn, 1922): Walter Donaldson was born in Brooklyn, NY in 1893, one of 11 children in a music-loving family. His mother was a classically trained pianist, but Walter preferred popular music. After high school, he found work as a song plugger on Tin Pan Alley. He served in the army during the war and was stationed at Camp Upton where he met and befriended Irving Berlin (five years his senior). After the war, Berlin asked him to join his new publishing business, Irving Berlin Inc., and Donaldson stayed for ten years, leaving to establish his own firm in 1928.

In 1922, Donaldson teamed up with lyricist Gus Kahn to begin a collaboration that would produce more than 100 songs. "My Buddy" was their first effort, and the song remained Donaldson's most personal. While the sentiment of a buddy who has departed might seem like a reference to a fellow soldier lost in the Great War, Donaldson actually wrote it to express his grief over the death of his fiancée. The melody, with its repetitious lilting rhythm in three-quarter time, evokes profound sadness and longing, with or without lyrical support. Amazingly, the opening measures are exactly the same as another tune Donaldson wrote that same year, one with a totally different expressive feel: "Carolina in the Morning." The ability to rework musical materials in subtle ways is the mark of a master tunesmith. This could explain how he managed to turn out so many great songs without ever seeming to have a dry spell. With an output of some 600 songs, one could only imagine what he would have produced had he lived to 101, as did Irving Berlin. Tragically, Donaldson died at the age of 54; coincidentally, so did Gus Kahn.

Paul Dresser died without knowing that his last song, "My Gal Sal," would become one of the biggest hits of its era. (Courtesy Lilly Library, Indiana University, Bloomington, Indiana.)

My Gal Sal (music & lyrics: Paul Dresser, 1905): Paul Dresser (1857-1906) ran away with a travelling show when he was 16 and became a successful entertainer and songwriter. At the height of his fame, in the 1890s, he ran his own publishing house and was one of the most popular tunesmiths on Tin Pan Alley. His "On the Banks of the Wabash" (1897), which eventually became the state song of Indiana, was the second most successful song of the 19th century in terms of sheet music sales. Many people compared him to Stephen Foster, and alas, the comparison went deeper than intended—Dresser, like Foster, died an alcoholic and a pauper. As the new century came in, Dresser's tunes no longer appealed to the public as they once had. His fortunes began to turn, made worse by his habits of lavish generosity and reckless spending. By 1905, his firm had gone bankrupt and he was forced to leave his hotel. He died in January of the following year while living with his sister, not knowing that the last song he published, "My Gal Sal," was destined to become his most successful, eventually selling some three million copies of sheet music, a feat achieved by only a handful of songs in history.

Dresser, who had changed his name from the original spelling "Dreiser," was the older brother of the famous novelist Theodore Dreiser, who wrote a biographical story about him called "My Brother Paul." That story became the basis for the 1942 film *My Gal Sal* starring Rita Hayworth and Victor Mature.

And who was Sal? No one knows for sure what was in his mind, but we can guess. In the 1880s Dresser had made Evansville, Indiana his home base. While there, he became friends with a Sally Walker, who owned and operated a brothel. They had a long-term relationship but never married.

For a recent recording that combines the tune's original waltz character with its jazz possibilities, hear pianist Steve Pistorius on his 2013 album *New Orleans Shuffle*.

> They called her frivolous Sal
> A peculiar sort of a gal
> With a heart that was mellow
> An all 'round good fellow, was my old pal
> Your troubles, sorrow and care
> She was always willing to share
> A wild sort of devil, but dead on the level
> Was My Gal Sal.

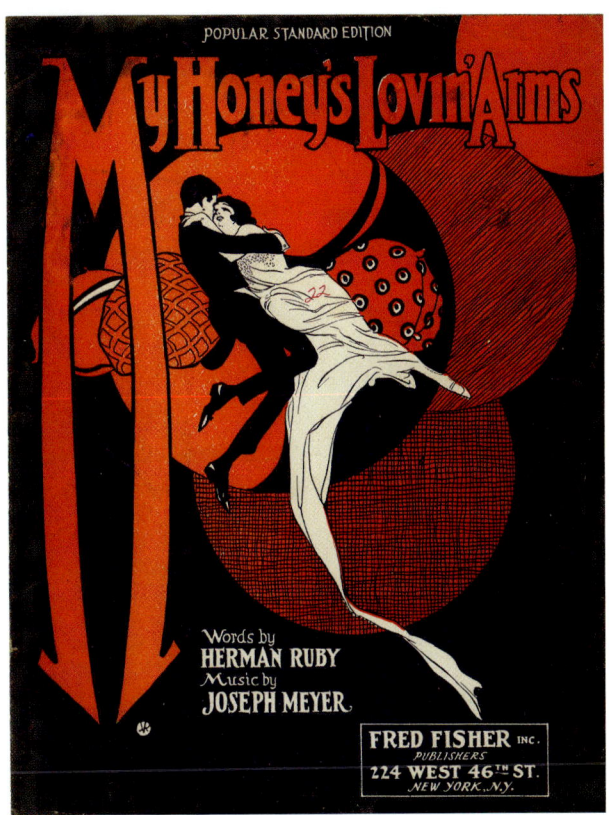

"My Honey's Lovin' Arms," by Joseph Meyer and Herman Ruby. Despite the early copyright date, the song has a swing feel, and was successfully revived by Benny Goodman during the Big Band Era. (Courtesy Lilly Library, Indiana University, Bloomington, Indiana.)

My Honey's Lovin' Arms (music: Joseph Meyer; lyrics: Herman Ruby, 1922): It's likely that most jazz aficionados would not recognize the name Joseph Meyer, but if you mentioned a few of his tunes: "California Here I Come," "Clap Hands Here Comes Charlie," "Crazy Rhythm," and "Street of Dreams," for example, they would certainly know his work. There is something particularly appealing about Meyer's style to the jazz musician. His melodies often resemble riff tunes, containing simple repeating phrases that are just perfect for jamming. "My Honey's Lovin' Arms" is no exception: the opening phrase presents a melodic shape and rhythm that holds throughout the tune, adapting to the changing harmonies much like a jazz improviser would.

Like many popular musicians of that time, Meyer had a formal music education, including a year abroad, studying harmony and counterpoint in Paris. After serving in the army during World War I, he went into business for a while, but his heart was in music. Finally he decided to go to New York and see if he might make a living as a composer. "My Honey's Lovin' Arms," one of his first songs, became a hit, as did "California Here I Come," published the same year. He went on to compose many notable tunes and contributed to, or supplied the score to, several Broadway musicals. His tunes can be heard in more than 100 film scores.

"My Honey's Lovin' Arms" was a 1922 hit for both Isham Jones and the California Ramblers, and was successfully revived by Benny Goodman in 1939. A fine recording from 1929 by Joe Venuti's Blue Four showcases Jimmy Dorsey on the baritone saxophone rather than his usual instrument, the alto saxophone. Not surprisingly, he handles the larger instrument with finesse and dexterity. The recording contains a slight blooper near the end, which only demonstrates how good these guys were at thinking on their feet. It seems that Eddie Lang played through the first couple of beats of Dorsey's four-bar break, but fixes his mistake by repeating it on the third bar—as if it had been planned that way!

For a charming rendition of more recent vintage, listen to singer/banjoist Cynthia Sayer on her album *Forward Moves* (2010), featuring Kenny Davern on the clarinet and Vince Giordano on bass saxophone.

By the way, as with "All By Myself" (see entry), the lyrics to "My Honey's Lovin' Arms" also refer to a "cozy Morris chair." It makes you wonder if the company was giving out free furniture in return for endorsements!

> I love your lovin' arms
> They hold a world of charms
> A place to nestle when I'm lonely
> A cozy Morris chair
> Oh, what a happy pair
> One caress, happiness
> Seems to bless my little honey
> I love you more each day
> When years have passed away
> You'll find my love belongs to you only
> 'Cause when the world seems wrong
> I know that I belong right in my honey's lovin' arms.

"My Melancholy Baby, by Ernie Burnett and George A. Norton. Notice how the writers and publisher get top billing, not the singer. (Courtesy Lilly Library, Indiana University, Bloomington, Indiana.)

My Melancholy Baby (music: Ernie Burnett, lyrics: George A. Norton, 1912): The old cliché is that this is the tune everybody requests, and for good reason—it was the song that just wouldn't go away: Walter Van Brunt had a hit in 1915, Gene Austin revived the song with a Number 3 hit in 1927, and Teddy Wilson with Billie Holiday had a Number 6 hit in 1936. But we're just getting started: Bing Crosby had a hit in 1939, tenor saxophonist Sam Donahue in 1947, and Tommy Edwards in 1959. Judy Garland sang it in *A Star Is Born* (1954) after a drunk yells out "play Melancholy Baby." And in *Some Like it Hot* (1959) Marilyn Monroe's character, Sugar Kane, says at one point: "All they have to do is play eight bars of 'Come to me My Melancholy Baby' and my spine turns to custard, I get goosepimply all over and I come to 'em!"

According to Edward Shanaphy, it was "My Melancholy Baby" that was responsible for the term "torch song" as a reference to a sentimental love song. An American singer named Tommy Lyman liked the number and adopted it as his theme song sometime around 1915. During a show one night during the early 20s he supposedly announced, "and now my famous torch song: 'Come to me My Melancholy Baby.'"

The song was originally published in 1911, with the music by Burnett but lyrics by his wife, Maybelle E. Watson. The publisher liked the song but not the lyrics, so Norton supplied new words and the song was republished. Early interpretations treated the song as a fast dance number, but by the mid 20s it was generally considered a ballad.

The song prompted another piece of history, which might have helped make it a popular request: Composer Ernie Burnett fought in France during the First World War and was wounded in battle. When he was found, he had lost his dog tags and had total amnesia. No one could determine who he was and he remained in an army hospital for an undisclosed period of time. At some point, the name Ernie Burnett had appeared on the list of soldiers killed in action. One day a piano player who was entertaining the patients announced that he would play "Melancholy Baby" in honor of the dead composer, which he did. Upon hearing the number, Burnett sat up and said, "I wrote that song!" and his memory returned.

One of my favorite recordings is by the Dorsey Brothers Orchestra from 1928. That was the year the famous but ever-quarreling brothers first began recording under that name, though they didn't appear in public as an ensemble until 1934. Their recording of "Melancholy Baby" contains excellent solos from the brothers, as would be expected, but the driving force behind it all is the superb bass saxophone work of Adrian Rollini, who also takes a fine solo on the number. The ten-piece ensemble also includes a name that is familiar to saxophone players—Arnold Brilhart, who would go on to become a legendary manufacturer of saxophone mouthpieces.

My Monday Date (Earl Hines, Sid Robin, 1928): The great pianist Earl Kenneth "Fatha" Hines (1903-1983) grew up in Pittsburgh, relocating to Chicago in 1923. By 1926, he was hailed as the hottest piano player in jazz—his swinging "trumpet" style supplanting the older Jelly Roll Morton approach. He and Louis Armstrong met in 1926 and quickly became best friends. By 1927, they were working together steady at the Sunset Café and Armstrong recruited him into his Hot Five and Hot Seven recording ensembles, replacing Louis' wife Lil. In 1928, Hines recorded his first piano solos and started his big band, which he would lead until 1948. For three years after that, he joined Louis Armstrong's All Stars, then moved to the West Coast, where he led his own small ensembles. In 1975, an acclaimed documentary film was made on the life of Earl Hines.

Hines explains the origin of "Monday Date": "'My Monday Date' got its title as a sort of gag. Louis would sometimes forget we were going to meet, or Lil, his wife, would take him off somewhere, and I'd wait and he wouldn't show up. So the next time we would be going to get together, I'd say something like, 'Don't forget our Monday date that You promised me last Tuesday.' Out of that we got a tune and a title for one of our record sessions."

Hines recorded "Monday Date" as both a piano solo and a piano roll in 1928, and also with Louis Armstrong's Hot Seven that same year. In 1973, he remade the piano roll for QRS, along with all of the numbers dating from his 1928 sessions. Incidentally, Armstrong entitled the number "A Monday Date" on his Hot Seven recording. When he recorded the number in 1939 and again in 1947 he called it "Our Monday Date." Evidently, not only couldn't he remember his dates with Hines, he couldn't even remember the name of the tune Hines wrote about them!

Nagasaki (music: Harry Warren, lyrics: Mort Dixon, 1928): Never heard of Harry Warren? How about "I Only Have Eyes for You," "Jeepers Creepers," "That's Amore," "The More I See You," "At Last," or "Chattanooga Choo Choo," (which became the first gold record in history)? You're not alone. Wilfred Sheed, in his wonderful book *The House That George Built,* sums up the problem quite well: "Insofar as Harry Warren is famous for anything at all, it's for not being famous."

Warren's real name was Salvatore Antonio Guaragna, but the Anglicization of his Italian name did little to promote his popularity. When talking pictures came in, which really meant musical pictures, the black hole of Hollywood began sucking the musical life out of Broadway. One by one the Tin Pan Alley publishers were bought out, and one by one the songwriters too succumbed to the inevitable gravitational force. Warren was one of the first of the great songwriters to write primarily for film, and his reward was to be forgotten. To quote Wilfred Sheed once again: "So [Warren] disappeared into Warner Bros.' studio, and was never heard of again—until, that is, he eventually became an archivist's delight as the king of the unknowns and the prototype to the point of caricature of all the New Yorkers who went West in the 1930s, kicking and screaming, and stayed there moaning and groaning, and vanishing one by one from public view, like a pack of Cheshire cats, leaving behind not smiles but forgettable movies and unforgettable music." Did this bother him? If it did he never let on: "Michelangelo didn't sign his paintings. If they don't know my work then the hell with them."

But we're getting ahead of ourselves. The tune under discussion dates from Warren's Tin Pan Alley days, which were indeed short. The title "Nagasaki" was simply a grab for some exotic place, and this thriving Japanese port city seemed the perfect choice.

(The events of August 1945, of course, put this frivolous tune on the shelf for many years.) Warren's bouncy melody is complemented by some delightfully ridiculous lyrics by Mort Dixon. (Who? How about "Bye Bye Blackbird" or "I'm Looking Over a Four Leaf Clover"? Yeah, that guy.)

A final note on the lyric that goes, "Back in Nagasaki where the fellers chew tobaccy and the women wicky wacky woo." Surprisingly, the goofy verb was not coined by lyricist Mort Dixon but had actually been used in a song title before. In 1916, Albert Von Tilzer with Stanley Murphy and Charles McCarron had a Number 1 hit with a song entitled "Oh How She Could Yacki Hacki Wicki Wacki Woo (That's Love in Honolulu)." As far as what a Hawaiian is doing in a song about Japan—well, let's just call it artistic license.

"Nagasaki" can be heard on the 1990 album *Piano Players and Significant Others*, featuring Dick Hyman and Ralph Sutton playing some great piano. For an earthier version recommended is a 2009 recording by the New Orleans-based Cottonmouth Rhythm Kings. This group swings like mad, with a somewhat unusual instrumentation of clarinet (Bruce Brackman), trumpet (Charlie Fardella), violin (Matt Rhody), bass saxophone (Tom Saunders), guitar (John Rodli), and bass (Robert Snow).

New Orleans (music and lyrics: Hoagy Carmichael, 1932): There are so many songs with New Orleans in the title that musicians often refer to this number as "Hoagy Carmichael's New Orleans," and deservedly so, since he penned both the music and the lyrics. Although Hoagy supplied the words to relatively few of his songs, his lyrics are something more than serviceable and display the same unmistakable homey quality as his melodies: "It will remind you of old-fashioned lace; a glass of wine will greet your smiling face."

The tune is only 16 bars long, but the harmony is fast-moving and unusual, presenting a significant challenge for the performer. The chord scheme is adapted from the bridge to "You Took Advantage of Me" (Rodgers & Hart, 1928), except that Hoagy uses this harmony for the main part of the tune. (Musicians recognize the chord sequence as a "cycle of fifths.") The melody is somewhat instrumental in character (it must be to negotiate the rapid harmonic motion), but this impression goes away when the song is sung slowly. Unfortunately, musicians didn't realize this at first (or perhaps they did but dancers would have none of it), and performed the song as a brisk foxtrot. Both Bennie Moten and the Casa Loma Orchestra recorded the song in this fashion and their records went nowhere. "New Orleans" never did have a hit recording, but as musicians began performing it at slower tempos its inner qualities became apparent, and it eventually became a jazz standard. Bobby Hackett and Jack Teagarden recorded a superb rendition in 1955, and Hoagy can be heard singing the song himself on a 1956 recording with the Johnny Mandel Orchestra.

Songwriter Johnny Mandel told a curious story that involves "New Orleans." He recalled that when he wrote the theme for the film *The Sandpiper* (1965), the studio wanted a version with a title and lyrics. He approached Johnny Mercer, who heard the theme and turned down the offer. Mercer told Mandel "I couldn't do that to Hoagy." He felt that the opening phrase was a direct copy of the opening phrase of "New Orleans." Mandel then turned to Paul Francis Webster, maybe even at Mercer's suggestion, who came up with "The Shadow of Your Smile."

The song went on to become a big hit and won the Academy Award. When Johnny Mercer later told Hoagy Carmichael the story, Hoagy said that he "never noticed" the similarity between the two songs!

There is no shortage of recordings of "New Orleans." All the greats have done it. An interesting version to check out was recorded by New Orleans trumpeter/vocalist Leroy Jones (from the album *'Mo Cream from the Crop*, 1994). Jones is a fascinating player whose improvisations draw from a deep vocabulary of musical ideas adapted to a hard-swinging New Orleans feel. He's also among the few jazz singers performing today who know how to embellish a melody without losing the melody.

Nobody Knows You When You're Down and Out (music and lyrics: Jimmy Cox, 1923): Jimmy Cox (1882-1925) is remembered for this perennial song, but he never lived to enjoy its success. Perhaps the beginning of the Roaring Twenties was the wrong time for a song bemoaning the fortunes of a millionaire who had lost all his money, but those words would ring true a few years later. Cox introduced the song himself in vaudeville, and it went pretty much unnoticed for several years. It wasn't until 1927 that it was recorded, by blues singer Bobby Leecan, who went by the name of Blind Bobby Baker. Then in January 1929, boogie-woogie pianist Pine Top Smith recorded the song, just two months before he died. It was one of only 11 known recordings he made. In May of that year Bessie Smith recorded the number with a small band. The record was released in September, just weeks before the stock market crash. Whether it was the right artist, the right arrangement, the right time, or all three, the song finally had an impact, becoming a major hit.

Understandably, considering the bluesy nature of the song and its hard luck lyrics, it has been recorded in every genre imaginable, including folk, soul, rock and blues versions. Solid traditional jazz versions can be heard by Eddie Condon (1943, 1944), Sidney Bechet (1949) and Kenny Ball (1951).

Nobody's Sweetheart Now (music: Elmer Schoebel and Ernie Erdman, lyrics: Billy Meyers and Gus Kahn, 1924): A favorite of jazz musicians since it first came out, this song features a catchy harmonic progression and a four-square melody that stays out of the way. It was written for the Broadway show *The Passing Show of 1923* and introduced by Ted Lewis. Isham Jones had a hit in 1924, Whiteman revived the song for a Number 2 hit in 1930, and the Mills Brothers had a Number 4 million seller in 1934. But more to the point are the plentiful jazz recordings that began appearing early on.

Significant among these is the first recording made by the legendary clarinetist Frank Teschemacher, a leading member in the cadre now referred to as the Austin High Gang. This group of young White jazz musicians from the West Side of Chicago emerged with a new take on New Orleans jazz, emphasizing more solo space, more energy and a hard driving beat, which began to be referred to as Chicago Style Jazz. Teschemacher in particular was noted for his daring, energetic solos, and is credited as an important influence on players such as Benny Goodman and Pee Wee Russell. In December 1927, a band led by Eddie Condon and Red McKenzie went into the studio to make the first recording by these musicians. In addition to Condon, McKenzie and Tesch, the musicians included Jimmy McPartland on cornet, Bud Freeman on saxophone, and Gene Krupa on drums. "Nobody's Sweetheart" was one of four songs recorded that day, and this song in particular would remain a favorite of jazz musicians who played in this style.

For a recent recording, listen to New Orleans reedman Ryan Burrage on his 2004 album *Toulouse Street Blues*, which also features some nice stride piano work by Richard Scott.

"Oh By Jingo," by Albert Von Tilzer and Lew Brown, suggests an earlier era, but has proven itself a splendid jazz number as well. (Courtesy Lilly Library, Indiana University, Bloomington, Indiana.)

Oh by Jingo, Oh by Gee, You're the Only Girl for Me (music: Albert Von Tilzer, lyrics: Lew Brown, 1919): Albert Von Tilzer (1878-1956) was one of the leading songwriters and publishers on Tin Pan Alley during the first couple of decades of the 20th century. The son of Jewish immigrants (an apparent requirement for songwriters of the time), he was born Albert Gumm, but later took his mother's maiden name and added the "Von" just because it sounded impressive. His brothers, also in the music business, thought it was a good idea and did the same. "Take Me out to the Ballgame" is one of his most famous compositions.

"Oh by Jingo" is a novelty song pure and simple, and any effort to make sense of the lyrics misses the mark and loses the fun:

> Oh! by Gee! by Gosh, by Gum, by Juv
> Oh by Jingo, won't you hear our love
> We will build for you a hut
> You will be our fav'rite nut
> We'll have a lot of little Oh by Gollies,
> Then we'll put them in the Follies
> By Jingo said, By Gosh, By Gee
> By Jiminy please don't bother me
> So they all went away singing
> Oh by Gee, by Gosh by Gum, by Juv by Jingo,
> by Gee, you're the only girl for me.

Introduced in the Broadway show *Linger Longer Letty*, it became a popular Tin Pan Alley song of the post-World War I Era, with hit recordings by Frank Crumit (1920) and Billy Murray (1920). If this song weren't silly enough in its own right, Spike Jones had a Number 20 hit with it in 1943 and it was sung by "Mertz and Kurtz" on the *I Love Lucy show* (season 4 episode 2, 1954).

But my favorite novelty performance of the song has to be the one by Hugh Laurie and Stephen Fry in *Jeeves and Wooster* (season 4, episode 5, 1993). Any fan of the 20s will want to watch this series, which aired from 1990 through 1993, adapting the humorous stories of P.G. Wodehouse to the screen. Sir Pelham Grenville Wodehouse (1881-1975) was a prolific author and one of the most widely read humorists of the 20th century. Although most of his fiction takes place in England, Wodehouse spent much of his life in the United States and wrote Broadway musical comedies early in his career.

So why is this novelty tune a traditional jazz standard? Because it makes a great jam tune, with an effective chord progression, catchy, straight-forward melody, and a change-up in rhythm, harmony, and melody for the last eight bars to add interest and kick off the next chorus. Von Tilzer might have intended to write a bouncy parlor song, which he did, but he unknowingly also provided a romping swing vehicle.

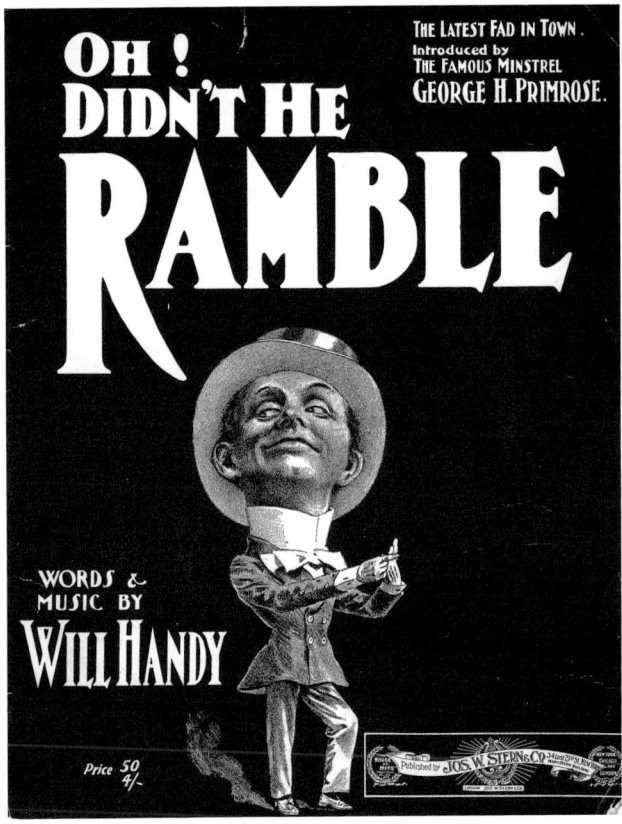

"Oh Didn't He Ramble," by Will Handy, was adapted from an English folk song with roots dating back hundreds of years. (Courtesy Sandy Marrone, Cinnaminson, NJ.)

Oh Didn't He Ramble (Will Handy, 1902): There was no Will Handy. It is certainly not a reference to W.C. Handy, who was still leading bands in Mississippi at the time and not yet recognized as a composer. Rather, it was a pseudonym adopted for unknown reasons by some of the hottest tune writers on Broadway—the Cole-Johnson trio.

James Weldon Johnson and John Rosamond Johnson were two African-American brothers who came from a well-established family in Jacksonville, Florida. They each had a thorough education: James completed a B.A. from Atlanta University, where he studied Latin and Greek, and took a special interest in English composition. Rosamond, an excellent pianist, studied for six years at the New England Conservatory of Music in Boston. They settled in New York, where they teamed up with Bob Cole, who was already an experienced performer and songwriter. The combination was magic, and their songs began turning up all over town. In 1901 they signed an exclusive three-year contract with Joseph Stern, one of the leading firms on Tin

Pan Alley. It is puzzling that the publisher used a fictitious name for "Oh Didn't He Ramble," since the Cole-Johnson team was well known to the public.

"Oh Didn't He Ramble" is a reworking of the old folk song "The Darby Ram." The song is so old that its origins cannot be identified, traces of it dating back to Renaissance England. The song made its way to America and was frequently performed by African-American songsters. At some point the opening words to the chorus became "Oh, didn't he ramble," which the Cole-Johnson team chose as their title. The song, as stated on the sheet music cover, was "introduced by the famous minstrel George H. Primrose," and was soon performed in minstrel shows throughout the country. In New Orleans, where the original song was surely known, "Oh Didn't He Ramble" quickly became a staple in the brass band repertoire and has remained so to this day. Along with "The Saints" and "Closer Walk with Thee," it is one of the songs most closely associated with a New Orleans funeral. To hear present-day New Orleans musicians performing the song, listen to *The New Orleans Moonshiners* (2009).

"On the Alamo" by Isham Jones and Gus Kahn, is one of many songs that refer to the Alamo as a place for romantic encounters. (Courtesy Sandy Marrone, Cinnaminson, NJ.)

On The Alamo (music: Isham Jones, lyrics: Gus Kahn, 1922): Isham Jones (1894-1956) was a master tunesmith whose name is all but forgotten but whose songs are not. What is truly remarkable about Jones' output is not that he wrote more than 200 songs, but that at least 40 of them became hits. Batting .200 in the majors isn't very impressive, but it is an astonishing achievement in the music business. Moreover, these hits were not temporary flashes in the Tin-Pan-Alley hit list—many of them went on to become some of the most recorded and enduring tunes in the great American songbook. "Wabash Blues," "I'll See You in My Dreams," "The One I Love Belongs to Somebody Else," "There Is No Greater Love," and "It Had to Be You" are just a few of his classic songs that have earned a permanent place in the repertoire. What's more, Jones led one of the most popular bands in the country during the 20s and 30s.

"On The Alamo" was a tremendous success for Jones, charting first place in record sales for four weeks in 1922. The tune was one in a long history of songs about the San Antonio fortress. In the decades following the defeat of March 1836, many songs were written about the epic battle. By the early 20th century the location still fascinated Americans, but was more likely to be considered the scene of a romantic rendezvous. Examples include "When It's Moonlight on the Alamo" and "Across the Alley from the Alamo." Gus Kahn's lyrics follow this sentiment: "Where the moon swings low, On the Alamo, In a garden fair where roses grow ..."

The tune entered the jazz repertoire early on, and survived the transition to modern jazz as well. Traditional jazz versions can be heard by Red Nichols (1929), Benny Goodman (1941), Wild Bill Davison (1984), Vince Giordano (1994), and the Atlantic City Jazz Band (2010).

Oriental Strut (Johnny St. Cyr, 1926): Johnny St. Cyr (1890-1966) was a guitar and banjo player from New Orleans, mostly remembered for his recordings with Louis Armstrong's Hot Fives and Sevens as well as Jelly Roll Morton's Red Hot Peppers. St. Cyr is not known as a songwriter and the tune was probably assembled on the spot for the February 1926 Hot Five recording session, perhaps with input from other band members. There isn't much of a melody to speak of, but the form and harmony are both unusual and somewhat complicated. It isn't surprising that a "chord man" was largely responsible for its composition. It begins with a minor section supported by an exotic rhythm, but soon gives way to a multipart structure typical of New Orleans tunes.

The highlight of Armstrong's recording of "Oriental Strut" is his stop-time chorus, which must have thrilled and mystified musicians at the time. His execution is not flawless (it would be nearly so just a year or two later), but he is soloing in a way no one ever had before. This was the laboratory in which Armstrong was experimenting and formulating the principles of solo improvisation that would guide the entire future of jazz. Through these recordings, we can be in his workshop and hear him reaching for the sky. Trumpeter Wingy Manone told the story that Jack Teagarden was so taken with this recording that he thought it should be preserved for posterity. So they drove out on the plain, dug a big hole and buried a copy.

As with several of the songs associated with the Hot Five and Seven recordings, most musicians avoided playing this song for decades to come, whether out of fear or reverence. Only in recent years has the tune re-entered the repertoire, and it is commonly performed by traditional jazz bands. A smoking version can be heard on the 2014 album *Owl Call Blues* featuring the New Orleans-based ensemble Tuba Skinny.

Original Dixieland One-Step (Nick La Rocca, 1937): The copyright date is totally misleading. This was actually the first commercially released jazz song, recorded on February 26, 1917 by the Original Dixieland Jass Band, under the title of "Dixieland Jass Band One-Step." (Toward the end of 1917 they changed the spelling to "Jazz.") Unfortunately, copyright infringement difficulties resulted in publication being delayed for two decades. Only when the band reassembled to celebrate the 20th anniversary of their initial recording were they able to see the music in print.

It seems that the third section of this multipart tune bears a strong resemblance to the trio of a 1910 composition by Joe Jordon entitled "That Teasin' Rag." A lawsuit resulted with the expected complications. The settlement required that the records be recalled and relabeled with "Introducing That Teasin' Rag by Joe Jordan." The name was also shortened to "Dixie Jass Band One-Step." When La Rocca gathered his band members together in 1936, the sheet music was finally published, with a cover that read "Original Dixieland One-Step, by D.J. (Nick) La Rocca, composer of 'Tiger Rag'; A new arrangement of the familiar jazz favorite, with vocal refrain." Whatever lyrics La Rocca added for this publication were soon forgotten. Nobody ever sings this number.

"Original Dixieland One-Step" is an exemplary New Orleans march-derived tune, complete with introduction, trombone slides, built-in breaks, and trio section. Its historic importance, in addition to its solid construction, has made it a Dixieland classic. For a recent performance that remains historically respectful without trying to re-create the past, listen to Jerry Rife's Rhythm Kings in a live performance from 2002 entitled *In Concert at the Yardley Community Center*.

Ory's Creole Trombone (Kid Ory, 1921): Edward "Kid" Ory (1886-1973) was the premier trombone player during the early years of New Orleans jazz. Born in La Place, Louisiana, he moved to New Orleans in 1907 and led one of the best bands in the city, employing the finest musicians available, including King Oliver, Louis Armstrong, Johnny Dodds, and Sidney Bechet. In 1919 he moved to Los Angeles and in 1921 he made the first recording by an African-American band from New Orleans. Although his regular band was called Kid Ory's Creole Orchestra, they recorded under the name of Spike's Seven Pods of Pepper Orchestra. Ory moved to Chicago in 1925, retired from music during the depression, and made a come-back in 1943, leading bands until 1961.

"Ory's Creole Trombone" was one of the songs recorded at the historic 1921 session, and it features Ory demonstrating his "tailgate" style trombone. Ory is primarily responsible for the invention of this technique, which is characterized by the playing of long glissandi in the lower register underneath the other instruments. The name derives from the necessity that the trombonist sit at the back of the wagon, on the tailgate, in order to have room to operate his slide.

For many years, few recordings were made of "Ory's Creole Trombone." Ory went on to record the tune twice more—once with Armstrong's Hot Five in 1927, and again with his newly formed Kid Ory's Orchestra in 1945. Perhaps the tune was passed over in deference to Kid Ory, but more likely it was simply considered out of date as the older tailgate style was replaced by a more lyrical approach to the instrument, such as that exemplified by Jack Teagarden. In recent years, traditional bands have rediscovered the song and it is frequently heard at jazz festivals.

Paddlin' Madelin' Home (music and lyrics: Harry Woods, 1925): Harry Woods (1896-1970), composer of such beloved melodies as "Side by Side," "I'm Looking Over a Four Leaf Clover," and "Try a Little Tenderness," had to be the oddest character on Tin Pan Alley. He was born without fingers on his left hand yet his mother, a concert singer, encouraged him to study piano, which somehow he mastered. He worked his way through Harvard playing recitals and singing in church choirs. He then settled down in Cape Cod to be a farmer. During his service in the army during World War I, Woods began to write songs, and early in the 20s he began to have hits. But the city did not appeal to Woods; he preferred fishing, farming, hanging with sailors at the docks, and being an all-around tough guy. Eventually, however, the lure of success got the best of him, and he became a reluctant member of Tin Pan Alley.

In sharp contrast to his heartwarming lyrics, Woods had a reputation as a fighter (he would sometimes challenge anyone in the bar to wrestle with him) and a dangerous alcoholic. In a legendary story, one night when Woods was drunk he got into an argument with another bar patron who was also half loaded. When the fight turned into a physical brawl, the establishment, knowing Woods' reputation, called the police immediately. They arrived to find Woods pinning the man down with his right hand while pummeling him with his left stump. As the police hauled him off, a startled woman asked, "Who was that horrible man?" to which somebody answered, "That's Harry Woods. He wrote 'Try a Little Tenderness.'"

"Paddlin' Madelin' Home" was an early hit for Woods; a recording by Cliff Edwards reached Number 3 in 1925. It is one of the few tunes that Woods wrote his own lyrics for, and of course, they're charming, with lines such as: "First I kiss her a while, and when I get through, I paddle for one mile and drift back for two."

"Palesteena," by J. Russell Robinson and Con Conrad, was one of many jazz standards introduced by the Original Dixieland Jazz Band. (Courtesy Lilly Library, Indiana University, Bloomington, Indiana.)

Palesteena (music: J. Russell Robinson, lyrics: Con Conrad, 1920): J. Russell Robinson (1892-1963) was an accomplished Ragtime and early jazz pianist as well as a composer of jazz and popular tunes. Well-represented as a creator of piano rolls, the QRS company referred to him in their catalog as "the White boy with colored fingers." In 1919, he joined the Original Dixieland Jazz Band, replacing Henry Ragas, who had died from influenza the year before. He contributed a number of compositions to the organization.

"Palesteena" is a typical novelty tune of the period, evoking some exotic place with humorous lyrics and just a hint of something in the music to make the point, whether geographically accurate or not. To complement Conrad's words about Lena, "the Queen o' Palesteena" who "plays the concertina," Robinson writes a melody with a strong Klezmer influence, actually quoting a well-known Klezmer tune called "Nokh A Bisl." The ODJB recorded the song in December 1921, with "Margie" paired with "Singin' the Blues" on the other side. Robinson composed all three songs, and all three became hits. The record was a huge seller.

"Panama," by William Tyers, attempts to evoke a South American spirit through various Latin rhythms. (Courtesy Sandy Marrone, Cinnaminson, NJ.)

Panama (William H. Tyers, 1911): William Henry Tyers (1876-1924) was an African-American musician who became a prominent arranger and composer on Tin Pan Alley, serving as a staff arranger for the prestigious Joseph W. Stern publishing house from 1897-1913. Starting in the early 1900s, he began to turn his attention to purely instrumental numbers incorporating Latin-based pieces with habanera rhythms, the "Spanish tinge" that Jelly Roll Morton believed to be an essential part of jazz. Tyers had a natural feel for such rhythms and there is some evidence that his family history on his father's side reached back to the Caribbean or South America.

By 1911 the Panama Canal was on everyone's mind. American had taken over construction in 1904 and completion was only three years away. It was the perfect title for a piece to evoke a Central American spirit. Moreover, this was the middle of the Tango rage that was sweeping American music and "Panama" contributed to the momentum. Tyers wrote the song for a vaudeville act, *Aida Overton Walker and her Panama Girls*, but it was a natural for dance bands (and later jazz bands) to play and soon became a staple of the repertoire.

"Panama" is a long tune, containing many sections, but many recordings of the song are heard in truncated versions. In part, the reason has to do with the limitations of recording technology. The 78 rpm record, which was virtually the only recording medium available until the late 1940s, could hold approximately three minutes and twenty seconds of music per side. If a song was too long, something had to be cut. Since jazz musicians needed to leave space for soloing, sections of multi-part tunes were sometimes omitted. Bob Crosby's 1937 recording, which became extremely popular, does exactly that, and many musicians learned the tune from this recording, not even realizing there were other parts to the tune. It was the revivalist bands who began playing the song in its entirety, as can heard from Turk Murphy (1953). The full version can also heard on a fine recording by New Orleans clarinetists Tim Laughlin and Jack Maheu on their 1997 album *Swing that Music*.

But by far, the majority of recordings take liberties with the long structure of the tune, mixing up the order of the sections and leaving some out. A very clever arrangement was recorded by Luis Russell and his orchestra in 1930, capturing that moment in history when hot jazz was transitioning into swing. A modern rendition of the same arrangement can be heard on the 2014 album *Do Something*, by Tom Saunders and the Tomcats. This New Orleans-based, 12-piece ensemble plays jazz arrangements from the 1920s and 30s, capturing just the right spirit.

Incidentally, the tune "Panama" has no connection with the 1904 tune by Charles Seymour called "Panama Rag."

The Pearls (Jelly Roll Morton, 1923): The early 20s found Jelly Roll working for an old friend in Tijuana who owned a place called the Kansas City Bar. He recalled, "There was a very pretty little waitress at the Kansas City Bar and I dedicated a new composition to her. This was 'The Pearls,' consisting of several sections, each one matching the other and contributing to the total effect of a beautiful pearl necklace. There are very, very few pianists, if any, that can play 'The Pearls,' it being the most difficult piece of jazz piano ever written, except for my 'Fingerbuster.'"

It would be easy to dismiss these words as mere braggadocio, coming from the man who also claimed to have invented jazz himself. Surely by 1938 (the date of the interview), more challenging piano pieces must have been written. And he was aware of the monstrous technical capacity of the Harlem Stride players, and the razzle-dazzle pieces of Zez Confrey. But Jelly Roll chose his words carefully, and his recordings bear out the fact that flamboyant virtuosity never appealed to him. It is also apparent that nobody makes his compositions sound the way he does. He had a sense of rhythm and a capacity to swing that was unequalled. So it is not farfetched to suggest that many may be able to play "The Pearls," but few will be able to bring the music out.

Alas, Jelly Roll's happy days at the Kansas City Bar were about to come to an end. It seems that the owner had murdered a former partner when he lived in Oklahoma, and the authorities finally caught up with him. "With all his millions, he had to go to jail for twenty years."

Jelly Roll can be heard playing "The Pearls" on piano solos from 1923 and 1926, a Vocalstyle piano roll from 1924, and with the Red Hot Peppers in 1927. He recorded it as a piano solo twice again in 1938.

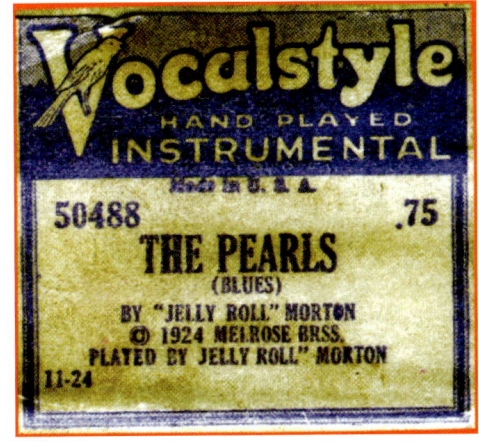

The label from Jelly Roll Morton's piano roll of "The Pearls," played on November 24, 1924. (Public domain.)

168 | THE SONGS

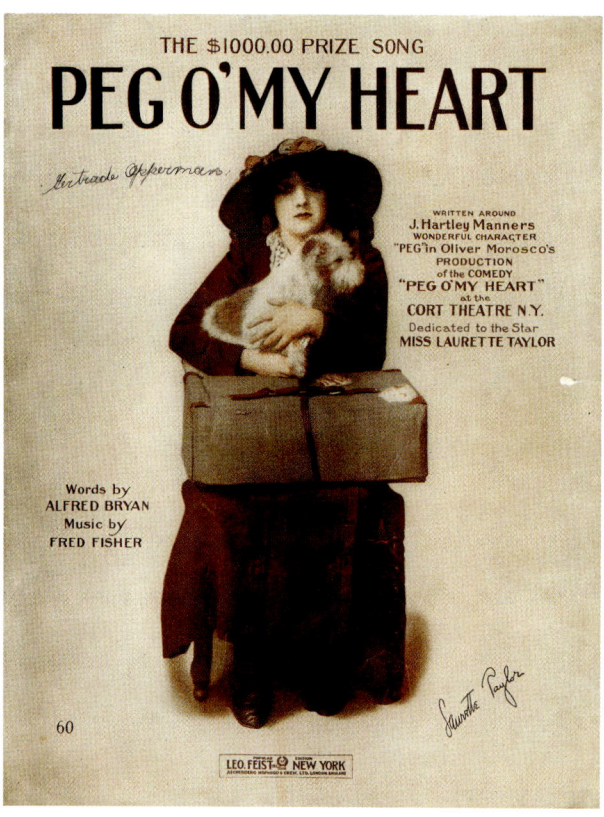

"Peg o' My Heart," by Fred Fisher and Alfred Bryan, had an amazing revival in 1947 with six individual recordings charting in the top ten. (Courtesy Lilly Library, Indiana University, Bloomington, Indiana.)

Peg o' My Heart (music: Fred Fisher, lyrics: Alfred Bryan, 1913): The music business is a strange place, or maybe America is a strange place, or both. It's hard to believe that the composer of this charming classic got his start by writing a song called "If the Man in the Moon Were a Coon" (1905), which became a hit and sold three million copies of sheet music, launching Fisher's career as a songwriter.

Fisher (1875-1942) had a colorful life, at least until success came along and made him settle down. Born in Germany, he ran away from home at age 13 to join the navy and later the French Foreign Legion. Around 1900, he found his way to the U.S. and went to Chicago, where he met a saloon musician who taught him how to play the piano. He then founded a publishing company, began to write songs, and hit pay dirt with "If the Man in the Moon." He topped that several years later with "Peg

O' My Heart," which became a Number 1 hit for Charles Harrison, a Number 2 hit for Henry Burr, and almost unbelievably a Number 1 hit for three separate artists in 1947: the Harmonicats, the Three Suns, and Buddy Clark. Other well-known songs by Fisher include "Come Josephine In My Flying Machine" (1910), "Dardanella" (1919), and "Chicago, That Toddling Town" (1922).

The song "Peg O' My Heart" was inspired by a successful play of 1912 called *Peg O' My Heart*, which ran for an incredible 603 performances. The comedy starred Laurette Taylor playing the part of a poor orphaned Irish girl who was forced to move in with unloving relations. The relatives gradually warm to Peg, and an inevitable Romantic encounter soon arrives to complicate matters. "Peg o' My Heart" was not part of the play, yet Laurette Taylor's photograph appears on the original sheet music cover. "Peg O' My Heart" was actually featured in the 1913 *Ziegfeld Follies*, sung by José Collins. The original lyrics are somewhat different from later versions:

> Peg o' my heart, I love you,
> We'll never part, I love you,
> Dear little girl, sweet little girl,
> Sweeter than the Rose of Erin,
> Are your winning smiles endearin',
> Peg o' my heart, your glances,
> With Irish art entrance us,
> Come be my own,
> Come, make your home in my heart.

Petite Fleur (music: Sidney Bechet, lyrics: Sidney Bechet and Fernand Bonifay, 1952): Bechet's most famous composition, "Petite Fleur" features a haunting, winding melody in a minor key that continuously extends itself in unpredictable ways. Bechet recorded several versions of the song, the first dating from 1952. But it was British clarinetist Monty Sunshine who had a million seller with it in 1956. He relates his nearly accidental discovery of the song: "I was on holiday in Spain, and an accordionist in a bar I went to always seemed to be playing 'Petite Fleur.' The melody stuck in my head as 'holiday tunes' sometimes do, but I never even asked what the piece was called. Months later I was driving home from a gig and heard on the car radio Bechet's version of 'Petite fleur.' It was my 'holiday tune' so I got the record and learnt the melody." Band-mate Chris Barber continues: "Monty hadn't quite got the structure of the tune right, so our version had an extra bar—one more than the Bechet version. And because Monty's record player went at a fast speed he learnt it in A flat minor instead of Bechet's key of G minor. We found out later, but never bothered to change it." In early 1959, dying and too ill to play, Bechet sent a note to Monty Sunshine saying, "To Monty, who made 'Petite Fleur' in the sunshine."

"Petite Fleur" is heard in the AMC television series *Mad Men* (season 7, episode 5, 2014).

Please (music: Ralph Rainger, lyrics: Leo Robin, 1932): The beloved songwriting team of Ralph Rainger (1901-1942) and Leo Robin (1900-1984) came to an abrupt halt with the tragic death of Rainger in a plane crash when he was only 41 years old. But the decade they spent together was long enough to produce "June in January" (1934), "Love in Bloom" (Jack Benny's theme song, 1934), "I Wished on the Moon" (1935), "Easy Living" (1937), "Blue Hawaii" (1937), and "Thanks for the Memory" (Bob Hope's theme song, 1938).

Rainger had early schooling in music and was playing the piano professionally by the time he was in high school. His parents discouraged him from music, so he went to law school and became a lawyer. But when it occurred to Rainger that he was making more money playing the piano than from his law practice, he decided to go to New York and pursue music full time. In 1929 Rainger was working as rehearsal pianist for a musical revue entitled *The Little Show*, with music by Arthur Schwartz and lyrics by Howard Dietz. At one point in the show, another song was needed that had not been planned for. Rainger improvised one on the spot (or perhaps he had a few already "written" in his ear), which everyone agreed was just perfect. Dietz supplied the lyrics, and "Moanin' Low" became Rainger's first published song. But he didn't remain in New York for long. With the onset of the depression and the rise of movie musicals, scores of songwriters made their way to Hollywood and so did Rainger, teaming up with Leo Robin to compose a series of successful songs.

Coincidentally, Leo Robin's career started out on the same trajectory as Rainger's. He was from Pittsburgh, where he studied both drama and law until he decided to save up all he could and move to New York to try to make it as a songwriter. Making the rounds, he managed to meet some very influential people but was getting nowhere. George S. Kaufman (known for his witty remarks) advised him to take the money he had saved, "have a helluva good time, and go back to Pittsburgh." Finally, in one final desperate act to try to get someone's attention, Robin wrote a set of spoof lyrics to Buddy DeSylva's tune "Look For The Silver Lining" and sent it to him. You might think that DeSylva would have been insulted; instead he was so impressed with Robin's wordplay that he arranged to have him contribute a song to the *Village Follies* for $200. Robin had the break he'd been waiting for.

"Please" was written for *The Big Broadcast of 1932*, starring Bing Crosby (who played himself). Bing sang the tune and had a Number 1 hit with it, charting for 16 weeks. He re-recorded it in 1941 and again had a hit. John Lennon admired the song so much that he claimed it inspired the Beatles tune "Please Please Me" which was also the title of their debut album.

"Poor Butterfly," by Raymond Hubbell and John Golden, was so popular in its day that its success became the subject of jokes. (Courtesy Lilly Library, Indiana University, Bloomington, Indiana.)

Poor Butterfly (music: Raymond Hubbell, lyrics: John L. Golden, 1916): Adapted from the plot of Giacomo Puccini's opera *Madame Butterfly*, the song tells the story of a young Japanese girl, wed by an American sailor, who has left her "with a promise to return." Raymond Hubbell (1879-1954), who was an active theater composer during the first three decades of the century, did not create many hits but found the magic with this one. The verse is imitative of traditional Japanese music and also manages to quote from Puccini's opera, while the chorus works in a conspicuous chord with an augmented fifth a la Puccini.

The song was not received well when premiered in *The Big Show of 1916*, but soon became a Number 1 hit when the Victor Military Band recorded it in 1917. That year, four other artists had hit records with the tune, reaching oddly enough Number 3, Number 5, Number 7 and Number 9. Sheet music sales topped two million. The song became so popular that people began to joke about it, prompting Arthur Green and William Jerome to write a song entitled "If I Catch the Guy Who Wrote Poor Butterfly."

Listening to the original recordings from 1917 is a bit of a shock; typical of period, the rhythm bounces along at a brisk fox trot tempo. Only decades later, when musicians began slowing the tune down to ballad tempo did the subtle nuances of the song become evident. Fine recordings can be heard by Benny Goodman (1944) and Teddy Wilson (1958). Goodman is no longer with us, but to hear one of the most impressive Goodman-style clarinetists active today, listen to Joe Midiri play "Poor Butterfly" on the album *Together* (2010), which also features his brother Paul on vibraphone.

Potato Head Blues (Louis Armstrong, 1927): From November 1925 through March 1929, Louis Armstrong recorded a series of landmark recordings released as either Louis Armstrong and his Hot Five or Louis Armstrong and his Hot Seven. It would be impossible to overstate the impact these records had on the future of jazz. Armstrong was creating the vocabulary that would lie at the core of jazz improvisation to the present day, and fellow musicians were following his every move. Players who didn't even play the trumpet learned his solos by heart. For example, drummer Ray McKinley once told the story of how he and Tommy Dorsey met in a restaurant and amused each other by singing Louis Armstrong solos to each other.

"Potato Head Blues" was recorded on May 10, 1927 with the Hot Seven. Evidently the tune was written for the session, or perhaps improvised on the spot, and the copyright wasn't filed until November of that year. Louis' solo on "Potato Head" has been hailed as one of the finest moments in jazz history. Yet the tune seems to have never entered the repertoire—following Louis' recording, the next rendition of the song is by Louis himself in 1957. Only in recent decades have other musicians dared to attempt it. An excellent recreation of Armstrong's solo can be heard and seen on a live recording by Wynton Marsalis (2012).

"Potato Head" is a 32-bar tune, and therefore not a blues in the strict sense, but it certainly is blues-influenced. It contains a verse and a chorus, the latter beginning with a chord sequence that resembles Jelly Roll Morton's "Froggie Moore Rag" (which Armstrong had played and recorded with Joe Oliver). The highlight of the recording is Armstrong's stop-time chorus, which follows an excellent clarinet solo by Johnny Dodds. (Stop-time was a common rhythmic device among early jazz bands. Generally, the band plays one short note at the beginning of each measure, or every second measure, and then drops out, leaving the soloist unaccompanied until the next hit.)

Woody Allen's character Isaac Davis mentions "Potato Head Blues" in the 1979 movie *Manhattan*. Attempting to answer the question, "Why is life worth living?" Davis lists many things, including: "Willie Mays. and um, the second movement of the Jupiter Symphony, and ummmm... Louie Armstrong's recording of 'Potato Head Blues' ..."

"Pretty Baby," by Tony Jackson, Egbert Van Alstyne and Gus Kahn, was revised from an old tune that Jackson used to play in New Orleans during the early years of the century. (Courtesy Lilly Library, Indiana University, Bloomington, Indiana.)

Pretty Baby (music: Tony Jackson and Egbert Van Alstyne, lyrics: Gus Kahn, 1916): Jackson wrote the song, Kahn "cleaned up" some of his lyrics, and Alstyne cut in on the royalties. Tony Jackson (1882-1921) was hailed by New Orleans musicians as the best pianist and entertainer in town. Jelly Roll Morton, who was anything but modest, praised him as a man who "could play and sing from opera to blues in its correct formation and knew everything that probably was ever printed." It was said that he would know a tune after hearing it only once, could play any song requested, and had a tremendous singing voice. Jackson wrote many of his own songs, but none were published while he was in New Orleans. He left for Chicago in 1912.

Jackson had been performing "Pretty Baby" for years while he was still in New Orleans, but the song wasn't published until it became popular. First, "Pretty Baby" was interpolated into the Broadway musical *A World of Pleasure* (1915), and then it appeared in *The Passing Show of 1916*, along with the first Gershwin songs to be included in a Broadway show. "Pretty Baby" became a Number 1 hit for Billy Murray and sold over one million copies of sheet music.

Billy Murray (1877-1954) was probably the most prolific recording artist of his generation, making more than 200 hit records between 1903 and 1927. Unfortunately for Murray, his career was winding down just as electronic recording was getting started (that is, recording into a microphone instead of a horn). If his hit records had been recorded with the vastly improved sound quality that was soon to come, he would certainly be better remembered than he is.

For a dynamic recent recording of "Pretty Baby" that highlights its Ragtime Era roots, hear Dan Levinson and his Canary College Jazz Orchestra on their 2005 album *Crinoline Days*.

P.S. I Love You (music: Gordon Jenkins, lyrics: Johnny Mercer, 1934): The age-old question is "What comes first, the music or the words?" Oftentimes it's the music, ideally it's a collaboration, but in this instance it was the words. Mercer came up with the lyric while writing a letter to his wife, describing the mundane things that were happening at home while she was away, and thought it would make a good song. He decided to take it to Gordon Jenkins.

Jenkins was primarily an arranger and conductor, but in 1933 he had a hit record with "Blue Prelude" and in 1934 Benny Goodman adopted his "Goodbye" as his closing theme. Around this time he befriended Johnny Mercer and they became drinking buddies. As Gordon explains, "I met Johnny in the Brill building in New York, where people used to come in and write. We'd hang around there in the afternoons, just sit at the piano and fool around. On 'P.S. I Love You,' he just walked in with the lyric and said, 'Write me a tune for that.' I did, and we sold it in an instant. It's not a particularly good melody, I don't think; it's very derivative. But it's been a hit three times."

Rudy Vallee had a hit with "P.S. I Love You" in 1934. Vallee (1901-1986) was a singer, actor, saxophonist, and one of the biggest stars of the early 30s. He started performing on the radio in 1928, and by the end of 1929 was a national sensation with well over a dozen hit records. He has been called the first "crooner" (referring to a performer who sings gently into the microphone rather than singing in full voice) and the first teen idol. As he could be heard by anyone with a phonograph or a radio, his influence was widespread, impacting the style of countless singers. His saxophone playing was also significant, and even the great Charlie Parker, credited with changing the course of jazz history, claimed that Rudy Vallee inspired him to play the saxophone.

Puttin' on the Ritz (words and music: Irving Berlin, 1929): Copyrighted in 1927, the song was not published until 1929. In 1930 it appeared in the film of the same name, where it was introduced by Harry Richman. Richman had a Number 1 record with it that same year and adopted it as his theme song. But it is Fred Astaire whom we associate with "Puttin' On the Ritz." Astaire had a successful recording of it in 1930, but staked his claim to the song when he sang and danced it in *Blue Skies* (1946), with new lyrics, again by Irving Berlin.

The two versions of the lyrics reflect changes in race relations that were slowly taking shape in America. The 1929 version depicts African Americans parading down Lenox Avenue in Harlem. It contains racial references that have long been relegated to the past, such as "high browns" (Blacks with lighter skin who think they are better than most) and "Lulu-Belle" (referring to a Black maid). By 1946, when it was decided that the song would be used in the film *Blue Skies*, the minstrel overtone of the lyrics was no longer acceptable, and much of the slang verbiage was simply obsolete. Berlin deftly moved the scenario from Lenox Avenue to Park Avenue, changed the subject from African Americans to wealthy New Yorkers, and brought the terminology up to date (complete with a reference to Gary Cooper, rhyming with super-duper!).

Incidentally, the expression "putting on the Ritz," meaning to dress pretentiously, predates the song and refers to the Ritz Hotel in London, which remains a symbol of wealth and grandeur today just as it did in the 20s.

The appeal of the song as a jazz number derives in part from its rhythm, which is unique among popular songs. Berlin managed to mix up the accents of the opening phrase in such a manner as to give the impression of changing meters and a shifting downbeat. The magic is that he does this while instilling a sense of irresistible swing. It's no wonder Fred Astaire loved the number.

A final footnote: In 1983, at the age of 95, Berlin had the honor of having his number become a hit all over again. Dutch singer Taco Ockerse included a synthesized version of "Puttin' On the Ritz" on his album *After Eight*. It became a hit and sold over a million copies.

Red Sails in the Sunset (music: Hugh Williams, lyrics: Jimmy Kennedy, 1935): The writers of this song were European and so was their inspiration. Hugh Williams (aka Wilhelm Grosz, 1894-1939) was born in Vienna, but fled to England with the Nazi takeover. He was a classically trained composer, but found little interest in the avant-garde style, so he turned to pop music. He is also the writer of "Isle Of Capri" (1934) and "Harbour Lights" (1937). Jimmy Kennedy (1902-1984) was an Irish lyricist who also wrote "Teddy Bears' Picnic" (1932), and "My Prayer" (1939).

"Red Sails" is an unassuming number about a young "fisher girl" waiting for her lover to return safely from sea. And there actually was a boat with red sails that inspired the song. Lyricist Kennedy often saw a particular yacht off the northern coast of Ireland whose bright red sails caught his attention. The boat was called *Kitty of Coleraine*, and today it stands on display in the city of Portstewart in Northern Ireland, where Kennedy was staying when he wrote the song.

"Red Sails" was introduced to Americans in the revue *Provincetown Follies* (1935). Several hit recordings soon followed, including Number 1 records by both Bing Crosby and Guy Lombardo. Sheet music sales exceeded one million, and the song has been revived many times. Louis Armstrong had a hit with his 1936 recording of the song.

By far, pop versions of "Red Sails" outnumber jazz renditions many times over, but the tune provides a great bluesy jazz number in the right hands. Highly recommended are recordings by pianist Erroll Garner (1949), pianist Dick Wellstood (1971), and pianist/singer/bandleader Jay McShann (1983). Surprisingly, McShann (1916-2006) is the granddaddy in this prestigious lineup. He led widely influential bands, and some of the greatest names in the business passed through his ranks, including Charlie Parker and Ben Webster. McShann's style of music became known as the "Kansas City sound," which can distinctively be heard on his recording of "Red Sails."

Riverboat Shuffle (music: Hoagy Carmichael, lyrics: Irving Mills, Dick Voynow, and Mitchell Parish, 1924): Hoagland "Hoagy" Carmichael (1899-1981) was a student at Indiana University when he befriended Bix Beiderbecke, then playing with the Wolverines. Carmichael, a decent piano player who worked his way through college playing several nights a week, could not read or write music at the time, but was so enthralled with Bix and the Wolverines that he vowed to write a song for them. "I just had to write a tune ... I got a phrase and played it. Played it again. And again and again and again ... But before supper I had it! Well, I had something." What he had was rather vague, but very good. He played it for Bix, who loved it (but not Hoagy's suggested title "Free Wheeling"), and promised to record it on his next record session. The Wolverines worked out an arrangement, impromptu and without music, and recorded "Riverboat Shuffle" on May 23, 1924.

Partly on its own merit, and partly because of its association with Bix, the tune quickly became a staple of the White jazz band repertoire. It became Hoagy Carmichael's first published song. Dick Voynow, who assisted with the lyrics, was the pianist and leader of the Wolverines. Mitchell Parish was a prominent Tin Pan Alley lyricist. He later supplied the words to Hoagy's "Stardust." Exactly how the collaboration worked on this song is suspicious. It was written as an instrumental. Most likely, Voynow helped Hoagy put the song together, Mitchell Parish wrote the lyrics (in 1939, which is the copyright date), and the publisher, Jack Mills gave partial credit to his brother Irving.

Following Bix's landmark recording of "Riverboat Shuffle" there have been too many great records made on this number to count. Muggsy Spanier's 1938 recording deserves mention. Also, Eddie Condon and his boys can be heard and seen playing this number on some rare film footage from 1958. More recordings include those by Vince Giordano (1994) and Emily Asher's Garden Party (2013).

Hoagy later described "Riverboat Shuffle" as a number that "had a harmonic structure not far removed from the blues and yet had a happy sound and plenty of opportunity for breaks," which sums it up pretty well. He would go on to write many more songs in his lifetime. Incidentally, Hoagy is the composer of "Heart and Soul," the number that every child likes to tap out on the piano.

Rockin' Chair (music and lyrics: Hoagy Carmichael, 1929): Hoagy wrote both the music and lyrics for this one and it shows. A personal favorite among his own songs, it is set as a father-and-son dialog with spaces built in for the son's improvised responses. The unusual form (ABCA) complements the meandering, reminiscing nature of the lyrics. The inspiration for "Rockin' Chair" is not entirely clear, and multiple people or images might have sparked his creativity. In his autography he writes: "'Old Rockin' Chair,' thought of that one early one morning swimming in the Bloomington reservoir after all night drinkin' of Granny Campbell's home brew." Granny Campbell was an elderly African-American woman who lived a few miles outside of Bloomington and was noted for her corn-mash liquor.

As with "Star Dust," Hoagy didn't realize how popular the tune would become when he wrote it. He remembered that when he tried it out on his mother, "she, too, was not overly impressed." But as recordings of the song were made its stature steadily rose. Hoagy recorded a landmark version with Bix on cornet in September 1929, and then a version with Louis Armstrong in December that became a hit record. The Mills Brothers had a Number 4 hit in 1932 and Mildred Bailey recorded the song three times, adopting it as her theme song. But the song is probably remembered best as performed by Louis Armstrong with Jack Teagarden, with Teagarden as the father and Armstrong supplying the banter.

"Rose of Washington Square," by James Hanley and Ballard MacDonald, was the theme song of Fanny Brice. (Courtesy Lilly Library, Indiana University, Bloomington, Indiana.)

Rose of Washington Square (music: James F. Hanley, lyrics: Ballard MacDonald 1920): There very well may have been a real Rose of Washington Square. Rose O'Neill (1874-1944), artist and creator of the "Kewpie" doll, author, women's rights advocate, "The Queen of Bohemian Society," had an apartment in Washington Square Park where she hosted gatherings of poets, actors, dancers, and "great thinkers" of her day. She was rich, beautiful, outspoken, and certainly well known. It is likely that she was the inspiration for the song that Hanley and MacDonald wrote for singer Fanny Brice, who put her stamp on it and made it her own.

Franny Brice (1891-1951) was an influential American stage personality who got her start in the productions of the extravagant Florenz Ziegfeld. He discovered her in 1910, and the occasion of her hiring was typical of Ziegfeld's precipitous actions and total confidence in his personal judgment. Brice was a relatively unknown comic songstress singing in a small revue when Ziegfeld heard her and decided he must hire her at once. He had her summoned to his office and asked her how much she wanted to appear in the *Follies*. When she said forty dollars a week Ziegfeld frowned. Thinking her request was too high, she began to cower, offering to take less when Ziegfeld abruptly cut her off and barked "We'll make it seventy-five, and you'll get a year's work."

Brice sang "Rose of Washington Square" in the 1919 and 1920 editions of *Ziegfeld's Midnight Frolics*, and it became a smash hit. (Hanley followed up with a similar song in 1922 called "Second Hand Rose," which became an even bigger hit.) "Rose of Washington Square" saw a significant revival when it appeared in the 1939 film of the same name, and inspired a hit by Benny Goodman that same year. Since then, the song has remained a solid staple in the traditional jazz repertoire. Incidentally, the film, though obviously based on Fanny Brice's career, was never cleared with her. She subsequently sued MGM, settling out of court for an undisclosed amount.

There's no shortage of recordings of "Rose of Washington Square," but it's surprisingly hard to find interpretations with a real 20s jazz feel. There's a splendid recording from 1929 under the leadership of Red Nichols that features trombonist Jack Teagarden, clarinetist Pee Wee Russell, and saxophonist Bud Freeman prominently. A curiosity about this recording (and others from this period) is that Russell had not yet developed the avant-garde (yet somehow traditional) jazz style that would define him. In fact, he's barely recognizable. To hear the mature Pee Wee, listen to him playing the same number solo in 1944. Now that's the Pee Wee we know!

Jazz vocal recordings of the number are even more difficult to come by. One of the best I've heard was recorded by Banu Gibson on her 2006 album *Vintage Banu*. Banu swings hard, sings great, and knows how to interpret in a style appropriate for the period.

"Rose Room," by Art Hickman and Harry Williams," is named after a room in the St. Francis Hotel. (Courtesy Lilly Library, Indiana University, Bloomington, Indiana.)

Rose Room (music: Art Hickman, lyric: Harry Williams, 1918): Art Hickman (1886-1930) was a pioneering orchestra leader and one of the first to use saxophones in a dance band. He started his first successful band in 1913. The press hailed his ensemble as a "jazz band" but in truth it was what later would be known as a "sweet band." (Eddie Condon referred to such ensembles as "violins and soft saxophones.") During the teens especially, but even during the 20s, there was much confusion about what "jazz" really meant, and some just used it as a term for any peppy music that could be danced to. By the 20s, Art Hickman had one of the best-paid and most successful orchestras in the United States, rivaling that of Paul Whiteman. Hickman died at the age of 43, leaving several unfinished projects.

The St. Francis Hotel in San Francisco, where Art Hickman played with his famous "jazz band." (Author's personal collection.)

"Rose Room" takes its name from a venue in the Hotel St. Francis in San Francisco. (In turn, the venue itself may have taken its name from the room in the White House called the Queens' Bedroom, which was called the Rose Room from 1902-1963.) The St. Francis opened in 1904, and miraculously survived the San Francisco earthquake of 1906, receiving little serious damage. The hotel went on to host many celebrities in the coming decades, becoming a favorite destination for the well-to-do. A major attraction of the St. Francis was its "jazz orchestra," led by Art Hickman, which appeared in the Rose Room of the hotel. In 1917, Hickman composed a song named after the band's residence, and it went on to become his most enduring hit. "Rose Room" has a harmonic structure conducive to jazz improvisation, and quickly became a favorite of jazz bands. Duke Ellington's hit recording of "Rose Room" in

1932 strengthened the tune's link with jazz musicians, as did Ellington's composition on the same chord sequence, "In a Mellow Tone" (1940).

"Rose Room" was the tune that led to the discovery of the legendary pioneer of electric jazz guitar Charlie Christian (1916-1942). As Scott Yanow relates, "In 1939, while working with Leslie Sheffield, Christian was heard by producer John Hammond, who flew him to Los Angeles in August for a tryout with Benny Goodman. The clarinetist was not impressed by Christian's flashy clothes. But he called out 'Rose Room' and 45 minutes later they were still playing the song! Christian immediately became a regular member of BG's sextet/septet. Very soon Charlie Christian was the talk of jazz, a sensation among musicians ..."

"Roses of Picardy," by Haydn Wood and Frederick Weatherly," is named after a region in northern France. (Courtesy Lilly Library, Indiana University, Bloomington, Indiana.)

Roses of Picardy (music: Haydn Wood, lyrics: Frederick Weatherly (1916): Wood (1882-1959) was a classically trained violinist and prolific composer of orchestra music who also wrote for the stage. Weatherly (1848-1929) was an accomplished author and lawyer with more than 3,000 popular songs to his credit. His lyrics include "Danny Boy" and "The Old Brigade." Wood said that the melody to "Roses" came to him one evening when travelling home on a London bus. He immediately got off the bus and jotted down the music on the back of an old envelope while standing under a street lamp. Weatherly received his inspiration for the lyric while visiting France. Picardy is a historic region in northern France, and was the scene of some of the fiercest battles of World War I. "Roses of Picardy" quickly became popular throughout Britain and served as a rally song for British soldiers. Some 50,000 copies of sheet music were sold each month.

"Roses" has remained popular through hundreds of recordings in many languages. Red Nichols had one of the early jazz versions in 1929, and after World War II the song really took off as a swing number. Notable recordings include those by Eddie Condon (1945), Pete Kelly's Big 7 (Dick Cathcart, 1951), Sidney Bechet (1954), and Kid Ory (1954). For a more recent recording, listen to the Midiri Brothers sextet on their 2004 album *Trees*.

Rosetta (music and lyrics: Earl Hines and Henri Woode, 1933): Earl Hines (1903-1983) was a brilliant and highly influential jazz pianist. His recordings with Louis Armstrong as part of the Hot Seven ensemble are considered classics. For decades he fronted a big band that was famously acclaimed for its outstanding musicianship. Many musicians who would go on to become luminaries in the jazz world passed through its ranks, including Charlie Parker, Dizzy Gillespie, Billy Eckstine, and Sarah Vaughan.

Henri Woode was the arranger for Earl Hines' band. Woode was crazy about a girl named Rosetta, and every time Hines was looking for him someone would say, "Oh, he's with Rosetta." Hines became so curious that he told Woode he should bring her to the gig and offered to pay her tab, just so he could meet her. One night Woode heard a phrase Hines was playing and thought it might be the beginning of a tune. They collaborated on it, and the result was "Rosetta." They recorded the song with a singer named Walter Fuller, and the song became a hit. Fuller even named his daughter Rosetta. Hines recalls "We wrote it as a ballad, but later it was played in all kinds of ways." Earl Hines can be heard playing "Rosetta" on a splendid solo piano recording from 1939.

"Royal Garden Blues," by Spencer Williams and Clarence Williams, references a famous Chicago nightclub where the famous Joe "King" Oliver performed. (Courtesy Sandy Marrone, Cinnaminson, NJ.)

Royal Garden Blues (Spencer Williams and Clarence Williams, 1919): The Royal Gardens Café was a famous nightclub in South Chicago, located on East 31st Street. The establishment was said to accommodate more than 1000 dancers, and adopted a jazz policy during the late 1910s. In 1922, Joe Oliver began a steady job there (by this time the club was renamed the Lincoln Gardens), fronting a band called The Original Creole Jazz Band, and sent for his protégé Louis Armstrong to join him. This landmark ensemble remained there for nearly two years, making a set of historic recordings in 1923, and was a significant force in presenting jazz to a wider audience.

Spencer Williams wrote "Royal Garden Blues" in 1919, at which time he was publishing with Clarence Williams. Clarence was a tireless promoter of Spencer's music, and shared writer credits on them, although it is doubtful that he contributed much if anything to the music or lyrics. The tune didn't attract much attention until 1921, when several recordings appeared, including a Number 3 hit recording for the Original Dixieland Jazz Band. Blues Singer Mamie Smith also had a hit with the tune in 1921, while Bix Beiderbecke's recording of 1927 is one of the most revered of all renditions of the song.

"Royal Garden Blues" is a curious but effective number that adapts to various treatments. It is structured into two 24-bar sections (12-bar blues repeated) with a four-bar modulating interlude in between. Thus it resembles the multi-part march structures of New Orleans jazz bands, but also incorporates the blues. Additionally the final section incorporates a riff structure (a la "In The Mood"), quite unusual for its day, which accounts for the song's resurgence in the 1930s as a favorite of the big bands. "Royal Garden" certainly shows no signs of going away and can be heard on Jim Cullum's 2013 album *The Real Stuff*. A powerful and inventive cornet player, Cullum is based in San Antonio and for years had led one of the most exciting jazz bands in the country. Broadcasts featuring Cullum's band and distinguished guests have been heard on Public Radio's *Riverwalk Jazz* since 1987.

"Runnin' Wild," by A. Harrington Gibbs, Joe Grey and Leo Wood, represents one of the few instances when a show was inspired by a song with the same name. (Courtesy Lilly Library, Indiana University, Bloomington, Indiana.)

Runnin' Wild (music: A. Harrington Gibbs, lyrics: Joe Grey and Leo Wood, 1922): With its streamlined melody and straightforward harmony, the tune is built for speed. A perfect vehicle to appear at the beginning of the Roaring Twenties, the song took off with a spate of recordings, spawning the Broadway revue *Runnin' Wild* (1923) in one of the rare instances where the show is named after the song that appears in it. The lyric extols the carefree spirit of a jilted lover who vows to live reckless and free. "Runnin' wild, lost control, runnin' wild, mighty bold."

Ted Lewis had a hit with a hokey version in 1923, and Glenn Miller had one with a killer-diller version in 1939. The song is probably best known to the general public from the film *Some Like It Hot*, set in the Prohibition Era, where it is sung by Marilyn Monroe. "Runnin' Wild" was briefly the theme song for the comic duo Laurel and Hardy prior to their adoption of "The Ku-ku Song." As entertaining as all of these interpretations are, none of them gets us close to a real jazz rendition. For that we can listen to Django Reinhardt (1937), Art Tatum (1938), and Eddie Condon (1957). Finally, for proof that the tune really does work as a jazz vocal number, listen to the excellent performance by Banu Gibson on her 2006 album *Vintage Banu*.

"Sailing down the Chesapeake Bay," by George Botsford and Jean Havez, didn't catch on with jazz bands until the 1950s. (Courtesy Lilly Library, Indiana University, Bloomington, Indiana.)

Sailing down the Chesapeake Bay (music: George Botsford, lyrics: Jean Havez, 1913): George Botsford (1874-1949) made his mark as a composer of piano rags. His compositions might not have been the most innovative of the era, but they were compelling and well crafted, earning them a lasting place in the repertoire. Among his best known works are "Black and White Rag" (1908), "Texas Steer" (1909), "Grizzly Bear Rag" (1910), "Chatterbox Rag" (1911), "Honeysuckle Rag" (1911), and "The Incandescent Rag" (1913).

By 1915 Tin Pan Alley was in full swing, but the piano Ragtime Era was winding down. Not that Ragtime was going away—quite the contrary. It was having a significant effect on popular song as well as on the next generation of pianists who would lead the transition of Ragtime into Harlem Stride. But composing rags as solo piano compositions was no longer a lucrative business. Botsford, as well as many other rag composers, were able to preserve their Ragtime ideas and apply them to popular song. He had already had tremendous success with adapting his "Grizzly Bear Rag" (1910) into a popular song and he had another hit with "Sailing down the Chesapeake Bay." Though not a rag per se, the song incorporates typical Ragtime syncopation, an instrumental-style melody, and a lyric with a "let's go!" spirit so evocative of the Progressive Era:

> Come on Nancy, put your best dress on
>
> Come on Nancy 'fore the steamboat's gone
>
> Everything is lovely on the Chesapeake bay
>
> All aboard for Baltimore
>
> And if we're late they'll all be sore
>
> Now look here captain, let us catch that boat
>
> We can't swim and listen, we can't float
>
> Darkies humming a good old tune
>
> Up on deck is the place to spoon
>
> Cuddle up close beneath the silvery moon
>
> Sailing down the Chesapeake bay

The formula clicked, and Botsford had the biggest hit of his career. In 1913 Henry Burr had a Number 2 record with the song while the American Quartet had a Number 5. Early jazz bands seem to have neglected the song, which was somewhat out of step with the spirit of the 20s, but the song was brought back into the repertoire by the revivalists of the 1940s and 1950s. Bob Scobey recorded it in 1951 with Clancy Hayes on vocals. The song is performed frequently today and is a favorite among banjo players, perhaps because of its vague similarity to other banjo classics such as "Alabama Jubilee" or "Floatin' down to Cotton Town."

"San," by Lindsay McPhail and Walter Hirsch, combines exotic imagery with silly lyrics. (Courtesy Sandy Marrone, Cinnaminson, NJ.)

San (music and lyrics: Lindsay McPhail and Walter Hirsch, 1920): The meaning of the song, in so far as it has one, is best revealed in the lyrics, which are charmingly silly enough to quote in full:

> King San of Senegal Sat on the shore At Bulamay,
> Singing a sad refrain. To his dear queen who'd gone away, This was his lay.
>
> One day the queen came home Saw San in sadness on the shore, Told him she'd no more roam. Only her San would she adore, Then came this lore.
>
> Oh, sweet heart Lona, my darling Lona, Why have you gone away? You said you loved me, But if you loved me, Why did you act this way? If I had ever been untrue to you, What you have done would be the thing to do; But my heart aches, dear, And it will break, dear, If you don't come back home again to San!
>
> Oh, sweet heart Lona, my darling Lona, Have you come back to stay? You said you loved me, I knew you loved me, I knew you'd come some day. If I had ever been untrue to you, What you have done would be the thing to do; But now you're mine, dear, For all the time, dear, And you're forgiven by your loving San!

This hit song appears to be a one-time success effort for McPhail and Hirsch—their names are virtually absent in any other song references.

The tune has a pared down melody and a repeating harmonic shift meant to invoke distant lands. It was played by the George Olsen Orchestra in the *Ziegfeld Follies of 1924*. Four recordings of the song became hit records but unfortunately, each exaggerates the "exotic" nature of the tune without exploring the possibilities it offers as a jazz vehicle. Most musicians know the song from Paul Whiteman's 1928 recording featuring Bix Beiderbecke and Jimmy Dorsey. It was this instrumental version that was responsible for the song's entrance into the traditional jazz repertoire, and for most jazz bands it has remained an instrumental ever since.

But the lyrics, silly as they may be, are too much fun to ignore. And in recent years some bands have returned to them. Listen to the New Orleans-based Jumbo Shrimp Jazz Band on their 2014 release, *Louder Than Last Time*, with Mike Fulton on trumpet and Colin Myers on trombone. Vocalist Joseph Faison is fantastic, delivering an entertaining mix of Eddie Cantor and Cab Calloway (did I just say that?), which captures the light-hearted spirit of the tune perfectly.

St. James Infirmary (music and lyrics: Joe Primrose, 1930): Joe Primrose did not write this song; in fact there was no Joe Primrose. Publisher Irving Mills used this pseudonym one time, when filing the copyright for this traditional folk tune. The song, entitled "The Unfortunate Rake," derives from the British Isles, and the story and lyrics can be traced back hundreds of years. It appears in a 1927 publication called *American Songbook*, a compilation of the music and lyrics to 280 folk songs, assembled by poet Carl Sandburg.

The first recording seems to be one by Fess Williams and His Royal Flush Orchestra, naming the song "Gambler's Blues" (1927). This recording attracted little attention, but one by Louis Armstrong the following year did. For the first time the song is entitled "St. James Infirmary Blues" and Armstrong's interpretation became the model for all future renditions of the song. It was a hit for him in 1929 and by 1930 at least 18 other versions appeared. King Oliver followed up with an even bigger hit in 1930, and Cab Calloway topped that with a Number 3 hit in 1931. Jack Teagarden adopted the song as a feature number, recording it more than 20 times. It also appears in the 1933 Betty Boop animation *Snow White*, sung by Cab Calloway, who also appears as an animated character. (This production has been hailed as one of the finest cartoons ever made.)

And where is St. James Infirmary? That question can't definitively be answered. The oldest sources for the lyric refer to "St. James Hospital." There was such a place in London, but it was demolished in 1532 and replaced with St. James Palace. This was long before the oldest versions of the lyrics. There was however an infirmary in an establishment called the St. James Workhouse, which was in operation during the 18th and 19th centuries, contemporary with the advent of the song. This is probably the best guess for the proper reference.

The interior of the St. James Workhouse, as depicted by the artist Thomas Rowlandson in 1809. Constructed in the Soho area of London, England in 1725 for the able-bodied poor, the establishment also contained in infirmary, which may have been the inspiration for the song "St. James Infirmary." (Public domain, via Wikimedia Commons.)

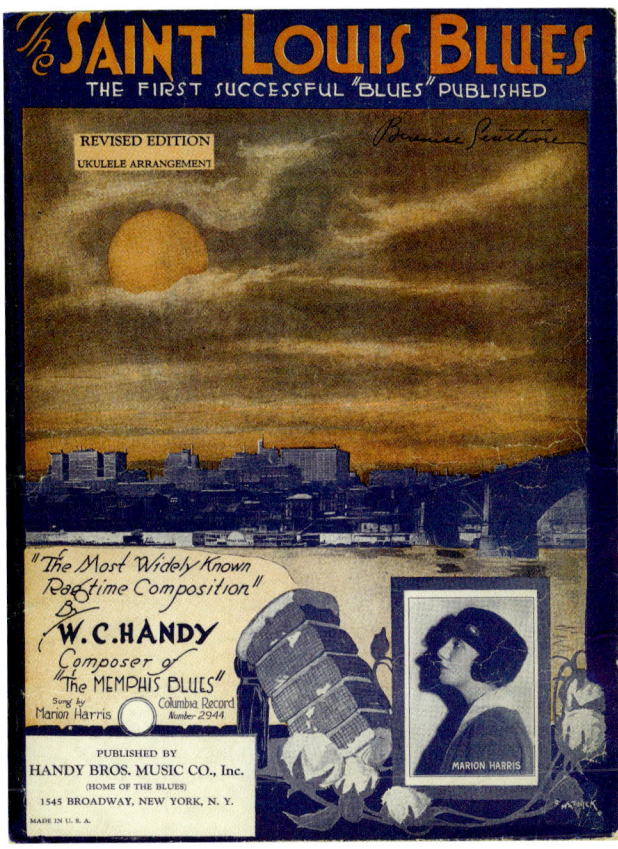

"St. Louis Blues," by W.C. Handy, is by far the most famous blues song in history. (Courtesy Lilly Library, Indiana University, Bloomington, Indiana.)

St. Louis Blues (music and lyrics: W. C. Handy, 1914): What distinguishes a tune and makes it famous? Record sales? Airplay? Sheet music sales? Number of recordings made? Continued appearance on stage and in film? Number of requests by dancers? Its place in history? Having a sports team named after it? It's not at all clear what the criteria are, but however you measure it, St. Louis Blues is the most famous blues number ever written, and ranks among the most enduring classics in the American songbook. It resulted in at least 15 hit records and for nearly half a century was the second most recorded song in history (second only to "Silent Night"). Its influence was not confined to the United States; this was the song that introduced the blues to the world.

W.C. Handy was down on his luck when he struck gold with this one. Having been cheated out of the royalties on "Memphis Blues," which should have made him rich, he was now 40 years old and wracked with disappointment. "There was the picture

I had of myself, broke, unshaven, wanting even a decent meal, and standing before the lighted saloon in St. Louis without a shirt under my frayed coat." Encountering a destitute woman with pain seemingly greater than his, he heard her muttering the phrase that would inspire his song: "My man's got a heart like a rock cast in de sea." Intrigued by this line (which appears in the chorus of "St. Louis Blues"), the opening phrase of the song came to him: "I hate to see de evenin' sun go down." Thus Handy came to write his masterpiece.

Handy was an accomplished musician, had thoroughly assimilated the language of the blues, and was a shrewd businessman. He knew that pure blues, at that particular time, were too unfamiliar to be accepted by a wide audience. But the tango was all the rage. "I tricked the dancers by arranging a tango introduction, breaking abruptly into a low-down blues." It worked. According to Handy, "dancers were electrified." But success was not assured. Handy failed to find a large publisher willing to accept his work so he published it himself with his small and struggling firm, the Pace and Handy Music Company. With their limited resources and influence, the battle was uphill, but the song began to catch on and within a few years the momentum was unstoppable.

Notable recordings of "St. Louis Blues" are too numerous to list, but among the most highly acclaimed are those of the Original Dixieland Jazz Band (1921), W. C. Handy (1923), Bessie Smith with Louis Armstrong (1925), Fats Waller (1926), and Louis Armstrong (1929). And, of course, the organist for the St. Louis Blues ice hockey team plays the song in its entirety before every game.

Shake That Thing (music and lyrics: "Papa" Charlie Jackson, 1925): By the mid-20s, the blues craze was well underway, and it was dominated by women—the "blues queens." Beginning with Mamie Smith's "Crazy Blues" in 1920, many hundreds of successful recordings flooded the market, and dozens of capable singers graced the stage, none of them more lauded than Bessie Smith, "Empress of the Blues" (1894-1937). Early male blues singers were considered crude, inelegant, and amateurish. They learned their craft in the honky-tonks or on street corners, and their delivery was rough and raw. But by mid-decade some came to feel that men had something to offer to the genre. Their music was earthy, and they accompanied themselves on their own idiosyncratic instruments, but they seemed to bring something authentic to their performances—as if giving a glimpse into the very origins of the blues.

Little is known about the life of Papa Jackson (1887-1938). He was born in New Orleans and moved to Chicago in 1920. An executive for Paramount Records discovered him on a street corner and decided to book him as a novelty act. Papa Jackson was one of the first male blues singers to be recorded, and found success with his first record "Papa's Lawdy Lawdy Blues," followed by "Shake That Thing" the following year. Jackson played a six-string banjo tuned like a guitar (as did Johnny St. Cyr—banjoist with Louis Armstrong) and was possibly the first self-accompanied blues artist to record. He went on to make 66 sides. Though his fame would soon be eclipsed by other artists, his place in blues history is indisputable.

"Shake That Thing" is a representative blues of its genre, with its 12-bar structure, stop-time chorus (see entry on "Potato Head Blues"), and characteristic opening line, "I woke up this mornin' 'bout half-past four, I told my baby couldn't use her no more." Besides Jackson's 1925 recording, other notable versions include those of Ethel Waters (1925) and Kid Ory (1954). "Shake That Thing" is heard in the 2004 film The *Aviator*, performed by Vince Giordano and the Nighthawks.

She's Funny That Way (music: Neil Moret, lyrics: Richard Whiting, 1928): Richard Whiting (1891-1938) was a fantastic composer who died much too young. Among his hit songs are "Ain't We Got Fun," "Hooray for Hollywood," "My Ideal," "Too Marvelous for Words," and many others. He once gave this advice to his daughter Margaret Whiting, when she was just starting her career: "[Composing is] something I love to do, but it is a job, it is work, and we work very hard to write a song. You must sing this song with great affection and feeling. It takes the men who write the lyrics a long time. Just believe in their words. Do them simply and honestly. That's how a singer should interpret a song."

"She's Funny That Way" seems to be the only time that Whiting wrote the lyrics to a song with someone else contributing the music. And it is fitting that it allegedly stemmed from a real-life experience. Moret and Whiting both worked in Detroit, for the Remick publishing company. Whiting was recently married, but he and his wife realized that his burgeoning career would require them to relocate to either Hollywood or New York. Reluctantly, Whiting chose New York, but soon after arriving it became clear that his future lay with the movies in Hollywood. While still in New York, Whiting and Moret wrote "She's Funny That Way," and according to Margaret, it was a love song to Whiting's wife back in Detroit, with the specific reference in the last line, "I'm only human, coward at best, I'm pretty certain, she'd follow me west."

Neil Moret was the name that Charles N. Daniels (1878-1943) used for his creative works, though he used his real name for his business ventures. He was equally successful as a composer and a music industry executive. In his early years as a publisher he was an avid promoter of Ragtime, contributing significantly to the continuing popularity of the genre. He composed the song "Hiawatha" in 1901, whose success initiated the trend of "Indian songs," which were all the rage during the early years of the 20th century. Among his many famous songs are "You Tell Me Your Dream, I'll Tell You Mine" (1908), "Moonlight and Roses" (1925), "Song of the Wanderer" (1926), "Chloe" (1927), and "Sweet and Lovely" (1931).

"The Sheik of Araby," by Ted Snyder, Harry Smith and Francis Wheeler, was inspired by the famous silent film of the same name, starring Rudolph Valentino. (Courtesy Lilly Library, Indiana University, Bloomington, Indiana.)

The Sheik of Araby (music: Ted Snyder, lyrics: Harry B. Smith and Francis Wheeler, 1921): Ted Snyder (1881-1965) was a pianist and songwriter for several music publishers in Chicago and New York before setting up his own Tin Pan Alley firm in 1908. He gave Irving Berlin his first break, hiring him as a lyricist in 1909. (Berlin hadn't yet begun to write his own melodies.) The Berlin/Snyder team clicked; they wrote several successful songs together, and Berlin supplied lyrics to some of Snyder's piano rags. When Berlin achieved instant fame with "Alexander's Ragtime Band," he was made a partner in the firm, now called Waterson, Berlin, and Snyder. Berlin stayed until 1919, when he left to start his own publishing business. After his departure the company reverted back to its original name of Waterson and Snyder.

It has been said that "The Sheik of Araby" was written in order to capitalize on the tremendous success of the 1921 silent film *The Sheik*, starring Rudolph Valentino, but it seems that the connection was mostly good fortune. Snyder explains, "I had the melody of the chorus of the 'Sheik' written and I couldn't get any kind of verse that suited me ... I finally went into the Oriental and at last completed the song under the title of 'My Rose of Araby.' Mr. Waterson [Snyder's partner] had just read the book of The Sheik ... and wanted to call my song '*The Sheik*.' However, I couldn't connect the Sheik of the story with my 'Rose of Araby,' as we had written it. Mr. Waterson showed the way and a few days after the song was written the moving picture was announced. So it was an all-round fortunate combination of circumstances."

The timing was perfect, and certainly audiences had Valentino in mind when hearing the lyrics: "I'm the Sheik of Araby, your love belongs to me. At night when you're asleep, into your tent I'll creep." Don Albert's band recorded the song in 1936 with the now-familiar addition of "with no pants on" between lines. It got his recording banned from both airplay and record sales, but his routine lives on. Jack Teagarden's 1930 recording demonstrated the jazz possibilities inherent in the song, and his recording of 1939 became a hit.

A historically significant (but musically questionable) "one-man-band" recording of "The Sheik" was made by Sidney Bechet in 1941. One by one, he overdubbed himself, eventually laying down tracks on six different instruments: soprano saxophone, tenor saxophone, clarinet, piano, string bass, and drums. This is significant because it was before tape recording. Each new track had to be recorded on a fresh 78 rpm original. A mistake meant starting the track all over again!

Coincidentally, "Araby" is pronounced the same way as the name of the small town of "Arabi" just outside of New Orleans, making the song especially appealing to regional listeners. Arabi, Louisiana was an active center for illegal gambling activities during the first half of the 20th century.

Shine (music: Ford Dabney, lyrics: Cecil Mack and Lew Brown, 1924): Unfortunately, this nimble jump tune dates from the "coon song" era, and the lyrics show it. (During the early years of the 20th century it was considered great sport for songwriters to deride and stereotype various racial and ethnic groups.) But its history is a bit more involved than that. The song first appeared in 1910 in the traveling Black show *His Honor the Barber* under the title of "That's Why They Call Me Shine." As was common at the time, even though the lyrics are degrading, they were written by African-American songwriters, doing what they needed to do for public acceptance. But this tune gets still more complicated. In addition to blackface there was a bit of cross-dressing going on, as can be seen on the original sheet music cover, showing a picture of a woman dressed in a man's suit, complete with top hat and cane. The lady is Aida Overton Walker, dressed as her husband, famous comedy performer George Walker, who had fallen ill and would die in 1911. At various times, she would continue to dress in his costume as a tribute to him.

If there is any saving grace to the lyrics, it is found in the second verse, which turns the tables on the stereotype, choosing to rise above it all. Referring to the insults he has to put up with, the victim sings, "I simply smile, and smile some more, and vote them all a joke," adding later, "What is there in a name?" Unfortunately, even with the caveat (which comes after the first verse and chorus), the imagery of the rest of the song is disagreeable to many listeners. Revised lyrics have been attempted, with lines such as "Shine away your blues-ies, shine, start with your shoes-ies," which only seem to mock the clever rhymes concocted by Mack and Brown—creations that reflect their times and attitudes.

The pity is that the original lyrics really were expertly crafted, largely (if not completely) by one of the greatest African-American lyricists of the early 20th century, R.C. McPherson, better known as Cecil Mack (1883-1944). Mack was also a composer and a publisher, serving as president and co-founder of the Gotham-Attucks Music Company, which operated from 1904-1911. He remained active for several decades, and is probably best known for his compositions "The Charleston" and "Old Fashioned Love," both co-written with James P. Johnson for the 1923 show *Runnin' Wild*.

The California Ramblers had a number 10 hit record with an instrumental version of "Shine" in 1924. During the mid 20s, the Ramblers had one of the hottest dance bands on the East Coast. As jazz historian Richard Sudhalter noted, "No society cotillion, no college prom, was complete without them. ... In all, they're as much a part of the popular image of the 20s Flaming Youth as raccoon coats, hip flasks,

TUNES OF THE TWENTIES

and the cartoons of John Held, Jr." The band owed much of its energy and spirit to Adrian Rollini, a virtuoso of the bass saxophone, who provided agile and sparkling bass lines that just couldn't be matched by a tuba or string bass.

Both Louis Armstrong (1931) and Ella Fitzgerald (1936) recorded "Shine" early in their careers, then dropped it from their repertoire. The tune lives on as a solid instrumental number, and has also been recorded by modern jazz players. Outstanding recordings include those by Jack Teagarden (1940) and an unexpectedly relaxed interpretation by Benny Goodman (1945). By contrast, a 1945 recording by cornetist Wild Bill Davison and Sidney Bechet, under the leadership of Art Hodes, is totally unrestrained and frenetic.

Shreveport Stomp (Jelly Roll Morton, 1925): Most of Jelly Roll's piano works move along at a pretty fast clip, and it would be easy to overlook the fact that they contain great melodies. Slowing down the theme from the first strain of "Shreveport," for example, reveals how lyrical and Romantic his melodic conception was. The French opera that he heard in his youth left a lasting impression on his composing style. Typical Ragtime compositions are often based on boxy, chord-based themes. On the contrary, Jelly Roll's melodies tend to rely on smooth melodic contours in a manner reminiscent of operatic aria.

The primacy of melody was also central to Jelly Roll's conception of improvisation. Many jazz musicians, then as now, base their creations primarily on the harmony. Not Jelly Roll. "My theory is to never discard the melody. Always have the melody going some kind of way." This is evident in his performances. He never plays the melody strictly yet never ignores it entirely. The effect is one of continual invention and embellishment, start to finish.

Another of Jelly Roll's principles, evident in "Shreveport," was that the piano should sound like an entire jazz band. Thus, his bass lines sometimes sound like a tuba or string bass, left hand figures sound like a trombone, while the right hand played the melody like a trumpet with embellishment from the clarinet. "There's no jazz piano player can ever really play jazz unless they try to give the imitation of a band."

Jelly Roll recorded "Shreveport" in June of 1924 and made a piano roll shortly thereafter. In 1928, as part of his Red Hot Peppers series, he recorded a trio version with Tommy Benford on drums and Omer Simeon on clarinet. Jelly Roll, who was very particular about his musicians, considered Omer Simeon the finest jazz clarinet player around.

Recordings of "Shreveport" are somewhat scarce. It can be heard on Jim Cullum's 2006 album *3 Kings of Jazz*, with some fine clarinet work by Allan Vache.

Sidewalk Blues (Jelly Roll Morton, 1926): What do George Gershwin, Duke Ellington, and Jelly Roll Morton have in common? All three were egocentric geniuses with the ironic capacity to accept advice willingly regarding their own compositions. From Jelly Roll's incessant boasting and self-aggrandizing comments, you'd never think that he would allow musicians to make additions or changes to his own creations, but he did. This was quite apparent, and it surprised some people, when he assembled his famous Red Hot Peppers Orchestra. Between 1926 and 1930 this band made a series of records that constitute some of the most treasured monuments in jazz history. Jelly Roll hand-selected the musicians, rehearsed them thoroughly, and recorded at the famous Victor studios.

This was not to be some free-for-all jam session. On the contrary, Jelly Roll wrote intricate arrangements, leaving the right amount of space for individual expression, and tinkered with the music as they rehearsed. Omer Simeon recalled: "The reason his records are so full of tricks and changes is the liberty he gave his men. Sometimes we ask him—we get an idea, see—and we ask him to let us play a certain break, and he was always open for suggestions." The results speak for themselves. The Red Hot Pepper recordings are celebrated as the epitome of small band New Orleans jazz.

"Sidewalk Blues" was recorded in September 1926, at the second of the Red Hot Peppers sessions. This tune is one of several that contain effects reminiscent of Jelly Roll's vaudeville days. It should be noted that he not only played the piano in vaudeville—he also worked as an actor and comedian. "Sidewalk Blues" opens with a whistle and a car horn (ahooga, of course) and Jelly Roll shouting, "Hey, get out of the way. What are you trying to do, knock a streetcar off the track? You're so dumb you should belong to the Deaf and Dumb Society!" Another band member responds: "I'm sorry boss, but I got the sidewalk blues." Following a short piano intro, the band enters, following the formula that Jelly Roll believed was essential to jazz: "sweet, soft, plenty of rhythm."

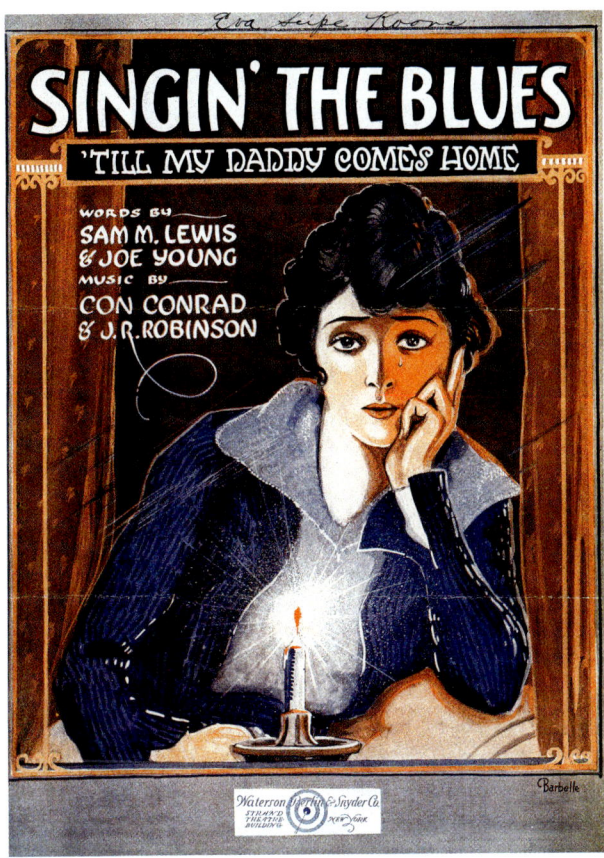

"Singin' the Blues," by Con Conrad, J. Russell Robinson, Sam Lewis, and Joe Young, is best known to jazz fans from the famous Bix Beiderbecke recording of 1927. (Courtesy Sandy Marrone, Cinnaminson, NJ.)

Singin' the Blues (music: Con Conrad and J. Russell Robinson, lyrics: Sam Lewis and Joe Young, 1920): The song was a decent hit for Aileen Stanley in 1921, and an instrumental version of it made into a medley with "Margie" with "Palesteena" on the flip side was a million-seller for the Original Dixieland Jazz Band. But the song might have been forgotten, or a least placed in the back of the closet, had not Frankie Trumbauer turned his attention to it. On February 4, 1927, Trumbauer recorded the song with Bix Beiderbecke, with "Clarinet Marmalade" on the reverse side, and had a Number 9 hit. "Singin' the Blues" in particular, with fine solos by Trumbauer, Bix and Eddie Lang had a profound influence on musicians, both Black and White. Lester Young claimed to have worn out several copies of the record learning all of the solos by heart, and for decades to come musicians would pay tribute to the recording by quoting from it in their own improvisations.

When Louis Armstrong's Hot Five recordings came out, it seemed that he had said it all. What else could be done? Range, technique, brilliant ideas—he was the hot player par excellence. But Bix quietly and modestly followed his own path. His solos utilized a limited range, relative scarcity of notes, and restrained emotional content. He found his own sounds, unexpected but right, that instilled a sense of inevitability—as if the way he played a phrase was the only way it possibly could have gone. He rarely missed notes, and found dissonant tones in the chord that didn't sound dissonant when he played them. In short, he wasn't really a "hot" player, which was the term usually applied to jazz musicians. He had invented the cool. Trumbauer's C-melody saxophone style blended so well with Bix that in short passages you might have difficulty determining which one is playing. No wonder Lester Young loved this record.

Smile (music: Charlie Chaplin, lyrics: John Turner and Geoffrey Parsons, 1936): Did the actor Charlie Chaplin really write this? Absolutely. To suggest that Chaplin (1889-1977) was multi-talented is a gross understatement: he produced, directed, starred in, edited, and composed the music for most of his films, and some of those films are among the most highly acclaimed in movie history. "Smile" is based on the love theme from *Modern Times* (1936). This fascinating film was an anachronism for its day in that it was almost completely silent except for music and sound effects. It was the last appearance of the Little Tramp, whose character would have been changed with the inclusion of dialogue. Following this, Chaplin produced only full-fledged talkies like everyone else, and the Little Tramp was no more.

If Chaplin didn't publish popular songs it was not for lack of melodic invention but simply because he occupied his talents with other matters. Nor did he have anything to do with the adaptation of this *Modern Times* theme into a song. Nearly 20 years later, in 1954, Turner and Parsons added words to the melody, Nat "King" Cole had a top-ten hit with it, and the popular song was born. Several of the lyrics are taken directly from the film, where they appeared in on-screen titles. The subject matter and name of the song were not hard to deduce from the context of the film. Curiously, it was modern jazz musicians and pop performers who first brought the song into their sphere. Traditional jazz bands were slow to discover the tune, despite the fact that its sound and sentiment clearly date back to the early Jazz Age.

"Smile" was used as the theme song for *The Jerry Lewis Show* from 1967-69. Audiences were re-introduced to the song when Michael Jackson included it on his 1995 album *HIStory: Past, Present and Future, Book 1*. It was one of Jackson's favorite songs and was sung at his funeral.

"Smiles," by Lee S. Roberts and Will J. Callahan. Roberts was one of the leading creators of piano rolls, issued under the name of Stanford Robar. (Courtesy Lilly Library, Indiana University, Bloomington, Indiana.)

Smiles (music Lee S. Roberts, lyrics: Will J. Callahan, 1917): There is certainly no shortage of "smile" songs in the American Songbook, either because we like to or because we need to. This one has remained a favorite since it first came out. Prompting three top-ten hit records in 1918, the song sold over two million copies of sheet music within six months. It would go on to sell an additional million copies in years to come. "Smiles" was interpolated into the Broadway revue *The Passing Show of 1918*, remained popular through the Big Band Era and was performed in more than two dozen films, including *Rose of Washington Square* (1939), *For Me and My Gal* (1942), *Is Everybody Happy* (1943), and *Pete Kelly's Blues* (1955). In 1980 it was used as the finale in the Broadway revue *Tintypes*. Clearly, there is something appealing about this song!

As a songwriter, Lee Roberts (Leland Stanford Roberts, 1884-1949) is known primarily for this one song. But as a pianist, he was admired as a highly prolific and capable creator of piano rolls that were issued under the name of Stanford Robar. Roberts was president of QRS, one of the leading producers of piano rolls in the 20s (and still in business today). He was considered one of leading authorities on the subject.

"Some of These Days," by Shelton Brooks, became Sophie Tucker's theme song and remained so throughout her long career. (Courtesy Lilly Library, Indiana University, Bloomington, Indiana.)

Some of These Days (music and lyrics: Shelton Brooks, 1910): It's always wise to use the connections you have, and it paid off for Shelton Brooks when he did just that. In his early 20s, Brooks was working clubs and theaters in Chicago and had gained some reputation as an imitator of Bert Williams (which Williams himself spoke of favorably when he saw his act). Brooks only had one previous song published when he came up with "Some of These Days." He knew the way to make a song successful was to plug it to someone famous. Sophie Tucker happened to be appearing in Chicago at the time, but she was constantly barraged by songwriters peddling their wares and it was very difficult to gain access to her. Fortunately for Brooks, he was friends with a girl named Mollie Elkins, who happened to be Sophie Tucker's maid. Elkins persuaded Sophie to grant Brooks a few minutes to play his song, and she loved it. She put it in her act immediately, made it her theme song and sang it in nearly every show she did for the rest of her life.

"Some of These Days" is a remarkable tune, especially considering when it was written. Melodically, it is nearly through-composed, meaning that very little of the melody returns later in the song. Similarly, the harmony travels quite a distance through the course of the tune, and it's not always clear why we're going to certain places, but there is a sense of inevitability when we get there. But for all of this complexity, it doesn't sound complicated; on the contrary, the tune is catchy and accessible on first hearing, as was Sophie Tucker's experience. In her autobiography (which is, of course, entitled *Some of These Days*) she praises the tune: "It had everything.... I've turned it inside out, singing it every way imaginable, as a dramatic song, as a novelty number, as a sentimental ballad, and always audiences have loved it and asked for it. 'Some of These Days' is one of the great songs that will be remembered and sung for years and years to come." The song entered the traditional jazz repertoire early on with a hit 1923 recording by the Original Dixieland Jazz Band, and has remained a staple ever since. It can be heard on trumpeter Norbert Susemihl's 2012 album *Night on Frenchmen Street*.

Somebody Loves Me (traditional): Not to be confused with the George Gershwin tune with the same name, this is a southern gospel hymn with a lyric that begins "Somebody loves me, answers my prayers." As with many hymns, the basic form, melody, and concept of the song most likely date back to the 1800s, and individual versions varied greatly. It was J.M. Henson, a 20th century musician and publisher of gospel music, who settled on the definitive version and included the song in a hymnal.

The 16-measure structure of the song uses a common harmonic framework that bears a casual resemblance to other traditional jazz tunes, such as "Ja-Da" and "How Come You Do Me." Ironically, the hymn is much closer in both melody and chord structure to a modern jazz classic by Horace Silver (1954) entitled "The Preacher." Considering the gospel-like quality of Silver's tune as well as the near-identical melodic contours, "Somebody Loves Me" most likely provided the inspiration for the later song. Both are now part of the traditional jazz repertoire.

"Somebody Stole My Gal," by Leo Wood, was written in the teens, but became a big hit in the 20s. (Author's personal collection.)

TUNES OF THE TWENTIES

THE SONGS | 205

Somebody Stole My Gal (music and lyrics: Leo Wood, 1918): The quaint title is enough to send you back a century, but a look at the sheet music is a dead giveaway that this is another era entirely. The cover of the original sheet music (not shown) is of a pretty girl—the stolen merchandise apparently, and the composer gets top billing, not a performer. In fact, no performer is mentioned—only the catalog numbers of a Victor recording, a Columbia recording, and a QRS piano roll, indicating where the song can be heard. In today's world, when alternate recordings of a song are so rare that they're called "covers," as if somebody's trying to get away with something, it's hard to believe there was a time when the song was at least as important as the person who played or sang it. People bought a record or went to a show to hear the tune—who performed it really didn't matter. Also on the sheet music cover is a list of eight other arrangements that can be bought for the tune—everything from "hot" piano solo to male quartet. Tin Pan Alley was still experimenting with the market, and in 1918 it wasn't at all clear which way it was going to go.

Another curiosity on the cover is the tip "with ukulele accompaniment." This was a curious phase in sheet music history. In the 1915 Panama Pacific International Exposition held in San Francisco, Americans were introduced to the ukulele, and they loved it. It was light, inexpensive, easy to play, and all the rage. Sheet music publishers responded immediately, placing "chord grids" above the staff to show how to finger the accompaniment on the ukulele. Amazingly the ukulele chords remained for another 30 years, only being replaced by grids for guitar fingerings in the 1950s.

"Somebody Stole My Gal" took a few years to catch on, but began to hit its stride in 1922 with recordings by the Original Memphis Five and Ted Lewis. Then in 1924, Ted Weems had a colossal hit with the tune that charted at Number 1 for five weeks and sold a million copies. Many more versions of the song were to follow, none more revered than Bix's 1928 recording.

But for a version that's the most fun to listen to, I'm going to suggest a 1928 recording by Fred Elizalde and his Anglo American Band. This was arguably the hottest jazz band in England during the late 20s, and Elizalde was always looking for American talent. In 1928 he persuaded the famed bass saxophonist Adrian Rollini to leave the California Ramblers and join his band.

This excerpt from "Somebody Stole My Gal" shows chord grids for ukulele above the staff. The instrument was all the rage in the late teens, and publishers were aiming to widen their market. (Author's personal collection.)

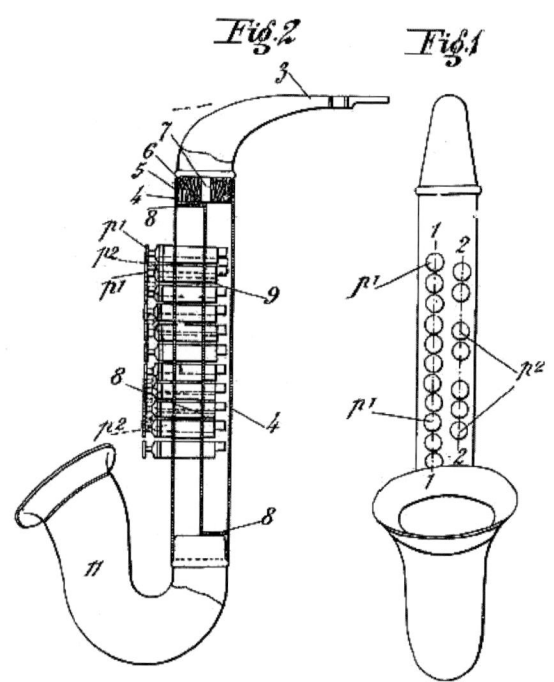

Adrian Rollini was known for playing many unusual instruments, including the "goofus" and the "hot fountain pen.(Images public domain.)

Rollini wasn't only a bass saxophone player. He played other instruments as well, including the vibraphone, piano, and instruments most people have never heard of, such as the couesnophone (usually called a "goofus") and the hot fountain pen. In truth, these two instruments were really intended as toys, but Rollini somehow managed to become a virtuoso on both of them.

Elizalde's recording of "Somebody Stole My Gal" must be heard to be believed. Rollini opens with a jazzy version of the melody on the hot fountain pen, which sounds something like a raspy clarinet that articulates like a trumpet. He then switches to the bass saxophone to underpin the cornet chorus, then lays out during the next half-chorus of piano. When the alto saxophone comes in at the half, Rollini accompanies him on the goofus. What's a goofus?! The real name of instrument is a couesnophone (that doesn't help, I know), which looks like a toy saxophone with umpteen buttons on the front of it. The reeds are inside, and the resulting sound is something like a cross between an accordion and a harmonica, if that makes any sense. But it sounds great in Rollini's hands. The recording finishes out with a band chorus with Rollini back to bass saxophone, and finally a short concluding statement by the hot fountain pen.

Someday You'll Be Sorry (music and lyrics: Louis Armstrong, 1946): Officially, Armstrong wrote this song, but it might be a stretch to say that it was completely original. In fact, the melody, along with its rhythm and harmonic structure, are nearly identical to an earlier song, "Goodnight Angel" (1937), with music by Allie Wrubel and lyrics by Herb Magidson. Wrubel was an active composer for the Disney studios, having penned such numbers as "Gone with the Wind" (1937) and "Zip-a-Dee-Doo-Dah" (1947). Armstrong knew the earlier song and even recorded it himself once. Nevertheless, he wrote original lyrics and at least made enough alterations to avoid copyright violations.

He remembers writing "Someday" with his fourth wife, Lucille, and that he had his third wife Alpha in mind. Another unsubstantiated claim is that he had Dizzy Gillespie in mind, since he and the bebop movement were at odds at the time, trading insults in the press. (Some years later they became best of friends, regretting their harsh words.) The lyrics to the song certainly fit this story, and who knows, perhaps the thought did cross Armstrong's mind, with lyrics such as: "The way you treated me was wrong," and "I was the one who taught you all you know."

"Someday" came along at a crucial time in Armstrong's life. 1946 was the year the big bands officially died, and Armstrong had been fronting a big band for some 15 years. But he was not about to go down with the ship. On May 17, 1947, Armstrong's manager booked him in Town Hall to do a small-group concert, playing the New Orleans repertoire of his early years. The success of that concert was a pivotal moment—it marked a change of direction for Armstrong, and the birth of the All Stars, the group he would lead for the rest of his life. In June, Armstrong recorded a session with the core of his new band, and "Someday" was one of the numbers. Within a short time, the All Stars were the most popular jazz band in America, in spite of the fact that bebop was the dominant force in jazz. True or not, the song proved to be a prophetic reply to the moderns.

South (music: Bennie Moten and Thamon Hayes, lyrics: Ray Charles, 1924): Is that the Ray Charles who had a hit with Hoagy Carmichael's "Georgia On My Mind" in 1960? No, that was Ray Charles Robinson (1930-2004), the immensely popular soul/pop/gospel musician. It was Ray Charles Offenberg (born 1918), a highly successful musician in his own right, who added lyrics to this originally instrumental number in 1941. Among his many accomplishments, Charles was a pioneer in creating the genre now identified as "easy listening" and it is not surprising that he spent the greater part of his career working with Perry Como. Charles was particularly known for his direction of a choral group that Como dubbed "The Ray Charles Singers."

Today, some might only know Bennie Moten (1894-1935) from the eponymous jazz standard "Moten Swing" made famous with Count Basie's 1940 recording. But to be truthful, if there had been no Bennie Moten, there would have been no Count Basie, at least in terms of his musical contribution. In the 20s and early 1930s, Moten, based in Kansas City, Missouri, led the most important jazz orchestra in the Midwest. His blues-based riffing style was to become a defining feature of the Big Band Era. Count Basie worked for Moten, as did Walter Page, Oran "Hot Lips" Page, and Jimmy Rushing—all of whom would become central figures in the Basie band.

Bennie Moten wrote "South" with his trombonist Thamon Hayes. The band had a hit record with the song in 1925. That happened to be the year that electrical sound recording was invented—which meant that musicians would record into a microphone rather than a horn, resulting in much improved sound quality. Within a few years all major record companies had converted to the new technology, introducing the possibility of re-recording previous versions of hit tunes with the hope that they might be hits all over again. For "South" it worked. Moten recorded the tune once again in 1928, and "South" became a Number 10 hit the following year. This particular record, Victor 24893, has a distinguished history in that it never went out of print. RCA-Victor reissued the record in 1935 and for some reason (perhaps Kid Ory's version of 1944) Moten's "South" became popular once again in 1944, reaching Number 22 on the charts. It remained a juke box hit during the 1940s, was reissued again when RCA made the transition to 45s and remained in print until RCA stopped making vinyl records.

S'posin' (music: Paul Denniker, lyrics: Andy Razaf, 1929): Andy Razaf (1895-1973) was one of the most celebrated Black lyricists in Tin Pan Alley history. If you think his last name is unusual you should get over it, as his full name was Andriamanantena Paul Razafinkarefo. His parents were members of an aristocratic family in Madagascar and his father was nephew to the queen, but such a life was not to be for him: His father was killed in the French invasion of 1894-95 and his pregnant mother fled to the United States. He was raised in Harlem and taught himself poetry and songwriting. At the age of 16, he quit school and took a job as an elevator operator on Tin Pan Alley. According to his biographer, Barry Singer, Razaf remembered: "I studied my passengers as they came and went. I talked and made friends with them and soon they were telling me about themselves. They confided in me their joys and sorrows, their ambitions, disappointments, happiness.... These are the things that songs are made of." Meanwhile, he studied his craft and read "everything I could get my hands on." Soon his efforts paid off and his songs (and poetry) began to be published.

By the mid-20s, Razaf had teamed up with Fats Waller and the magic was working. The pair had a banner year in 1929 with two hit shows and a string of hits that included "Ain't Misbehavin'," "Black and Blue," and Honeysuckle Rose." Razaf was firmly established as a leading wordsmith on Tin Pan Alley, but for one caveat: Most saw him as a lyricist of limited scope—one who could write for the African-American stage, but lacked the flexibility to adapt to other topics and sentiments. "S'posin'" changed all that. Teaming up with White songwriter Paul Denniker, Razaf demonstrated that he could readily adapt to the "mainstream" of the day, penning such appealing simple rhymes as "caress you" with "would it impress you, or distress you?" Razaf had done his homework, knew the language of the day, and delivered accordingly. Appropriately, Rudy Vallee, just starting his career and very much in step with the times, had a hit record with the song.

In an ironic twist to the story, Razaf's publisher, Joe Davis, marshaled all of his forces behind "S'posin'," practically ensuring its success single-handedly, and then strong-armed Razaf into relinquishing his royalties. Reluctantly, Razaf agreed, but thought enough of Davis' power and influence vis-a-vis his own ambitions that he signed an exclusive two-year contract with him after Davis had cheated him!

You can hear a delightful rendition of "S'posin'" on singer Banu Gibson's 1998 album *Love Is Good for Anything That Ails You*.

Squeeze Me (music: Fats Waller, Lyrics: Clarence Williams, 1925): (Not to be confused with "Just Squeeze Me," the 1941 jazz standard by Duke Ellington.) This was Fats Waller's first major publication, but the story is more complicated than that. By his own admission, Fats took the basic tune from a well-known bawdy song of the day called "The Boy in the Boat." Every musician would have known the tune, but Fats put it in popular song form, reworked the melody and chords and presented it to Clarence Williams for publication. This was in 1923, and Waller happened to be in Boston at the time, accompanying a vaudeville act, so he called the song "Boston Blues." Williams saw the merit in the song but didn't quite know what to do with it. He first tried to reset it with a parody to the lyrics from Victor Herbert's "Kiss Me Again," but when Herbert's publishers learned of his effort they put a stop to it. The tune was shelved for two years.

In 1925 Williams finally published the song as "Squeeze Me" with the lyrics we know today, which don't contain a trace of the original risqué words, nor any reference to "Kiss Me Again." If fact, the lyrics are quite good, far better than the routine words that Clarence Williams added to the tunes he published. It seems likely that someone else was responsible for the lyrics, and that Williams simply claimed them. (It wouldn't be the first or the last time. His own cousin, Pops Foster, once called Williams "a real horse thief.") Finally Andy Razaf, who generally took the high road when speaking of fellow musicians, asserted in a 1960 interview that he was indeed the author of the lyrics to "Squeeze Me."

Although "Squeeze Me" was destined to be a jazz standard, it was never a popular hit and its beginnings were modest. But musicians liked the song and eventually most got around to recording it. Notable versions include those by Bessie Smith (1926, with Williams on piano), Louis Armstrong (1928), Sidney Bechet (1930), and Fats Waller himself (1937). For a recent New Orleans-style recording, hear Tuba Skunny on their 2012 album *Rag Band*.

Stealin' Apples (music: Fats Waller, lyrics: Andy Razaf, 1936): As with many songs of the era, the copyright date is misleading. Waller and Razaf actually wrote the tune in 1932 for a revue at Connie's Inn called *Hot Harlem*. The song evidently has words but no vocal recordings exist, and no one around today seems to have heard or seen any lyrics. Fletcher Henderson recorded it in 1936, but the song didn't attract much attention until Benny Goodman made a hit out of it in 1939. He included it in most of his performances after that and can be heard and seen performing it on films from 1948, 1961 and 1985. The 1948 clip is from a movie called *A Song Is Born* in which Benny Goodman plays the part of Professor Magenbruch.

"Stealin' Apples" has a riff structure typical of the Swing Era and is generally played at a pretty fast clip. Goodman "owned" the song to be sure, but there was a fellow who gave him a run for his money on this one, and that was clarinetist Michael Andrew "Peanuts" Hucko (1918-2003). Hucko played with Goodman on and off, and was also closely associated with Eddie Condon. He performed the song often and fortunately, live film exists from a 1961 television broadcast with Eddie Condon, in addition to live performances from 1981, 1990, and 1999.

Stompin' at the Savoy (music: Edgar Sampson, Chick Webb, and Benny Goodman, lyrics: Andy Razaf, 1934): It was said that there was so much dancing going on at the Savoy that the owners had to replace the maple dance floor every three years. Located at 596 Lenox Avenue in the middle of Harlem, with its 10,000 square foot dance floor, it was the hot spot for dancers in the 20s and 30s. It featured the house band of Chick Webb, and hosted the best bands of the day, often through good-natured "battles of the bands." Unlike many of the top nightclubs in town, it had no discrimination policy, and both Blacks and Whites were welcome. The Savoy opened in 1926 and closed in 1958.

Today, the placard on the site where the Savoy once stood reads:

> "Here once stood the legendary Savoy Ballroom, a hothouse for the development of jazz in the Swing Era.... It was a catalyst for innovation where dancers and musicians blended influences to forge new, wide-spread, and long-lasting traditions in music and dance. Whether they attended or not, all Americans knew the meaning of 'Stompin' at the Savoy.'"

The tune was written by alto saxophonist Edgar Sampson (1907-1958), who had other published songs to his credit, but in this instance it is likely that Webb and Goodman offered musical collaboration in addition to the promise to plug the song with their bands. Chick Webb had the first hit in 1934, followed by Ozzie Nelson and Benny Goodman in 1936. Goodman re-recorded the song in 1937 with his quartet and achieved a Number 4 hit.

"Savoy" is a riff tune in call-and-response form, and is ready made for duet or big-band performance. The opening section keeps the harmony steady, but the bridge moves off to foreign territory with some "side-stepping" along the way that can trip up even experienced musicians. Although most instrumental numbers don't fare very well when lyrics are added after the fact, "Savoy" is an exception and Razaf really showed his stuff. His strategy was to cast the opening in the third person, describing the Savoy: "Savoy, the home of sweet romance;" move to the second person for the next section: "Your lips so warm and sweet as wine;" the first person for the bridge: "How my heart is singing;" and a combination for the last 8, concluding with "Savoy, let me stomp away with you."

For a delightfully sensitive treatment of the song, hear guitarist John Pizzarelli sing and play "Stompin'" on his album *Let There Be Love* (2000).

"Strut Miss Lizzie," by Turner Layton and Henry Creamer, came from the show that caused the breakup of a successful writing team. (Courtesy Lilly Library, Indiana University, Bloomington, Indiana.)

Strut Miss Lizzie (music: Turner Layton, lyrics: Henry Creamer, 1922): This song is from the show of the same name that caused the break-up of the great songwriting of Creamer and Layton. After six years together and a string of successful songs including "After You've Gone," "Dear Old Southland," and "Way down Yonder in New Orleans," a rift developed between the two partners, and here's how it happened.

When Creamer heard Ziegfeld's new slogan "Glorifying the American Girl," he had a brainstorm, and came up with the idea to present an all-Black show called *Strut Miss Lizzie*, adapting Ziegfeld's promotional slogan to "Glorifying the Creole Beauty." It was a good idea, a good show, and it got good reviews, but just couldn't seem to get the traction it needed to catch on. Unwisely, Creamer took a series of desperate steps to keep the show afloat—changing venues, borrowing money, and wheeling and dealing with the copyrights to the songs. When the show finally closed after nine weeks, with unpaid actors and a pile of debt, Layton had had enough. The team never worked together again.

"Strut Miss Lizzie" is a number about a girl strutting the avenue and knocking the men dead. The form is unusual and effectively laid out by breaking into the "Hoochie-Coochie" dance at the end. This familiar melody is worth a moment's scrutiny. Variously known as the "snake-charmer," "Egyptian" or "belly-dancer" tune, the song has been around for a long time, and even shows up in the *Arban Trumpet Method* of 1864 (which has never been out of print since its publication—perhaps contributing to the survival of the "Arabian melody," as he called it). It was used to accompany a dancer at the 1893 Chicago World's Columbian Exposition, which prompted several song copyrights, such as "The Streets of Cairo" (1895). As can be imagined, cartoons of the 1930s and 1940s had great fun with it, using it to evoke Middle Eastern imagery.

The American Quartet had a hit record with "Strut Miss Lizzie" in 1921, but it was a 1920 recording by the Original Dixieland Jazz Band that put the tune in the jazz repertoire. Among the many excellent recordings are those by Bix Beiderbecke (1930), Eddie Condon (1939), and Jack Teagarden (1947). All of them use the "Hoochie-Coochie" dance as the introduction. For a swinging solo piano version, hear Neville Dickie (2011).

Struttin' with Some Barbeque (music: Lil Armstrong, lyrics: Don Raye, 1927): Lil Hardin Armstrong was Louis Armstrong's second wife. She was the pianist in Joe Oliver's band when Louis joined in 1922. Though her playing might not have been as hot as the top pianists of the day, her classical training and musical knowledge earned the respect of other band members. A few years later, when Louis began recording his Hot Fives and Sevens, he was breaking new ground that went beyond Lil's comfort zone. In 1927, he hired Earl Hines to replace her, a brilliant pianist who was experimenting along the same lines as Louis. But Lil's influence on Louis's career went far beyond her piano skills. It was she who urged him to quit Joe Oliver to go with Fletcher Henderson and then to strike out on his own and make a name for himself. Also, Lil was a competent songwriter and sometimes collaborator with Louis.

And there lies the difficulty in figuring out who wrote what. Lil received the copyright for "Struttin'" only after Louis attempted to copyright the song and she sued him. (Yes, they were still married; for the time being.) But he always maintained that he was the composer, as he said in this 1951 interview: "This tune was derived and thought of when Zutty Singleton and I were playing at the Savoy Ballroom on the South Side of Chicago.... And after the dance was over every night, Zutty and I would drive out to 48th and State Street.... There was an old man there who made some of the most delicious barbecue.... One night, while Zutty and I were manipulating those 'Chime Bones,' a thought came into my head... I said to Zutty ... I should write a tune and call it 'Struttin with Some Barbecue.'"

It certainly reeks of a story made up for the press, especially considering the double entendre of the title, which mainly refers to the act of parading about town with an attractive woman. But then again, the adventurous melody and its unusual note choices point to Louis. Most likely, it was composed on the spot as a collaborative effort, and it is likely that Lil was the one who wrote it down. (As with many of the songs recorded by the Hot Fives and Sevens, the copyright was not filed until several months after the session.) As for the lyrics, they were added many years later by Don Raye, who was writing for the Andrews Sisters at the time. (He wrote the words to "Boogie Woogie Bugle Boy.") Raye's lyrics add little to "Struttin'" and are seldom sung.

Sweet Sue (music: Victor Young, lyrics: Will J. Harris, 1928): This was written by one of the heavyweights; what's more, it was his first song. Victor Young (1900-1956) was born in Chicago into a musical family. When he was ten he was sent to Poland where he studied violin at the Warsaw Conservatory. After receiving his diploma and pursuing additional private study, he made his debut with the Warsaw Philharmonic and toured Europe as a concert violinist. With the outbreak of World War I he returned to the United States and began working as a violinist and arranger for dance bands. Beginning with "Sweet Sue," he continued to write songs, often collaborating with lyricist Ned Washington. Young began writing for Hollywood in the mid-1930s and composed more than 300 film scores in his 20-year career. His well-known songs include "Around the World," "My Foolish Heart," "Stella by Starlight," and "When I Fall in Love."

Whether or not actress Sue Carol was the inspiration for "Sweet Sue," she was soon associated with it and her picture appears on the sheet music cover. The tune caught on quickly: both Ben Pollack and Earl Burnett had hits in 1928, the Mills Brothers in 1932, Tommy Dorsey in 1939, and Johnny Long in 1949. Obviously, the song was here to stay. "Sweet Sue" is a compelling jam tune with its riff-like opening melody and subtle harmonic plan. A fascinating 1930 recording by Joe Venuti's Blue Four features some intricate duet work between Venuti on violin and Jimmy Dorsey on baritone sax.

The names Jimmy and Tommy Dorsey come up a lot in discussing music of the 20s through the 40s. They were among the most talented studio musicians of the 20s, each had one of the leading big bands of the late 30s and early 40s, and in the 50s they joined forces to front one of the last of the big bands, the only famous swing orchestra to have a regular television show (1955-56). (Elvis Presley made his television debut on their show.) Jimmy (1904-1957) was an excellent clarinet and saxophone player, while Tommy (1905-1956), who could also play the cornet, goes down in history has one of the most lyrical trombone players the world has ever heard. The 1947 film *The Fabulous Dorseys* gets a lot of the facts wrong, but has the right spirit, and showcases the brothers on screen presenting their fabulous music. Their personalities were said to be opposite from one another— Jimmy was gentle, kind, and understanding, loved by the musicians in his band. Tommy was a gruff, demanding taskmaster, respected but feared by his musicians. (Frank Sinatra, Tommy's featured singer, would go on to imitate both his boss's lyricism and leadership style.) But perhaps their most infamous trait was their tendency to fight—physically—when together on the bandstand. And woe to the unsuspecting sideman who dared try get between them!

Swing That Music (music: Louis Armstrong, lyrics; Horace Gerlach, 1936): There are songs that are so complete in themselves that the performer only needs to render them properly to bring them off. Then there are songs that give little more than a sketch or a plan, staying out of the way but requiring an expert musician to make them come to life. "Swing That Music" is that kind of song. The melody is little more than a riff, the harmony is brief, following well-worn paths, and the words are, quite frankly, pretty dumb. But Louis Armstrong's debut recording of the song on May 18, 1936, is arguably the most exciting record he ever made. It must be heard to be believed.

Before describing this performance (which is a futile endeavor, except to whet your appetite to go listen to it), it will be helpful to review where Armstrong was in his career at the time. After laying down the textbook on jazz improvisation in his Hot Fives and Sevens, he spent some time in Europe, returning home in early 1935. That year he hired manager Joe Glaser, who would stay with him the rest of his life, and signed with Decca Records. In the summer of 1936, he acted a prominent part in the film *Pennies from Heaven*, starring Bing Crosby, and in November of that year he published his first autobiography, *Swing That Music*, specifically named to cash in on the momentum of the tune. His career was flourishing.

Ironically, Armstrong said himself at the time that his bravura days were over—that he was going to concentrate on pleasing audiences instead of showing off how well he could play the trumpet. Perhaps his plan was to show his stuff one more time before cooling down, for "Swing That Music" presents a serious dose of trumpet razzle-dazzle. The recording starts off innocently with the band playing the melody for one chorus, followed by Armstrong's vocal chorus. It's fascinating to hear his vocal quality at this point when his signature gravely sound was not yet in place. The band plays another chorus, and Armstrong finally enters on the trumpet. What follows are four solid trumpet choruses, each hotter than the last, ending with literally dozens of high C's on the trumpet, capped off with a high Eb.

As an interesting contrast, Armstrong recorded the number just a couple of months later with the Jimmy Dorsey Orchestra (another best-selling ensemble for Decca Records). The band is obviously more polished than the previous ensemble, but the rhythm section doesn't have the same drive. Armstrong follows his same basic plan, but changes the ending. He would continue to record the song many more times in his career. Three live radio broadcasts, from 1937, 1938, and 1941, are excellent and have been preserved on record. During this critical time period we can hear the gradual development of the gravely quality of Louis' voice, which became his trademark in later years. Even more fascinating, an October 1938, "News of the Day" newsreel features Armstrong playing "Swing that Music." His performance is edited down to a brief excerpt, but to see and hear Louis play, even for a few seconds, is simply precious.

"Tain't Nobody's Biz-ness if I Do," by Porter Grainger and Everett Robbins, is based on a humorous lyric that invites endless possibilities for expansion. (Courtesy Lilly Library, Indiana University, Bloomington, Indiana.)

Tain't Nobody's Biz-ness if I Do (music and lyrics: Porter Grainger and Everett Robbins, 1922): The delightful words and simple but energized melodic sketch make this tune come alive. The lyrical plan sets up invitingly endless possibilities, such as "If I should take a notion to jump in to the ocean," and caps off each image with "Tain't nobody's bizness if I do." The original song had words for several choruses, but it has accumulated many more over the decades.

"Tain't" is one of the first blues standards (although it does not follow a typical 12-bar blues structure) and began to be recorded late in 1922 just as the blues craze was picking up steam. Bessie Smith, who did not arrive in New York until February 1923, attempted the song on her recording debut but couldn't get it to click after nine tries and scrapped it. She returned to it two months later and it became her fifth hit record of 1923. One year later, Clarence Williams' Blue Five also had a hit record.

In the late 1940s Jimmy Witherspoon revived the tune, renaming it "Ain't Nobody's Business" and adding some new lyrics. It became the biggest selling R&B record of 1949, inspiring dozens of other recordings by artists in various genres.

"That Da-Da Strain, by Edgar Dowell and Mamie Medina, found its place as a hot instrumental number. (Courtesy Sandy Marrone, Cinnaminson, NJ.)

That Da-Da Strain (music: Edgar Dowell, lyrics: Mamie Medina, 1922): Whether or not the composers were influenced by the sound of the word "Dada" as it relates to the art and cultural movement of the time, we'll never know. The nonsense lyrics of the song certainly have no statement to make, with a chorus that begins "Da-da-da-da-da-da-da-da, it's so appealing, starts me reeling." Strangely enough, an earlier song, "My Crooney Melody" (1914) begins with similar lyrics: "Tia-da-da, Tia-da-da, Tia-da-da, Tia-da-da, listen, listen, listen to that wonderful strain." Let's just conclude that lyric writing in popular music hadn't reached its full maturity yet.

Early blues singers including Ethel Waters and Mamie Smith recorded "That Da-Da Strain," but the song might have been all but forgotten had not instrumentalists latched onto it. It soon proved to be a great jazz number.

Ross Gorman and his Virginians made a fine recording in December 1922. (Ross Gorman, Paul Whiteman's virtuoso clarinetist, might not be known by name, but he left his mark in the world. In 1924, when rehearsing *Rhapsody in Blue* with the orchestra, Gorman decided to play a joke on composer George Gershwin by adding a huge, sweeping glissando to the opening clarinet solo. To everyone's surprise, Gershwin loved it, and insisted that he play it that way during the performance. It is now one of the most recognizable openings in music literature.)

Other notable recordings of "That Da-Da Strain" include those by the Louisiana Rhythm Kings, featuring Red Nichols, Jack Teagarden, Pee Wee Russell, and Bud Freeman (1929), and a driving version by Muggsy Spanier (1939). More recent versions include those by pianist James Dapogny and his Chicago Jazz Band (1997) and clarinetist Kenny Davern (2006). One of the features of "Da-Da" is a hot, minor key verse that is invariably included in all performances, providing an effective contrast with the chorus/solo section.

"That's a Plenty," by Lew Pollack, was a rag that became a traditional jazz classic. (Courtesy Lilly Library, Indiana University, Bloomington, Indiana.)

That's a Plenty (music: Lew Pollack, 1914): Television audiences were very familiar with this number in the 1950s and 60s. Jackie Gleason (1916-1987) used "That's a Plenty" as his famous "away we go!" number following his opening monologue.

"That's a Plenty" was one of the few piano rags to make the transition into a jazz standard, albeit with a few alterations to the melody. Pollack (1895-1946), who was only 19 when he wrote the number, went on to compose "Charmaine," "Diane," "Miss Annabelle Lee," and "Two Cigarettes in the Dark." Pollack also composed the score to the film *Captain January* (1936), starring Shirley Temple and Buddy Ebsen, including their famous dance routine "At the Codfish Ball."

As with all piano rags, "That's a Plenty" is a sectional tune with elements taken from the march, including a trio section and the "dogfight" leading to the solo chorus. A distinctive feature of the number is that the opening section is in a minor key. It has been suggested that the title is a follow-up on the popular rag "Too Much Mustard," but the sheet music illustrator chose (or was assigned) a more elegant interpretation: A well-dressed woman in a restaurant raising her hand in refusal to a waiter in full tails and wearing a monocle, who offers her another glass of Champagne.

"That's a Plenty" entered the jazz repertoire early on, mostly due to the 1923 recording by the New Orleans Rhythm Kings. Another noteworthy early recording is by the Louisiana Rhythm Kings (1929) with Red Nichols, Miff Mole, and Fud Livingston. Ray Gilbert supplied lyrics to "That's a Plenty," inspiring a duet performance by Bing Crosby and Connee Boswell, but the words add little to the number and are rarely if ever sung.

An outstanding 1943 recording of "That's a Plenty" deserves mention. When the musicians' union strike (1942-44) began to wind down at the end of 1943, there was a rush among smaller record labels to get musicians into the studios as quickly as possible. Among the first to record were members of the Eddie Condon circle. Producer Bob Thiele set up a date with cornetist Wild Bill Davison, Condon on guitar, Pee Wee Russell on clarinet, George Brunies on trombone, Gene Schroeder on piano, Bob Casey on bass, and George Wettling on drums. The tune was recorded onto a 12-inch disc, meaning there was more recording time than the usual limit of about three minutes and 20 seconds. On this disc Russell, Schroeder, Davison, and Brunies each take outstanding solos, and it's fascinating to hear them take a second chorus, with the rest of the horns playing background chords.

"That's a Plenty" has become practically a requirement at every traditional jazz concert nowadays. For a recent recording, listen to trumpeter Al Harrison on his 2011 album *Side by Side*.

There'll Be Some Changes Made (music: W. Benton Overstreet, lyrics: Billy Higgins, 1923): Higgins and Overstreet were a successful African-American vaudeville team of their day, yet this song is virtually their only surviving legacy. Unlike Bert Williams and a handful of others, they remained in Black theater circuits, not widely known by the general public, in spite of the fact that Overstreet was an active composer with many copyrighted songs to his credit.

"There'll Be Some Changes Made" is ingenious in its unusual construction: it is 36 measures long, with a barebones melody and not much rhythmic activity. But the chord sequence in relation to the melody is unique. Beginning on a note that is dissonant to both the key and the chord of the moment, the tune begins far back on the circle of fifths, like a clock spring tightly wound, and proceeds from the very first measure on its long journey. The opening chord sits for four long measures, only to move on to one that does the same thing—prolonging and intensifying the need to move forward. Only near the very end of the tune do we reach home base—arriving at the chord that defines the key of the whole song.

Early blues singers loved the song and so did jazz musicians. There were four top-ten hits on the number in the 20s and then four hits in 1941 alone, including a number one record by Benny Goodman. By 1947 interest in the tune had not abated, and when Ted Weems' hit record of 1939 was reissued (the same recording) it became a hit all over again. A fascinating recording of "There'll Be Some Changes Made" was made by guitarist Eddie Lang accompanied by pianist Frank Signorelli in 1928. Recognized as the best jazz guitarist of his day, Lang takes a quasi-classical approach to the tune, eliciting more depth of feeling from the song than might be expected.

There'll Come a Time When You'll Need Me (music: Fats Waller, lyrics: Joe Davis, 1927): Publisher Joe Davis (1896-1978) exerted an important influence on Waller, advancing his career and encouraging him to compose more. In 1929, Davis actually gave Waller a "day job," setting him up at his office with a little room to work in from 10:00-5:00 for a weekly salary. Waller was to be available to play for any songwriters or vocalists who visited the office and spend the rest of his time writing. This might seem an unlikely environment for the wild and fun-loving Fats, but he produced some fine compositions while the arrangement lasted.

Little is known about the origins of "There'll Come a Time." It is not to be confused with the Shelton Brooks tune of the same title (1911). The Waller/Davis number was copyrighted but not published. The most famous recording by far is that by Bix Beiderbecke (1928). Bix and Trumbauer are featured throughout in a small-band setting with plenty of breaks and solo space. Of the relatively few other recordings available, recommended are those by Red Nichols (1928), Joe Sullivan (1952), and Miff Mole (1959).

Thou Swell (music: Richard Rodgers, lyrics: Lorenz Hart, 1927): Perhaps more than with any other songwriter, it's hard to think of Rodgers without linking his name to one of his two famous lyricists, and if you're a jazz connoisseur, that name is probably Hart. (On the other hand, if you're simply in love with *Oklahoma!*, *Carousel*, *South Pacific*, *The King and I*, and *The Sound of Music*—and who isn't?—then Oscar Hammerstein is your guy.) The pathetic, alcoholic genius of Hart was an unlikely partner for the dictatorial, workaholic creativity of Rodgers, but when the collaboration produced (thanks to Rodgers), the result was magic.

"Thou Swell" is a song (some say the best song) from *A Connecticut Yankee* (1927), Rodgers and Hart's greatest Broadway success of the 20s and their only show to be revived. It is based on the Mark Twain novel *A Connecticut Yankee in King Arthur's Court*. The plot in the musical concerns a 20s character transported back (in a dream) to the court of King Arthur in the year of 528. The concept would have been a challenge for the most accomplished lyricist, but Hart seizes on Rodgers' rhythmically charged melodies and turns out dozens of clever nonsense rhymes. The language used is pseudo Elizabethan, with clichés and slang thrown in for spice. The very title of the song "Thou Swell" combines one of the most characteristic pronouns in Shakespearian imagery with one of the buzz-words of the 20s. Hart continues in this vein, stretching a little further at the close of the bridge: "Hear me holler I choose a Sweet lollapaloosa in thee." It's not surprising that Howard Dietz once said, "Larry Hart can rhyme anything—and does!" ("Lollapaloosa, also spelled lollapalooza, meaning something excellent, is a word of unknown origins that became popular in the 20s.)

Even without Hart's brilliant contribution, Rodgers' tune is solid and stands on its own with its punchy melody and unique chord structure. It became a jazz standard from the start, beginning with Bix Beiderbecke's 1928 classic, and made the transition to modern jazz while staying in the traditional jazz repertoire. Among the many different treatments "Thou Swell" has received over the years, one of the hardest swinging was recorded by pianists Dick Wellstood and Dick Hyman on their album *Stridemaster*. The title says it all.

Three Little Words (music: Harry Ruby, lyrics: Bert Kalmar, 1930): The song debuted in the 1930 Amos and Andy film *Check and Double Check*, which featured the Duke Ellington Orchestra in their first major film appearance. It was intended to be sung by Duke's drummer, Sonny Greer, who did sing on occasion in clubs but wasn't ready for Hollywood. Duke explains "He got mike fright, light fright, Hollywood fright, and all sorts of funny things, and he said, 'Man, I can't sing, I'm not a singer, I'm a drummer,' and he was just scared to death. So we said, 'Well, tell you what we'll do, let's go over and get Bing Crosby.' So we went over to the Cocoanut Grove and got Bing, and he came over and made the track." But that's not the end of the story. Evidently, the director didn't like Bing, declaring, "This guy can't sing a note by himself.... Go get the three of them." So they brought all three of the Rhythm Boys into the studio and made the final version.

In the film, Duke's three trumpet players pretend to sing to a sound track recorded by the Rhythm Boys, who never appear. Later that year the Ellington band recorded the song with the Rhythm Boys and it became Duke's first Number 1 record. As was customary in many recordings of the day, the vocalists are confined to one chorus near the end of the tune while the band is featured throughout, affording Duke ample space to work his magic. His creative arranging skills elicit remarkable color from what is a rather simple tune.

Tiger Rag (Original Dixieland Jazz Band, 1917): Members of the ODJB (who often shared or took turns taking credit for songs) assembled this number from fragments that had been floating around New Orleans for a number of years. It is a multipart number with several sections, including built-in breaks, and concludes with a chorus that shares the same harmony with several other songs, among them "Washington and Lee Swing," "Bill Bailey," and "Bourbon Street Parade."

The first recording the band made of "Tiger Rag" ran into some difficulties. In February, 1917, the ODJB had made their first record for Victor with "Dixie Jass Band One-Step" on one side and "Livery Stable Blues" on the other. The record was a smash hit but both songs prompted lawsuits, causing Victor and the ODJB to part company for a while. The ODJB then went to Aeolian-Vocalion for a series of recordings that summer and fall, and recorded "Tiger Rag" on August 7. Unfortunately, the company was still using the outdated hill-and-dale recording technology instead of the laterally cut grooves that had become the norm. (Hill-and-dale refers to the original Edison method of cutting a vertical groove in the record.) That meant that the records would not play on most contemporary phonographs. Sales were not good. Fortunately, in early 1918, the ODJB went back to Victor and recorded "Tiger Rag" again on March 25. This time they hit the mark. The record became a Number 1 hit, charting for nearly three months.

"Tiger Rag" entered the jazz repertoire immediately, and hundreds of recordings appeared in the coming decades. Notable versions include those by Ethel Waters (1922), The New Orleans Rhythm Kings (1922), featuring a famous clarinet solo by Leon Roppolo, Bix Beiderbecke with the Wolverines (1924), Louis Armstrong (1930), and pianist Art Tatum (1933). But perhaps the most unlikely (and strange) is a radio broadcast of 1947 with Charlie Parker and Dizzy Gillespie! "Tiger Rag" is frequently heard today as a fight song for institutions that have a tiger as their mascot.

The Art Tatum recording of "Tiger Rag" is historically significant. During the late 20s, Fats Waller, James P. Johnson, and Willie "The Lion" Smith" were the unrivaled masters of Harlem Stride piano. Their prodigious techniques instilled respect and fear in the hearts of other pianists and they were seldom challenged. That all changed one night in 1932 when twenty-two-year-old Art Tatum took on the mighty triumvirate in a cutting contest and soundly defeated all three of them. He soon began recording prolifically and was universally recognized as the most technically proficient jazz pianist of his day. One night Tatum walked into a room where Fats Waller was playing. Waller promptly stood up and announced, "Ladies and Gentlemen, I play piano, but God is in the house tonight." His brilliance is prominently displayed in his 1933 recording of "Tiger Rag."

Tin Roof Blues (New Orleans Rhythm Kings, 1923): Though not as well known to the general public, the New Orleans Rhythm Kings played a significant role in the development of early jazz that rivaled or surpassed that of the Original Dixieland Jazz Band. The OJDB came first, turning everyone's attention to the new sound of "jazz" (whatever that was). But they billed themselves as a novelty act, and their raucous performances, while inspiring, left little room for improvisation or individual expression. By contrast, NORK took their music seriously, and their cohesive ensemble playing and creative solos pointed the way for the future of the music. What's more, NORK musicians acknowledged their debt to African-American jazz pioneers, while ODJB leader Nick La Rocca denied any such influence.

Their time slot in jazz history was brief but brilliant. They formed in 1921 with a steady job at the Friars Inn in Chicago, which inspired their original name, The Friars Society Orchestra. Bix Beiderbecke (who was sent to a boarding school near Chicago to mend his wayward ways—what were his parents thinking?) showed up frequently to hear and sit in with the band. During 1922 and 1923, NORK made a series of recordings for Gennett Records. The impact of these records on the future of jazz is incalculable. Not until Louis Armstrong's Hot Fives and Hot Sevens would any group of jazz recordings become so influential on other musicians. Unfortunately, after making their legendary recordings, the band broke up in 1923, and a handful of half-hearted attempts to reorganize were not successful.

"Tin Roof Blues" started out life as a routine that NORK did under the title of "The Rusty Rail Blues." The publisher decided that "Tin Roof Blues" would evoke a better image. Accordingly, the drawing on the sheet music cover (still under copyright and not shown) depicts the Tin Roof Blues Café in New Orleans. However, it shows it at its original location at Washington Street and Claiborne Avenue. That establishment had closed in 1910, and the "Tin Roof Café in operation in 1923 was located on Baronne St. (Its name was later changed to Suburban Gardens.) In any case, the definitive recording of this simple tune that NORK laid down has become famous among jazz musicians.

Among the highlights of their recording is a solo by clarinetist Leon Roppolo that has become a classic. Clearly one of the most well-structured improvisations of early jazz history, generations of clarinetists have learned and studied it thoroughly. Even Benny Goodman, not one to give compliments freely, proclaimed his debt to Roppolo: "My idea of a great clarinet player ... was Leon Roppolo.... I did my best to sound like him."

As much as musicians were inspired by NORK's recording of "Tin Roof Blues," few jazz bands recorded their own versions. Jelly Roll Morton made a piano roll in 1924, Ted Lewis had a modest hit in 1925, and King Oliver recorded it in 1928, but after that the song was nearly forgotten. Finally, with the Dixieland revival of the late 1940s, "Tin Roof" begins to appear again with recordings by Sidney Bechet (1949), Lu Watters (1950), Louis Armstrong (1955), and Al Hirt (1957). A big boost in the song's popularity undoubtedly came with Jo Stafford's Number 1 hit on "Make Love to Me" (1954), which is based on the same melody.

"Tishomingo Blues," by Spencer Williams, became the theme song of A Prairie Home Companion. (Courtesy Lilly Library, Indiana University, Bloomington, Indiana.)

Tishomingo Blues (music and lyrics: Spencer Williams, 1917): The title refers to a small town in Mississippi, not the city in southern Oklahoma. Both locations are named after the Chickasaw chief who died on the Trail of Tears when American Indians were forcibly relocated during the 1830s. Tishomingo lies about 125 miles east of Memphis, in the heart of the original Chickasaw homeland.

This was one of Spencer Williams' first blues compositions, and he really demonstrates his command of the genre. His words mix nostalgic imagery with the vernacular of the day: "Way down in Mississippi among the cypress trees, They get you dippy, with their strange melodies." Similarly, the music combines disparate elements as well. The tune is actually in standard 32-bar form, like a popular song, yet the first 12 bars of each half exactly follow the blues structure. The effect is that of a blues with an extended ending, going to harmonic regions that are not quite expected.

"Tishomingo Blues" became a jazz standard early on. Duke Ellington had one of the first noteworthy recordings in 1928, featuring Bubber Miley on the cornet. The general public would be most familiar with "Tishomingo Blues" as the theme song of *A Prairie Home Companion*. Recommended versions include those by clarinetist Ed Hall (1943, with James P. Johnson), and clarinetist Matty Matlock (1957). For more recent interpretations, listen to an earthy version by *Charlie Fardella and His Sensation Jazz Band* (1999). Also, a relaxed swinging approach can be heard on the 2010 album *When Dreams Come True* with Tim Laughlin and Connie Jones.

"Tuck Me to Sleep in my Old 'Tucky Home," by George Meyer, Sam Lewis and Joe Young, was somewhat neglected after its initial success, but saw a revival in the 1950s. (Courtesy Lilly Library, Indiana University, Bloomington, Indiana.)

Tuck Me to Sleep in My Old 'Tucky Home (music: George Meyer, lyrics: Sam M. Lewis and Joe Young, 1922): George Meyer (1884-1959) was a prolific Tin Pan Alley songwriter whose hit songs, for the most part, came a bit too early to become permanent fixtures in the repertoire. One notable exception is "For Me and My Gal" (1917), which sold over three million copies of sheet music. "Mandy Make Up Your Mind" (1924) and "Where Did Robinson Crusoe Go with Friday on Saturday Night" (1916) are other Meyer tunes that were regularly played by jazz bands.

Tuck Me to Sleep" seems to have been forgotten for a while, but it sure started out with a bang. Al Jolson popularized the song (it's right up his alley) and Vernon Dalhart had a Number 2 hit with his recording in 1922. The song is believed to have sold more than a million records and several million copies of sheet music, yet it didn't survive the 20s. "Tuck Me to Sleep" is a coon song (although there's nothing offensive in the lyrics, nor on the sheet music cover), a genre that quickly fell out of favor after 1920. The opening line sets the tone: "Tuck me to sleep in my old 'Tucky home, cover me with Dixie skies and leave me there alone." It seems to have been the Firehouse Five Plus Two who revived the song in 1954. Since then, many other bands have put it in their repertoire and it is heard frequently.

"Twelfth Street Rag," by Euday Bowman, has proved to be one of the most enduring rags in history, with substantial hit recordings in each of five decades. *(Courtesy Lilly Library, Indiana University, Bloomington, Indiana.)*

Twelfth Street Rag (Euday L. Bowman, 1914): The song refers to Twelfth Street in Kansas City, Missouri, in case you've ever wondered. During the first few decades of the 20th century, Kansas City was a Mecca for sin, vice, and hot music (funny how those things go together). Bowman (1887-1949) became a professional pianist at an early age, mostly playing in bordellos in large towns, which would certainly have included Kansas City. In truth, Bowman never actually said he was referring to Kansas City, and both Dallas and Fort Worth, Texas (where he was from) had Twelfth Streets in their red-light districts as well. But the sheet music was published in Kansas City, depicts Kansas City on its cover, and when lyrics were added a few years later, they mention Kansas City, so the issue was settled with or without Bowman's input. The street-title approach must have appealed to him, for he followed up with "Sixth Street Rag" and "Tenth Street Rag" that same year, and, in 1917, "Eleventh Street Rag." The latter is pretty much a sister companion to "Twelfth Street," with a section that directly reverses the prominent three-note figure.

Ragtime had its most intense years from 1907-1911 and was certainly in decline by 1914, but "Twelfth Street Rag" changed all that, and the sensation was to last for at least another 40 years. Although "popularity" is always a hard thing to measure in music with record sales, sheet music sales, number of recordings made, and number of hits all in the mix, "Twelfth Street" may in fact be the most famous rag in history. It saw at least one hit record in every single decade from its release until Liberace's 1954 recording. Without a doubt the most famous (but certainly not the most musical) version is by Pee Wee Hunt (1948), which became a Number 1 record, selling more than three million copies. More importantly, the composition entered the jazz repertoire from the beginning, with exemplary interpretations produced by Bennie Moten (1927), Louis Armstrong (1927), Duke Ellington (1931), Fats Waller (1935, a hit record), Count Basie (1939), Sidney Bechet (1941), and many others.

Poor Euday Bowman missed out on most of the profits from all of this. He fell into the trap of selling his manuscript outright to a publisher, only to watch them make millions of dollars from it. Finally, after 28 years, copyright law allowed him to reclaim "Twelfth Street" in 1942. He immediately republished the number, this time with a royalty claim. He must have been elated when Pee Wee Hunt once again sent his creation to the top of the charts in 1948. Unfortunately, Bowman's time had run out and he died the following year.

Undecided (music: Charlie Shavers, lyrics: Sid Robin, 1939): During the late 1930s and early 1940s it seemed that everyone had a big band. Whenever a sideman gained some recognition with the public, he was off to lead a band of his own. Small groups were simply out of fashion, with one notable exception: The John

Kirby Sextet. Billed as "Biggest Little Band in the Land," this highly polished, hard-swinging ensemble played smart arrangements and featured some of the finest soloists of the day. Trumpeter Charlie Shavers played the lead and also composed original material for the band.

Nowadays there is much joking about the errors that can occur when texting messages to people. Back in the days when telegraph companies charged by the word, responses could sometimes be abbreviated to the point where serious misunderstandings could take place. When Charlie Shavers sent his manuscript to the publisher, he failed to include a title for the song, so they wired him asking what the name was. He hadn't picked one yet, so he responded UNDECIDED. Shavers had also forgotten to indicate the tempo for his song, which he intended to be a romping instrumental. Thinking that they had just received the manuscript for a medium tempo fox trot, the publisher asked Sid Robin to supply appropriate lyrics, so he did.

But sometimes the best-laid plans of mice and men don't go astray, or perhaps they do but the Fates smile anyway. The title was catchy, if unintentional, and inspired Robin to write some clever lyrics with the memorable opening line "First you say you do, and then you don't." Musicians loved the song, and so did the public. Both The Kirby Sextet and Ella Fitzgerald with Chick Webb had hits with it in 1939 and dozens of notable versions soon appeared. More than a decade later the song reached the charts once again for Ray Anthony and Guy Lombardo, while the Ames Brothers had a million-seller.

For a solid up-tempo swing version, which is what Shavers had in mind, hear cornetist Randy Reinhart on his 2008 album *For Basie*. And for a recording that may make you suspect that Benny Goodman is still alive, listen to clarinetist Joe Midiri on his aptly named album *Finger Bustin'* (1990).

"Wabash Blues," by Fred Meinken and Dave Ringle, was one of many songs inspired by the Wabash River. (Courtesy Kmusser, CC BY-SA 3.0 via Wikimedia Commons.)

Wabash Blues (music: Fred Meinken, lyrics: Dave Ringle, 1921): Few places have inspired more songs than the Wabash River. (The state river of Indiana, the Wabash flows across northern Indiana into southern Illinois.) Examples include: "On the Banks of the Wabash" (state song of Indiana, 1908), "Where the Grand Old Wabash River Flows" (1904), "Wabash Moon" (1931), "Where the Dreamy Wabash Flows" (1924), "Moonlight on the Wabash" (1919), "At Sunset on the Wabash" (1906) and the "Old Wabash College Song" (no copyright). But only "Wabash Blues" has become a jazz standard. It is a model of simplicity and an exemplar of "less is more." The melody consists of a short motive that is either repeated or presented at different pitch levels throughout the tune. The harmony is basic and straightforward, except for one unexpected shift just before the middle.

Isham Jones had his first Number 1 record with "Wabash Blues;" It sold more than a million copies and launched his career. Jones was born and raised in Michigan, displaying early ability on the piano, violin, and saxophone. In 1915 he made his way to Chicago to become a professional musician. His reputation grew quickly and by 1920 he was leading a band at the Rainbo Gardens (yes, that's how they spelled it!), a new and popular dance hall. His band found the right niche of keeping up with the developing sound of the Jazz Age while focusing on the social dance crowd. In September 1920, they began recording for Brunswick and soon became one of the most prominent dance bands in the country. "Wabash Blues" was their seventh hit record and most successful to date.

Jazz musicians took an instant liking to "Wabash Blues" and many fine recordings were made, including those by the Charleston Chasers, (1927), Fletcher Henderson (1927), Red Nichols (1927), and an excellent record by the Ted Lewis ensemble featuring Muggsy Spanier and Frank Teschemacher (1929).

Walkin' My Baby Back Home (music: Fred E. Ahlert, lyrics: Roy Turk, 1930): This light-hearted song became a hit for a number of artists over the years, and singers just can't seem to resist recording it. As can be imagined, there are plenty of abominable versions of the song out there but some excellent ones too.

Ted Weems had a 1931 hit with the song set to one of their peppy, well-crafted arrangements. The Charleston Chasers also had a hit that year with a version that features the early use of a flute in the woodwind section. Benny Goodman solos on the first half of the final chorus. Louis Armstrong recorded the song that same year. Not surprisingly, he found, the melody too fussy for his taste and you hear very little of it.

Of the hundreds of pop versions of the song, those by Jo Stafford (1945) and Nat "King" Cole (1952) are probably the most tasteful. Some good jazz recordings include those by Earl Hines (1957), Stephane Grappelli with Oscar Peterson (1973), and pianist Dave McKenna (1979). The song is also featured in the 1953 film *Walkin' My Baby Back Home*, starring Donald O'Connor.

"Wang Wang Blues," by Gus Mueller, Buster Johnson and Henry Busse, was a number 1 hit for Whiteman when released in December 1920, but was actually recorded on the band's first session together in August of that year. (Author's personal collection.)

The Wang Wang Blues (music: Gus Mueller, Buster Johnson and Henry Busse, 1921): Paul Whiteman was famous for both the size of his orchestra and the size of his waist, but you wouldn't suspect either from the photograph that appears on the cover of the sheet music to this song. A stout but well-proportioned Whiteman in tails appears with his orchestra of nine men, consisting of violin, trumpet, trombone, two reeds, piano, banjo, bass, and drums. This was the ensemble he took into the Ambassador Hotel in Atlantic City during the summer of 1920, which would make him the most famous bandleader in the country. On August 9, these men assembled at Victor Studios in Camden, N.J., and began to record a series of discs that would be heard around the world.

The first session was intended to be experimental: In the days of acoustic recording, balancing sound and positioning instruments to play into a horn was touchy business. Of the four songs they recorded that day only "Wang Wang Blues" was acceptable for release. The song had been put together by three band members: reed man Mueller, trombonist Johnson and trumpeter Busse. Among the things they learned on the first session were that the bassist must play tuba, not string bass, in order to be heard; the drummer must confine himself to woodblocks and cymbals so as not to overpower the equipment; and the banjo must be prominent with a steady rhythm to compensate for the missing percussion instruments. All of those features can be heard on this recording. The band went back to the studio shortly after and began to record regularly.

The Ambassador Hotel, Atlantic City, where Paul Whiteman created a huge sensation in the summer of 1920. The original structure was rebuilt into the current Tropicana Casino and Resort. The Ritz Carlton can be seen in the background.(Author's personal collection.)

"Wang Wang" was the band's first recording but not the first record to be released. A disc with "Whispering" from the third session paired with "Japanese Sandman" from the second session was released in September and sold two million copies. "Wang Wang" was released in December and it too became a hit, charting at Number 1 for six weeks. Obviously, Victor had a specific marketing plan and was quite particular about timing the release of their records.

"Wang Wang" is a sectional tune and is well crafted with melodic contrast and harmonic interest, as would be expected from three trained musicians. Additionally, on the original recording, it is surprising how much like the Original Dixieland Jazz Band the Whiteman ensemble could sound, except that they are more polished and the arrangements tighter. And that was exactly the formula that would characterize the future of the bandleader who "made a lady out of jazz."

Drum set, circa 1920. Capturing the drums in the studio was a tricky business in the early years of recording, and drummers would have to adjust what they played to accommodate the recording equipment. (Image public domain.)

Paul Whiteman soon began to be called the King of Jazz, a reference that disturbs some people today, since his music was primarily tailored to the audience and he wasn't himself a jazz musician. But those who knew him had the greatest respect for him, and his contribution to jazz is incontrovertible. In his autobiography, *Music is My Mistress*, Duke Ellington stated, "Paul Whiteman was known as the King of Jazz, and no one as yet has come near carrying that title with more certainty and dignity."

Paul Whiteman was well known as a congenial person. A musician had to go a long way to get fired by Whiteman (although Bing Crosby came very close), and when Bix Beiderbecke was struggling with alcohol during the final years of his life, Whiteman would send him home for extended periods on full salary. Paul also had a keen interest in young people and discovering new talent. (He gave Johnny Mercer his start.) Alice Schmidt of Collingswood, NJ related to me how she met Whiteman in 1939. As a ten-year-old saxophone student, her progress had so astounded her teacher that he asked Whiteman if the girl might appear on his radio broadcast. Paul agreed. He put her on the program and allowed her to play a solo live over the airwaves. Alice remembers him as a kindhearted man who put her completely at ease.

An early sketch of Washington and Lee University.(Artist unknown, public domain, via Wikimedia Commons.)

Washington and Lee Swing (music: Thornton W. Allen, and Mark W. Sheafe, lyrics: C.A. Robbins, 1910): The early 20th century brought a growing interest in college life as well as the newly invented sport of American football, which at time was only played by college teams. With the rise of college football came college fight songs, and this one was written for Washington and Lee University by Mark Sheafe (class of 1906), with words by C.A. Robbins (class of 1911), and additional music by Thornton Allen (class of 1913). By the 20s the song had become so popular that it was heard all over the country. Bandleader Meyer Davis had a hit record with it in 1925, and it eventually entered the traditional jazz repertoire. The lyrics begin with "Come cheer of Washington and Lee, We're going to win another victory!"

The song utilizes a common set of chord changes that would have been known from "Over the Waves," "Under the Double Eagle" and "Bill Bailey," and would later be used for "Tiger Rag," "Bourbon Street Parade," "Beer Barrel Polka," and many other songs. The melody bears a slight resemblance to "Chinatown, My Chinatown" (1906) but is much simpler and follows a different harmonic path. More than 50 schools and colleges have adopted songs that share the melody of "Washington and Lee Swing."

"Way Down Yonder in New Orleans," by Turner Layton and Henry Creamer, displays several unusual features, despite its deceptively simple design. (Courtesy Lilly Library, Indiana University, Bloomington, Indiana.)

Way down Yonder in New Orleans (music: J. Turner Layton, lyrics: Henry Creamer, 1922): The song was intended for the ill-fated show *Strut Miss Lizzie*, which bankrupted Creamer and led to the split-up of the famous songwriting team, but was cut from that show and salvaged for *Spice of 1922*. Vaudeville singer Blossom Seeley put the song in her act and had a hit recording in 1923. Paul Whiteman also had a popular recording that year with one of his jazzier arrangements featuring the trumpet work of Henry Busse. Following his split with Layton, Creamer teamed up with tenor singer Tandy Johnstone and the duo sold more than ten million records between 1924 and 1935. They can be heard singing "Way down Yonder" on a 1927 recording.

"Way down Yonder" is a highly individualistic song for several reasons. It features a strange form which jumps to the bridge four bars early, leading to a total length of 28 bars for the song. The middle section has built-in pauses, both over the word "stop," and the tune has an unexpected harmonic shift near the end. Finally, there is a habanera section that recalls "La Paloma" to the words "Orange blossoms' sweet aroma, And the strains of La Paloma, Seem to throw me into a coma." Jazz musicians seldom play this part, probably taking their cue from the famous Bix Beiderbecke recording of 1927, which includes the chorus only, with dazzling solos by both Bix and Frankie Trumbauer.

Recommended recordings include those by trumpet men Billy Butterfield (1959) and Jimmy McPartland (1965).

"Weary Blues," by Artie Matthews, was originally an instrumental number. (Courtesy Sandy Marrone, Cinnaminson, NJ.)

Weary Blues (music: Artie Matthews, 1915): Artie Matthews (1888-1958) was an important composer of rags and popular songs. He was chief arranger for the John Stark Company, one of the leading publishers of Ragtime music in the country. Jelly Roll Morton, who did not give compliments freely, thought him one of the best pianists he had heard. Matthews' most important rags date from the teens and are among the finest in the literature. They hold a place as logical successors to the earlier works of Scott Joplin, James Scott and Joseph Lamb, employing chromatic harmonies, chord clusters, melodies in unexpected voices, and a wide pallet of rhythmic variety.

Part of "Weary Blues" is indeed a 12-bar blues, but it is also a sectional number with an extended form and intricate piano arrangement. The middle section contains one of the first instances of a boogie-woogie bass line in a published composition. Although words were later added by Mort Greene and George Cates, "Weary Blues" was intended as an instrumental number and the original printing of the sheet music contains no lyrics. Many notable versions were recorded, including those by the Louisiana Five (1919), New Orleans Rhythm Kings (1923), Louis Armstrong's Hot Seven (1927), Tommy Ladnier (1938), and Kid Ory (1945). As could be expected, Ory utilizes the built-in breaks of "Weary Blues" to feature his tailgate trombone style. (See entry on "Ory's Creole Trombone.") Notable recent recordings include those by clarinetist Tom Fischer (2005) and cornetist Jon-Erik Kellso (2007).

You might notice that the last section of "Weary Blues" sounds very much like the song "Farewell Blues." George Brunies, trombonist with the New Orleans Rhythm Kings, recalled: "We were playing the "Weary Blues" one night and all of a sudden Rapp [clarinetist Leon Roppolo] takes a chorus, just playing himself, man. He didn't care nothing about the people, he's high.... So they made a number out of it, the 'Farewell Blues.'" The New Orleans Rhythm Kings recorded "Farewell Blues" in 1922, a year before they recorded "Weary Blues." In fact, "Farewell Blues" soon became the more popular number, and "Weary Blues" might have been all but forgotten were it not for Armstrong's spectacular recording of 1927.

"Weary Blues" received even more momentum when singers abandoned the original lyrics and substituted the opening lines of Charley Patton's "Shake it and Break It" recording of 1929:

> You can shake it, you can break it,
>
> you can hang it on the wall
>
> Throw it out the window, catch it 'fore it roll

Trumpeter "Wingy" Manone seems to have been the first to do this in his recording of "Weary Blues" from 1930. Because this memorable lyric became so popular, "Weary Blues" soon took on a second title and is sometimes referred to as "Shake it and Break It." It remains a core standard among New Orleans bands and can be heard on the 2013 album *Leroy Jones and Katja Toivola* as well as the 2011 album *Frenchmen Street Parade* featuring the New Orleans Moonshiners. The powerful front line in this band is led by Chuck Brackman on cornet, Bruce Brackman on clarinet, and Ronell Johnson on trombone.

The West End, situated in New Orleans on Lake Pontchartrain, was a thriving resort community during the early years of the 20th century. (Photographer unknown, public domain, via Wikimedia Commons.)

West End Blues (music: Joe Oliver, lyrics: Clarence Williams, 1928): The West End is a New Orleans neighborhood in the Lakeview District along Lake Pontchartrain. During the late 1800s and early 1900s a three-mile-long shipping canal began at this point, connecting Lake Pontchartrain with the uptown region of the city. The thriving commercial activity attracted developers and it became a renowned resort, with restaurants, hotels, amusement rides, and musical entertainment. The site was certainly well known to New Orleans musicians.

"West End Blues" is so closely associated with Louis Armstrong that many people think he wrote it. In fact, Joe Oliver was the composer, and he recorded it some two weeks before Armstrong. But the difference between these two records is staggering. Armstrong took Oliver's tune, added a fiery opening cadenza, worked his magic and transformed a ho-hum blues number into a musical tour-de-force. There has probably been more adulation cast on Armstrong's "West End Blues" than any other number in the history of jazz.

Armstrong sings on his recording, but his scat is improvised—Oliver intended the number as an instrumental. However, publisher Clarence Williams supplied serviceable lyrics, as was his custom when presented with instrumental numbers.

Although Williams has been accused of adding lyrics just to cut himself in on the royalties, the charge is unfair, as Williams was a frequent accompanist for singers and saw the value in publishing vocal versions of songs. He can be heard accompanying Ethel Waters on her recording of "West End" from August 1928.

Musicians have had difficulty figuring out what to do with "West End Blues." The song is so closely welded to the opening cadenza and Louis Armstrong's interpretation that it seems wrong to offer an alternative approach. But to play his opening requires a trumpet player par excellence, who is still likely to fall short on feeling and interpretation. On the other hand, there is certainly a thrill in hearing a live version of this famous piece and most audiences are more than forgiving to have just that.

When It's Sleepy Time down South (music and lyrics: Clarence Muse, Leon Rene and Otis Rene, 1930): It's hard to fathom just how hard the Great Depression hit the music industry. During the peak year of 1927, 104 million records were sold in the U.S. In 1932, only six million were sold. Even the mighty Paul Whiteman felt the crunch. For nearly a full year, from late 1930 through the summer of 1931, the band did not make a single record. Finally in the fall of 1931, the band went into Victor Studios to resume their recording activities. By this time Whiteman had acquired Mildred Bailey. Although she was a difficult personality and would eventually price herself out of a job with Whiteman, the collaboration was fruitful while it lasted. Among her several hits with Whitman was "Sleepy Time," which reached Number 6 in the charts in 1931.

While Louis Armstrong's 1931 recording didn't become an immediate hit, he adopted it as his theme song and went on to record it dozens of times during his career, ensuring the legacy of the song. Some African Americans were not pleased with this because the lyrics, while not immediately offensive, rely on a stereotype. The whole gist of the song seems to be that there was something unnatural about the Great Immigration of Blacks to northern cities. The attraction for the South, "Takes me back there where I belong" and "How I'd love to be in my mammy's arms." Nevertheless, when it came to his career, Armstrong clearly knew what he was doing and was not to be dissuaded.

For a recent recording of the number, listen to cornetist Connie Jones with pianist Tom McDermott in a relaxed duet setting on their 2008 album *Creole Nocturne*.

"When My Baby Smiles at Me," by Bill Munro, Andrew Sterling and Ted Lewis, was the first big hit for bandleader Ted Lewis, who was hailed as "The Jazz King." (Courtesy Lilly Library, Indiana University, Bloomington, Indiana.)

When My Baby Smiles at Me (music: Bill Munro, lyrics: Andrew B. Sterling and Ted Lewis, 1920): Ted Lewis, "The Jazz King," led a band during the 20s that was second in popularity only to that of Paul Whiteman, "The King of Jazz." Ironically, neither one was a real jazz musician. But both knew good jazz when they heard it and hired some of the top musicians of the day. Columbia signed Lewis in 1919 as their answer to the Original Dixieland Jazz Band, which recorded for Victor. He would become their top artist. Lewis played clarinet with a swooping novelty style that never changed much, and became increasingly outdated as the decade wore on. But he knew how to run a band, and he respected great clarinetists, hiring the likes of Benny Goodman, Jimmy Dorsey, Frank Teschemacher, and Don Murray.

Lewis also knew how to reach the public. In her 2005 memoir, *Me and My Father's Shadow*, his daughter Dawn Williams remembered: "The audience could not get enough of Ted Lewis and his music. He could sing or talk his songs. Or combine the two. He could twirl his cane or play his clarinet, or both. Talk to his audience. Lead his band. Say his famous 'Yes sir.' Let his hat drop from his head onto his arm and roll into his hand, or introduce his acts. It did not matter. Whatever Ted Lewis did, he created a rapport with his adoring audience. When he came to the edge of the stage and asked his promised question, 'Is everybody happy?' 'Yes' came from everyone."

"When My Baby" has Ted Lewis written all over it. It was his first big hit, charting for 18 weeks and reaching Number 1 for 7 weeks. He adopted it as his theme song and recorded it several more times. His recording of 1938, 18 years after his initial release, again became a hit record. That same year, at his famous Carnegie Hall Concert, Benny Goodman included "When My Baby" in the program, paying tribute to his old boss by tastefully imitating Lewis's clarinet style. For decades, few jazz musicians would touch "Ted Lewis's song," but in recent years traditional jazz bands have increasingly included the number in their repertoire.

When My Sugar Walks down the Street (music: Jimmy McHugh, lyrics: Irving Mills and Gene Austin, 1924): It's not clear exactly when Jimmy McHugh (1893-1969) decided that he would become one of the most popular songwriters in history, but he was still a child when he determined that he would be highly successful at something. His mother gave him piano lessons and encouraged him to develop his personal talents. His father was a plumber who insisted that he learn the family trade. He listened to his mother. When he was 17 he walked into the newly built Opera House in Boston and literally talked his way into a job. He started as an office boy and was soon moved to the publicity department. When the Opera Company folded four years later, he began working jobs as a pianist and poured all his energies into becoming one of Boston's best song pluggers. In 1920, he moved to New York and began working his way up as a manager on Tin Pan Alley. But all the while what he really aspired to do was be a songwriter. He knew the business, he had the connections, and he was confident in his abilities. Little by little he began to establish himself as a composer.

McHugh's big break came in 1924. "When My Sugar" was the first significant commercial success for both McHugh and singer Gene Austin, who had a Number 3 record with it in 1925. According to McHugh biographer Alyn Shipton, "It is unlikely that Austin actually contributed much, if anything, to the lyrics, and it is more probable that Mills added his name as lyricist (and gave him a cut of the royalties) as a sales device, known in the trade at the time as a 'cut-in,' simply to feature his name more prominently on the sheet music." If it was only marketing logic, it was astute logic, as Austin was to become one of the most popular recording artists in history, selling nearly 100 million records over the next 15 years.

"When My Baby" was originally written for a 1924 revue called *Grab Bag*, and several recordings appeared simultaneously. It is a catchy tune with a simple melody and just the sort of thing someone would whistle on the street corner. McHugh now had proof that he knew how to write hits. What's more, he knew how to write good tunes that work in a variety of contexts. A stark contrast to Austin's playful interpretation can be heard in Clara Smith's bluesy version (1924). Big-band vocalists also had their chance with it, including Ivy Anderson (1938) and Ella Fitzgerald (1944). Jimmy McPartland gave it the hot jazz treatment as early as 1924, and Eddie Condon keeps up the Chicago spirit in a 1944 Town Hall broadcast.

When The Saints Go Marching In (anonymous): This song is not to be confused with "When The Saints Are Marching In" (James Black and Katharine Purvis, 1896), which is a different tune altogether. "The Saints" is a relative newcomer to the repertoire—it was in no way a traditional New Orleans jazz tune. In 1938 Louis Armstrong, who had excellent musical instincts, got the idea to jazz up this simple hymn that he knew from childhood. It must have seemed like a strange idea to him too, for he introduces the song with a bit of hokum: "Sisters and brothers, this is Reverend Satchmo getting ready to beat out this mellow sermon for you. My text this evenin': 'When the Saints Go Marching In.'" Word is that Armstrong's sister chastised him for his musical setting, but the public sure liked it. He had a big hit with his recording in 1939 and the public's thirst for the tune continued to grow over the years. With the Dixieland revival of the late 1940s the song became all the rage, and when rock and roll artists pulled it into their repertoire, there was no stopping it. Most people only know it as a "hot" number and assume it has always been played that way. Traditional jazz musicians have come to know it as the most requested song in the book.

As if the song wasn't popular enough in its own right, in 1966 the city of New Orleans was awarded an NFL franchise, and the team was named after the popular hymn. The deal was announced on November 1, All Saints' Day. Trumpeter Al Hirt was part owner of the team, and his version of "The Saints" became the official fight song. "The Saints" became so popular that for years Preservation Hall—the historic New Orleans bastion of traditional jazz—had a sign over the bandstand that read: "Requests: Standard $1, Unusual $2, The Saints $5." The sign remains; the prices have been raised.

"The Saints" is a short and simple tune with a built in call-and-response pattern. A prominent element in African-American worship, call-and-response in jazz contexts is believed to have survived from African origins. It consists of musical phrases being echoed or answered by follow-up phrases: "Oh when the saints (oh when the saints), Go marching in (go marching in)." Oh when the saints go marching in (go marching in)."

There are no "official" lyrics to "The Saints," and the flexible construction lends itself to countless variations.

When You're Smiling (music and lyrics: Mark Fisher, Larry Shay, and Joe Goodwin, 1928): All three were successful songwriters, but this collaboration was the biggest hit for each of them. The previous year they had also had a hit with "Everywhere You Go." Fisher and Goodwin were a regular team with bandleader Fisher writing the melody and Goodwin supplying the lyrics. Larry Shay, a conservatory-trained pianist and successful songwriter, became musical director for MGM in the 1930s, where he was responsible for hiring Bing Crosby, who allegedly was paid $50 per day for his first film.

"Smiling" is an instantly appealing tune that's easy to remember and tends to linger in the ear. The repetitious melody displays a pleasing symmetry with a constant rhythm that invites rhyme and word play. The premise is that smiling is contagious but crying only brings on the rain, so why not be happy? The last line sums it up perfectly: "When you're smiling, the whole world smiles with you."

Several artists had hit records with "When You're Smiling" over the years, and it's insightful to compare some of them. The very first was by pianist/vocalist Seger Ellis, whose recording of 1928 charted for six weeks, peaking at Number 4. His version features his high tenor voice, a chorus of straight singing, a chorus of alto saxophone and violin sharing the melody, and another chorus of Ellis singing; a solid performance with a straight delivery, but it makes you wonder what all the fuss was about. Louis Armstrong also had a hit, though not as sizable as Ellis', but with a performance that is simply breathtaking. The orchestra plays the first chorus in a straightforward routine manner, followed by Armstrong's vocal chorus, which is anything but routine. His delivery is so personal and genuine, it doesn't seem like you're listening to someone in a recording studio—you feel like he's in the room with you telling you a story. He caps the tune off with a chorus of trumpet in the upper register, powerful and expressive, but also sweet and gentle.

Time has a way of sorting things out, and Armstrong's delivery of "When You're Smiling" eventually persuaded the public. Trumpet players were so stunned by his high note rendering of the melody that some accused him of playing a fake instrument. It was Armstrong's version that made the tune a perennial hit, and he would go on to record it several more times in his career. "When You're Smiling" has been used in countless movies, television shows, and commercials through the years. Just about everyone in the music business has recorded it.

"Where did Robinson Crusoe go with Friday on Saturday Night?" by George W. Meyer, Sam M. Lewis, and Joe Young, was from the show Robinson Crusoe, Jr., which featured Al Jolson in his first starring role. (Courtesy Lilly Library, Indiana University, Bloomington, Indiana.)

Where Did Robinson Crusoe Go with Friday on Saturday Night? (music: George W. Meyer, lyrics: Sam M. Lewis and Joe Young, 1916): This song with the awkward title holds a more prominent place in history than one might think. Not surprisingly it is from the Broadway musical *Robinson Crusoe, Jr.*, (1916), the first Broadway show in which Al Jolson was featured as the star. The plot involves a millionaire who falls asleep, dreaming he is Robinson Crusoe and that his chauffer (Jolson) is Friday. Jolson plays the chauffer's role in blackface. The show was a rousing success and led to two hit records for Jolson, "Robinson Crusoe" and "Yaaka Hula Hickey Dula."

Robinson Crusoe Jr. was one of the few Jolson shows to have a real plot; however, true to form, he appeared alone on stage when singing, selling the song, not the story.

The song's comic lyric follows the story's original concept, but has the boys out carousing on weekends. "One fine day" Robinson Crusoe is stranded on an island, "no rent to pay, no wife to obey." He lives in a little hut with his only friend Friday, until Saturday night, when they wander out, because "on this island lived wild men," and "where there are wild men there must be wild women." The melody of the song is high spirited and well constructed, but the tune is seldom heard as an instrumental—the novelty lyrics are pretty much a requirement.

"Whispering," by Vincent Rose, John Schoenberger, and Richard Coburn. Paul Whiteman's recording of this song sold nearly two million records. (Courtesy Lilly Library, Indiana University, Bloomington, Indiana.)

Whispering (music: Vincent Rose, lyrics: John Schoenberger and Richard Coburn, 1920): As a classically trained violist, Paul Whiteman might seem an unlikely candidate to lead a jazz band, but the new sound of jazz music became his passion early on. After playing with both the Denver and San Francisco orchestras, Whiteman attempted to become a "hot" violinist but was fired from his first job and told, "you can't jazz at all." (Evidently "jazz" was once a verb!) Whiteman remembered, "This made me mad, and I was determined to find out why." He made a study of the music, going to every venue where he could find jazz and listening closely to what he heard. A short stint with the Navy as a bandleader provided him with the experience and the contacts he needed. It also gave him a chance to try out some of his own orchestrations.

When he returned to civilian life at the end of 1918, the first thing he did was organize a jazz band. After a few false starts and small steps forward, he assembled a band at the end of 1919 that would become the original Whiteman Orchestra. In early 1920, he took a nine-piece ensemble into the Alexandria Hotel in Los Angeles for a three-month engagement. Whiteman was so successful that the band was then offered a summer job at the recently built Ambassador Hotel in Atlantic City, which was under the same ownership. Whiteman's subsequent discovery by Victor Records launched what would become the most popular band in America.

Hotel Alexandria, Los Angeles, where the Paul Whiteman Orchestra worked its first engagement. (Author's personal collection.)

Several bands had hits with "Whispering," but Whiteman had the huge one, selling nearly two million records by 1921, at a time when selling just one million was an extreme rarity. The recording was instrumental—Whiteman had no vocalist in the early years—which is hard to fathom by modern assumptions. But the fact was, in the early 20s, dancers preferred purely instrumental numbers, feeling that vocalists were a distraction from dancing.

"Whispering" has a somewhat inhibited melody that could not be called lyrical, but is very effective in its own way. The characteristic harmony of the number is the side-stepping shift on the second chord, which moves down and then back up, while the melody gradually wends its way down the scale, only to return to its starting note in the middle and at the very end. With or without the words, the melody portrays the imagery of whispering, and, of course, we know the topic, as revealed in the final line "Whispering that I love you."

"Wild Cherries," by Ted Snyder and Irving Berlin, dates from Berlin's early days when he worked as a lyricist for the Ted Snyder Publishing House. (Courtesy Lilly Library, Indiana University, Bloomington, Indiana.)

Wild Cherries (music: Ted Snyder, lyrics: Irving Berlin, 1909): Snyder published his own "Wild Cherries" piano rag just two months after starting his own company. It became phenomenally successful and sold a million copies of sheet music. To put that in perspective, the population of the United States was only 90 million at the time, and the average household had six members. That indicates approximately 15 million households, meaning that one in 15 owned a copy of "Wild Cherries." A rough estimate to be sure, but an indication of what a million-seller really meant at that time.

Irving Berlin started out as a singer, began writing lyrics, then composed his own tunes, and finally started his own publishing firm. "Wild Cherries" dates from his second period, when he was working as a lyricist for the Ted Snyder publishing house. This rag was among several written by Snyder that Berlin supplied words to. Unfortunately it belongs to the genre that was popular at the time known as "coon songs." This doesn't imply anything specific about Berlin, who also published lyrics making fun of Italians and Jews, adding to the host of songs stereotyping every race and profession imaginable. Accordingly, someone once remarked that the early 20th century was not so much a melting pot as a chafing dish.

"Wild Cherries" was introduced by Fanny Brice in the *Ziegfeld Follies of 1910*. It became a favorite of pianist and entertainer Jimmy Durante. The number is a fine rag that adapts well to a small band setting, with all of the expected parts, including a dogfight and trio section for solos.

Wolverine Blues (Jelly Roll Morton, 1922): This was the tune that brought Jelly Roll to Chicago. He had written the instrumental number several years before he published it with the Spikes Brothers, a fledgling publishing firm in Los Angeles. It had always been one of his most requested numbers. By 1923, perhaps because of King Oliver, it had become a hot tune in Chicago nightclubs. The Melrose Brothers, a small publishing house in that city, were interested in obtaining the song, so they wrote to Jelly Roll in care of the Spikes brothers. Without consulting Morton, the firm intercepted the letter and sold the copyright to the Melrose brothers for $3,000, after they had added lyrics, which would ensure that they received half the royalties. When Morton learned of this he was outraged and set off for Chicago. What he did when he got there gets even more interesting.

Lester Melrose gives his first-hand account: "A fellow walked into our store with a big red bandana around his neck and a ten gallon cowboy hat on his head and hollered, 'Listen, everybody, I'm Jelly Roll Morton from New Orleans, the originator of jazz!' He talked for an hour without stopping about how good he was and then he sat down at the piano and proved he was every bit as good as he claimed and better."

At the end of this musical blitzkrieg, Jelly Roll informed the Melrose Brothers of his reason for coming—he would not tolerate sharing authorship of his "Wolverine Blues" with the Spikes Brothers. Not only did the Melrose Brothers acquiesce, they became his primary publisher and negotiator of his recording tracks.

"Wolverine Blues" has become one of the most solid of New Orleans jazz warhorses, and there probably has never been a Dixieland band that didn't play it. Jelly Roll recorded the song in 1923 (solo piano), 1925 (with clarinet), 1927 (with clarinet and drums) and in 1938, a solo piano/vocal performance in the Library of Congress.

The World is Waiting for the Sunrise (music: Ernest Seitz, lyrics: Eugene Lockhart, 1919): The song was written by concert pianist Ernest Seitz (1892-1978), who used the pseudonym Raymond Roberts for his few popular compositions. The melody has a pleasing contour, consisting of long note values, a limited range and slow harmonic movement, making it adaptable to a variety of treatments, and it generally holds up very well. Isham Jones had a Number 2 hit in 1922 with an instrumental version, while John Steel slowed it down with a vocal recording that was a Number 4 hit that same year.

Jazz musicians seemed to have first noticed the tune in the late 1930s, usually playing it at a brisk tempo. A recorded broadcast of 1946 features opera singer Gladys Swarthout giving it the classical treatment with orchestra, and it sounds surprisingly appropriate. A few years later, the Firehouse Five Plus Two recorded it as a rousing banjo feature (1950), with a runaway tempo on the last chorus, which makes up for its bad manners with a dollop of genuine excitement. Les Paul and Mary Ford had a Number 2 million seller with their pop version of 1951. Stan Freberg charted with a novelty version the following year, and somewhere along the way country artists discovered the tune, as can be heard on an instrumental version by Les Paul and Chet Atkins (1976). It seems you can do anything with this tune and make it work.

Many jazz greats have recorded the "The World is Waiting." Among the best are recordings by Jimmy McPartland (1939), Jack Teagarden (1940), Benny Goodman (a dazzling performance preserved in the 1944 film *Sweet & Lowdown*), and Django Reinhardt with Stephane Grappelli (1949).

Wrap Your Troubles in Dreams (music: Harry Barris, lyrics: Ted Koehler and Billy Moll, 1931): Harry Barris (1905-1962) was a member of the vocal group the Rhythm Boys, along with Bing Crosby and Al Rinker. (For those familiar with the more modern jazz pianist Barry Harris, "Harry Barris" looks like a misprint and feels something of a tongue-twister! Harris once quipped that always meant to record an album called "Barry Harris plays Harry Barris.") Barris supplied original songs for the group and wrote some of Bing's early hits when he went on his own.

Paul Whiteman was responsible for assembling the Rhythm Boys. Crosby and Rinker were working as a duo when Whiteman discovered them, and he subsequently added Barris to the mix. They proved a very successful addition to the orchestra in spite of their wild shenanigans (a source of constant grief to Whiteman), but parted ways in 1930 to go on their own. They joined with the Gus Arnheim Orchestra for a while, making several recordings that year. The orchestra's version of "I Surrender Dear," featuring Bing, became a big hit, which prompted him to leave and set out on his own. "Wrap Your Troubles" was one of his first recordings under his own name, and it reached Number 4 in the charts. By the end of 1931, Bing had a record contract and a radio deal and would soon be the most popular singer in the country.

Ted Koehler (1894-1973) took a pause from his partnership with Harold Arlen to write the lyrics with Moll. The first line of the chorus begins with "When skies are cloudy and gray," an allusion to the weather that would characterize so many of Koehler's future songs with Arlen ("Stormy Weather," "Ill Wind" and "When The Sun Comes Out" for example). The bridge, which features the same harmonic path as the Rodgers and Hart song "You Took Advantage of Me," features a sinking melody that Koehler sets beautifully, beginning with "Your castles may tumble, that's Fate after all."

Louis Armstrong made a fine recording of "Wrap Your Troubles" (the same 1931 date on which he recorded his famous "Stardust" record), ensuring the song a permanent place in the jazz repertoire. The modernists also adopted the tune, but it remained a traditional staple as well. Bing recorded the song several more times. A funny "blooper" outtake from 1939 has him losing his place but continuing to improvise lyrics, including, "they cut out eight bars the dirty bastards; I didn't know which eight bars he was gonna cut."

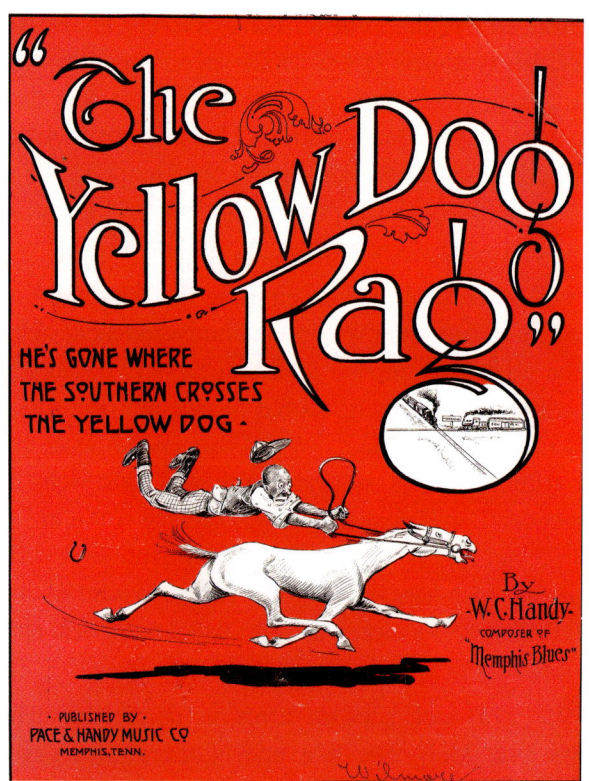

"The Yellow Dog Rag," by W.C. Handy received little attention when first published, but became a hit when he changed the name to "The Yellow Dog Blues." (Courtesy Sandy Marrone, Cinnaminson, NJ.)

Yellow Dog Blues (words and music: W.C. Handy, 1914): The subtitle reads "He's Gone Where the Southern Cross' the Yellow Dog." The title refers to the crossing of the Southern and Yazoo and Mississippi Valley railroads. In railroad slang, "dog" refers to a branch line. The Yazoo and Mississippi Valley Railroad was sometimes called the Yazoo Delta, abbreviated Y.D. From there, it assumed the name "Yellow Dog." The lyrics report the last sighting of a woman's missing lover: "Dear Sue, your Easy Rider struck his burg today, On a southbound rattler side door Pullman car."

Handy's tune, which was initially published as "Yellow Dog Rag," received little attention. In 1918 as Handy's publishing company was expanding, he opened a new office in New York City and reissued the song with the new title "Yellow Dog Blues." This time it began to get recordings. Curiously, as popular as Handy's blues numbers had become, New Yorkers preferred them as instrumentals and were initially put off by the down-home Southern references in the lyrics. Joseph C. Smith's Orchestra, a White ensemble, had a hit record with an instrumental version of "Yellow Dog" in 1920. That same year, Mamie Smith made her first blues vocal recordings and the blues craze was launched. The consummate rendition of "Yellow Dog" came in 1925, when Bessie Smith recorded it with Fletcher Henderson's Hot Six.

"Yellow Dog Blues" is heard in the 2004 film *The Aviator*, performed by Vince Giordano and the Nighthawks.

You Always Hurt the One You Love (music: Doris Fisher, lyrics: Allan Roberts, 1944): There weren't many female songwriters in the early days, but in consideration of the family Doris Fisher came from, it was nearly a requirement that she become one. Her father was the great Fred Fisher ("Peg o' My Heart," "Dardanella," "Chicago") and her brothers were Dan Fisher ("Good Morning Heartache") and Marvin Fisher ("When Sunny Gets Blue"). After singing with Eddie Duchin and other big bands in the 30s, she began achieving some success writing songs. Her best work came when she teamed up with lyricist Allan Roberts, whom she met in her father's office. Within one year of their partnership they had written "Into Each Life a Little Rain Must Fall," "That Ole Devil Called Love," "You Always Hurt the One You Love," and several other hits. This attracted the interest of Columbia Pictures, as was reported in *The Billboard*, May 26, 1945: "Harry Cohn, Columbia Pictures exec, last week signed tunesmith team Doris Fisher and Alan Roberts to a seven-year contract.... Team is unique in that it is the first signed as lot writers by Columbia, and the fact that they are young in the biz." In fact, Doris was 30 and Allan was 40.

The duo did about 20 films together, but alas, Doris Fisher decided it was not the life for her. In 1947 she married and quit the business to settle down and raise her family. She then became an expert on antiques and interior design serving as advisor to the Kennedys when they lived in the White House.

It's hard to think of "You Always Hurt" without hearing the Mills Brothers. This was a Number 1 hit for them, coming after "Paper Doll" and before "The Glow-Worm." The song was also a top-ten hit for Sammy Kaye. "You Always Hurt" was performed more by popular singers than by jazz musicians, but the tune makes a fine swing number as can be heard on recordings by Bunk Johnson (1945, reissued on the 2008 CD *The Roaring Forties*) and George Lewis (1959).

You Can Depend on Me (music and lyrics: Earl Hines, Louis Dunlap, and Charles Carpenter, 1932): This songwriting collaboration had an unlikely beginning. Earl Hines was having success and expanding his big band when his friend Louis Armstrong was about to leave Chicago for greater opportunities. Armstrong told Hines "I've got a boy here who is valeting for me. I want you to take care of him and look out for him." That was Charlie Carpenter, and Hines hired him as valet for his band. Carpenter proved to be so efficient that Hines soon made him secretary and hired his friend Dunlap as valet. Both men were aspiring songwriters, and before long Carpenter was Hines' manager, and Hines, Dunlap, and Carpenter were a songwriting team.

Louis Armstrong made the first recording of "You Can Depend" in 1931 and it became a Number 4 hit. Earl Hines didn't get around to recording it himself until 1940. Art Jarrett, who had recently taken over Hal Kemp's band after Kemp died in a car crash, had a hit with his version of 1941.

"You Can Depend" has an easygoing melody that bounces around quite a bit without going out of bounds, along with an upfront lyric that simply says what it means. The song readily adapts to practically any treatment. Armstrong, who recorded it again in 1951, treats it as a ballad, while Hines and Jarrett laid down solid swing versions. In 1960 Hines recorded it as a medium swing number, and does a fine job of singing a chorus as well. And then there was Brenda Lee's 1961 hit recording, which is anything but jazz, but truly demonstrates the flexibility of the number.

You Took Advantage of Me (music: Richard Rodgers, lyrics: Lorenz Hart, 1928): Richard Rodgers often said that you never know for sure if a song will succeed. He took particular care with the music to the show *Present Arms* (1928), and his music and Hart's lyrics were widely praised. The song they expected to be a hit and which was featured prominently in the show was "Do I Hear You Saying 'I Love You.'" Unfortunately, it never became a commercial success and is largely forgotten today.

Unexpectedly, "You Took Advantage of Me" became an instant hit. It's not an easy tune to sing or to play, but somehow the angular melody, wandering chords and busy lyrics come off disguised as simplicity and innocence and the formula worked. It is seldom remembered that the song was intended as a duet, introduced by Joyce Barbour and Busby Berkeley. (Berkeley, who would go on to become a celebrated choreographer and movie director, served as both dance director and second male lead in *Present Arms*.) Evidently Berkeley could remember steps better than words, for the story is that he flubbed his lines on opening night.

"I was awful," he recalled. "I can still see poor Larry Hart running up and down the wings almost apoplectic. He already had a reputation for witty, poetic lyrics, and here I was ruining his marvelous lines."

The song is rarely sung as a duet anymore, but coincidentally, the landmark recording of the tune includes a duet, at least an instrumental one. The Paul Whiteman band had a big hit with their recording of 1928, which featured Bix Beiderbecke and Frank Trumbauer trading off and a vocal chorus by Bing Crosby with the Rhythm Boys. The legendary Bix/Trumbauer chorus is still remembered and re-created by musicians to this day.

Another essential version of "You Took Advantage of Me" was recorded by Bunny Berigan in 1935. Most people, including musicians, remember Bunny as a dazzling trumpet player fronting a big band. (His memorable hit was "I Can't Get Started.") To hear him in a small group setting is an eye-opener. Odd as it seems, he somehow seems to combine the facility of Armstrong with the grace and tone of Bix with compelling results. Coming at the tune from another angle, Art Tatum recorded a beautifully structured solo piano interpretation of "You Took Advantage" in 1949.

"You Took Advantage" was performed by Linda Ronstadt on her Grammy Award-winning 1984 album *Lush Life*. More recently, Megan Mullally recorded a brassy version of the song on her 2007 album *Free Again*. Her version is also heard in the 2009 movie *Fame*.

You're the Cream in My Coffee (music: Lew Brown and Ray Henderson, lyrics: Buddy DeSylva, 1928): It was George White who first assembled this famous songwriting team. White was an impresario who produced an annual Broadway revue modeled after the *Ziegfeld Follies* that he entitled *George White's Scandals*. They were essentially variety shows, featuring singing, dancing, and comedy, and ran successfully from 1919 through 1939. For the first five years, White relied on George Gershwin to supply his music, but fresh off the success of his brilliant premier of *Rhapsody in Blue* in February 1924, Gershwin set his sights on loftier ambitions and parted company with White.

White responded by hiring Brown, Henderson, and DeSylva to replace him, and their first charge was to provide music for his *Scandals of 1925*. Within a short time they were producing hits on a regular basis, had formed their own publishing company, and DeSylva, Brown, and Henderson became the most popular and prolific songwriting team on Broadway, remaining so until their breakup in 1931. They broke no new ground and made no profound statements, but their optimistic, energetic music was just what the public wanted. Henderson recalled, "We usually roughed out the show in New York and then went to Atlantic City, where we took a suite at the Ritz for ten days and finished the score. We tried to write a balanced score—love songs, rhythm songs, comedy, low-down or torch numbers, and ensembles.

"You're the Cream in My Coffee" comes from the 1928 show *Hold Everything*. The plot (which generally counted for little in 20s musical comedy) concerned a welterweight boxer, "Sonny Jim Brooks," who loves his old girlfriend Sue, but is being pursued by a high society woman who is interrupting both his life and his training. Eventually his boxing rival insults Sue, invoking the fighting spirit in Sonny Jim, who goes on to win both the title and Sue's heart. Jack Whiting, who plays Sonny Jim, sings "You're the Cream" to his girl in the first act.

The show was made into a film musical of the same name in 1930, which was the first musical comedy to be set in Technicolor. The film is now lost. "You're the Cream" was the only song from the show to be used in the film version. Ted Weems, Ruth Etting, and Ben Selvin all had hit recordings of the song in 1929. For a recent recording that captures the original spirit of the tune, hear the vaudeville duo of Jesse Gelber (piano) and Kate Manning (voice) on their 2011 CD *Moonlight Picnic*.

The Ritz-Carlton, Atlantic City, where the famous songwriting team DeSylva, Henderson, and Brown did much of their writing. The establishment hosted many famous guests during the Roaring Twenties. During the height of his powers, political boss and racketeer Enoch "Nucky" Johnson (portrayed as Nucky Thompson in the HBO series Boardwalk Empire) conducted his business from a ninth-floor suite. Today the building operates as the Ritz Condominiums.

AFTERWORD

The great songs of the 1920s aren't about to go away, nor is the fascination with the era that led to their creation. Musicians continue to play these songs, and audiences continue to enjoy them. In recent years, the HBO series *Boardwalk Empire* has enjoyed tremendous success, as have movies based on F. Scott Fitzgerald's *The Great Gatsby*. Jazz Age-themed parties have become common, and "speakeasies" (whatever that means to people today) have been opening up in major cities across America. There is something enticing about the 1920s, and the fascination seems to be accelerating as the 2020s approach. And, as was the case nearly 100 years ago, music is at the center of the movement.

The music of the Jazz Age reflected the era. Times had changed. A horrible war was ended, women were liberated, sexual mores were loosened, and night life was thriving. Understandably, the music created for such an atmosphere was light-hearted, accessible, danceable, peppy, and happy. Formality, seriousness, and restraint were out; fun times were in. And aren't they still?

I wanted this book to be entertaining, and I certainly enjoyed writing it. But it also has a purpose—to bring this music to a wider audience and to enhance the experience of those who perform it, listen to it, and dance to it. (And yes, jazz is dance music. If there are bands that discourage dancing to their music, that's their loss.) The songs will endure without my help, but a little assistance along the way couldn't hurt. It is probable that many of the songs in *Tunes of the Twenties* would be recognized by someone under 30 today simply because they continue to be heard in films, on television, and on stage. But the songs take on a particular personality and individuality when their stories are told. Real people wrote them, and real people published, sang, and performed them.

The 20s was possibly the most prolific decade for popular music in the history of America. The number of songs written and live bands performing them was simply staggering. An average of more than 225 Broadway shows opened every year, each with more than a dozen original songs, not to mention all of the stand-alone songs, made popular by vaudeville performers or dance bands. And all of these songs—tens of thousands of them, were performed in theaters, cabarets, hotels, dance halls, movie houses, and speakeasies throughout the country.

But where can these songs be heard today? Fortunately, there are bands across the country that perform and record this music. An internet search of any song title in this book is likely to bring up an equal number of old and new recordings. There are hundreds of jazz societies across the country that schedule concerts and jazz festivals on a regular basis, and many establishments in major cities specialize in presenting hot jazz, often in a Roaring Twenties setting. And, of course, jazz thrives with a vengeance in its birthplace of New Orleans.

There is no shortage of bands that specialize in music of the Jazz Age, and increasingly they include young musicians. Just a few years ago, 20s jazz was somewhat neglected by music students, as many of them gravitated to more recently invented styles. In my 20 years of teaching music at the university level I've seen that completely change. "Everything old is new again," as the expression goes, and just when it seemed the last practitioners of the style had nearly disappeared, it was time for youth to rediscover it. The fascinating part is that they put their own stamp on the music, maintaining the spirit but infusing their own personalities and ideas. And that's just what was intended by the creators of this music. Yes, the songs were written to endure, but also to be rediscovered and re-created.

Obviously, the 250 songs in *Tunes of the Twenties* offer a small sampling of the musical treasures of the era. There is a nearly endless supply of great songs to be discovered and the well is not about to run dry. In the meantime, the drinks are cold, the music's hot, and *More Tunes of the Twenties* is just a publication away.

Chronology

Timeline

1870	*Edison invents phonograph*
1888	*Columbia Records founded*
1892	*First disc records*
1901	*Victor Talking Machine Company founded*
1903	*Caruso's "Vesti la giubba" becomes first million-selling record*
1904	*NYC subway opens* *First New Year's Eve celebration in Times Square*
1908	*Columbia introduces two-sided records*
1909	*Over 364,000 pianos are sold in the U.S.*
1910	*Sheet music sales top 30 million*
1912	*Titanic sinks*
1913	*Word "jazz" first appears in print* *Irene and Vernon Castle begin popularizing social dancing*
1914	*Introduction of the fox trot* *W.C. Handy publishes St. Louis Blues*
1915	*The ukulele becomes popular*

1917	Original Dixieland Jass Band records first jazz records Storyville, Red Light District of New Orleans, closes
1918	King Oliver goes to Chicago, promising to send for his protégé Louis Armstrong when he becomes successful
1920	Prohibition Begins Women win right to vote Station KDKA, Pittsburg, PA initiates first regular radio broadcasts Paul Whiteman Band becomes national sensation
1921	James P. Johnson makes earliest stride piano recordings First Miss American Pageant First radio broadcast of a baseball game Johnson and Johnson introduces the Band-Aid
1922	Louis Armstrong arrives in Chicago New Orleans Rhythm Kings begin recording Tomb of King Tut discovered Raymond De Walt invents the radial arm saw
1923	Louis Armstrong records his first fully improvised jazz solo on "Chimes Blues" Bessie Smith records "Down-hearted Blues" selling a million copies in six months James P. Johnson publishes "The Charleston," initiating the dance craze Yankee Stadium opens

1924 George Gershwin premiers Rhapsody in Blue with the Paul Whiteman Orchestra
First Macy's Thanksgiving Day Parade
"Disposable handkerchiefs" introduced under trademark of Kleenex tissues

1925 Advent of electronic recording dramatically improves sound quality of records
Louis Armstrong makes first "Hot 5" records
Bessie Smith and Louis Armstrong record classic version of "St. Louis Blues"
F. Scott Fitzgerald's The Great Gatsby is published

1926 Jelly Roll Morton makes first Red Hot Pepper records
Louis Armstrong sings scat chorus on "Heebie Jeebies"
Ford announces 40-hour work week
Route 66 established, stretching from Chicago to LA

1927 Al Jolson appears in the landmark talking film The Jazz Singer
Duke Ellington Orchestra opens at the Cotton Club
Phonograph industry sells 100 million records
Lindbergh crosses the Atlantic
Holland Tunnel opens

1928 Clarinetist Benny Goodman makes first records
Mickey Mouse appears in Steamboat Willie
Bubble gum invented
Sliced bread marketed

1929　*Saxophonist/crooner Rudy Vallee becomes a sensation*
　　　Stock Market crashes
　　　First Academy Awards

1930　*Paul Whiteman Orchestra makes film King of Jazz*
　　　First Philly Cheese Steak
　　　Pluto discovered
　　　Scotch tape invented

1931　*Fats Waller makes his first records as a singer*
　　　Empire State Building opens

1932　*FDR elected president*

1933　*Prohibition ends on December 5th*

1934　*Duke Ellington's Number 1 hit, "Cocktails for Two," celebrates the end of Prohibition*

BIBLIOGRAPHY

Anderson, Gene H. *The Original Hot Five Recordings of Louis Armstrong.* Hillsdale, NY: Pendragon Press, 2007.

Armstrong, Louis. *Satchmo: My Life in New Orleans.* London: Peter Davies, 1955.

Baldwin, Neil. *Edison: Inventing the Century.* New York: Hyperion, 1995.

Bergreen, Laurence. *As Thousands Cheer: The Life of Irving Berlin.* New York: Penguin Books, 1991.

Berton, Ralph. *Remembering Bix: A Memoir of the Jazz Age.* New York: Harper and Row, 19 74.

Bigard, Barney. *With Louis and the Duke: The Autobiography of a Jazz Clarinetist.* Ed. Barry Martyn. New York: Oxford University Press, 1980, 1985.

Block, Geoffrey. *Richard Rodgers.* New Haven: Yale University Press, 2003.

Bloom, Ken. *The American Songbook: The Singers, the Songwriters, and the Songs.* New York: Black Dog and Leventhal, 2005.

Brothers, Thomas. *Louis Armstrong's New Orleans.* New York: Norton, 2006.

Brunn, H.O. *The Story of the Original Dixieland Jazz Band.* Baton Rouge, LA: Louisiana State University Press, 1960.

Carmichael, Hoagy. *The Stardust Road.* Bloomington, Indiana: Indiana University Press, 1946, 1974.

Chilton, John. *Sidney Bechet: The Wizard of Jazz.* Boston: Da Capo Press, 1996.

Condon, Eddie, with Thomas Sugrue. *We Called It Music: A Generation of Jazz.* New York: H. Holt, 1947.

Dance, Stanley. *The World of Earl Hines.* New York: Scribner's, 1977.

DeLong, Thomas. *Pops: Paul Whiteman, King of Jazz.* Piscataway, NJ: New Century, 1983.

Ewen, David. *Popular American Composers.* New York: H.W. Wilson, 1962.

Feather, Leonard, and Gary Gitler. *The Biographical Encyclopedia of Jazz.* New York: Oxford University Press, 1999

Freeman, Larry. *The Melodies Linger On: 50 Years of Popular Song.* Watkins Glen, NY: Century House, 1951.

Feinstein, Michael. *Nice Work if You Can Get It: My Life in Rhythm and Rhyme.* New York: Hyperion, 1995.

Friedwald, Will. *Stardust Melodies: A Biography of Twelve of America's Most Popular Songs.* New York: Pantheon Books, 2002.

Furia, Philip, and Michael Lasser. *America's Songs.* New York: Routledge, 2006, 2008.

Gioia, Ted. *The Jazz Standards: A Guide to the Repertoire.* New York: Oxford, 2012.

Higham, Charles. *Ziegfeld.* Chicago: Henry Regnery Co., 1972.

Hilbert, Robert. *Pee Wee Russell: The Life of a Jazzman.* New York: Oxford, 1993.

Hischak, Thomas S. *The Tin Pan Alley Song Encyclopedia.* Westport, CT: Greenwood Press, 2002.

Jablonski, Edward. *Gershwin: With a New Critical Discography.* Boston: Da Capo Press, 1998.

Jablonski, Edward. *Harold Arlen: Rhythm, Rainbows & Blues.* Boston: Northeastern University Press, 1996.

Jablonski, Edward. *Encyclopedia of American Music.* New York: Doubleday, 1981.

Jasen, David A. *A Century of American Popular Music (1899-1999): 2000 Best-Loved and Remembered Songs.* New York: Routledge, 2002.

Jasen, David A., and Trebor Jay Tichenor. *Rags and Ragtime: A Musical History.* New York: Dover, 1978.

Jasen, David A., and Gene Jones. *That American Rag.* New York: Schirmer Books, 2000.

Jasen, David A. *Tin Pan Alley: An Encyclopedia of the Golden Age of American Song.* New York: Routledge, 2003.

Jasen, David A., and Gene Jones. *That American Rag: The Story of Ragtime from Coast to Coast.* New York: Schirmer, 2000.

Jasen, David A., and Gene Jones. *Spreadin' Rhythm Around: Black Popular Songwriters, 1880-1930.* New York: Schirmer Books, 1998.

Jasen, David A., and Gene Jones. *Black Bottom Stomp: Eight Masters of Ragtime and Early Jazz.* New York: Routledge, 2001.

Jasen, David A. *Tin Pan Alley: The Composers, the Songs, the Performers, and Their Times: The Golden Age of American Popular Music from 1886 to 1956.* New York: Donald I. Fine, 1988.

Kennedy, Rick. *Jelly Roll, Bix, and Hoagy: Gennett Studios and the Birth of Recorded Jazz.* Bloomington, IN: Indiana University Press, 1994.

Kernfeld, Barry, ed. *The New Grove Dictionary of Jazz. 2nd ed.* London: Grove's Dictionaries, 2001.

Kimball, Robert, and William Bolcom. *Reminiscing with Noble Sissle and Eubie Blake.* New York: Cooper Square Press, 2000.

Kirkeby, Ed. *Ain't Misbehavin': The Story of Fats Waller.* Boston: Da Capo, 1975.

Klamkin, Marian. *Old Sheet Music.* New York: Hawthorne, 1975.

Lax, Roger & Frederick Smith. *The Great Song Thesaurus, 2nd Edition.* New York: Oxford, 1989.

Lomax, Alan. *Mister Jelly Roll.* LA: University of California Press, 1950.

Marmorstein, Gary. *A Ship without a Sail: The Life of Lorenz Hart*. New York: Simon & Schuster, 2012.

Murrells, Joseph. *Million Selling Records from The 1900s to the 1980s: An Illustrated Directory*. London: B.T. Batsford, 1984.

Paymer, Marvin E., General Editor. *Facts Behind the Songs: A Handbook of American Popular Music from the Nineties to the '90s*. New York: Garland, 1993.

Reich, Howard, & William Gaines. *Jelly's Blues: The Life, Music, and Redemption of Jelly Roll Morton*. Boston: Da Capo, 2003.

Riccardi, Ricky. *What a Wonderful World: The Magic of Louis Armstrong's Later Years*. New York: Pantheon Books, 2011.

Shanaphy, Edward. *Piano Stylings of the Great Standards*. Los Angeles: Alfred, 2003.

Shapiro, Nat, and Nat Hentoff. *Hear Me Talkin' to Ya: The Story of Jazz as Told by the Men Who Made It*. New York: Dover, 1955.

Schuller, Gunther. *The Swing Era: The Development of Jazz, 1930-1945*. New York: Oxford, 1989.

Schwartz, Charles. *Gershwin: His Life and Music*. New York: The Bobbs-Merrill Co., 1973.

Secrest, Meryle. *Somewhere for Me: A Biography of Richard Rodgers*. New York: Applause Theater & Cinema Books, 2001.

Shaw, Arnold. *The Jazz Age: Popular Music in the 1920s*. New York: Oxford, 1987.

Sheed, Wilfrid. *The House That George Built: With a Little Help from Irving, Cole, and a Crew of about Fifty*. New York: Random House Trade Paperbacks, 2008.

Shipton, Alyn. *I Feel a Song Coming On: The Life of Jimmy McHugh*. Chicago: University of Illinois, 2009.

Simon, George T. *The Big Bands*. 4th ed. New York: Schirmer Books, 1981.

Singer, Barry. Black and Blue: *The Life and Lyrics of Andy Razaf*. New York: Schirmer, 1992.

Sudhalter, Richard M. *Bix: Man & Legend*. New Rochelle, New York: Arlington House, 1974.

Sudhalter, Richard M. *Stardust Melody: The Life and Music of Hoagy Carmichael*. New York: Oxford University Press, 2002.

Suskin, Stephen. *Show Tunes, 1905-1991: The Songs, Shows, and Careers of Broadway's Major Composers*. New York: Oxford, 2000.

Teachout, Terry. *Pops: A Life of Louis Armstrong*. Boston: Mariner Books, 2010.

Tucker, Mark. *The Duke Ellington Reader*. New York: Oxford, 1993

Tucker, Sophie. *Some of these Days*. Garden City, New York: Doubleday, Doran, 1945.

Tyler, Don. *Hit Songs, 1900-1955: American Popular Music of the Pre-rock Era*. Jefferson, North Carolina: McFarland & Company, 2007.

Waller, Maurice, and Anthony Calabrese. *Fats Waller*. New York: Schirmer Books, 1977.

Whitcomb, Ian. *Irving Berlin and Ragtime America*. New York: Limelight Editions, 1988.

White, H. Loring. *Ragging It: Getting Ragtime into History (and Some History into Ragtime)*. Lincoln, NE: iUniverse, 2005.

White, Mark. *You Must Remember This: Popular Songwriters 1900-1980*. New York, Scribner's, 1985

Whorf, Michael. *American Popular Song Composers: Oral Histories, 1920s-1950s*. Jefferson, NC: McFarland, 2012.

Wilder, Alec. *American Popular Song: The Great Innovators, 1900-1950.* New York: Oxford, 1972.

Wilk, Max. *They're Playing Our Song.* New York: Atheneum, 1973.

Williams, Dawn. *Me and My Father's Shadow: A Daughter's Quest and Biography of Ted Lewis "The Jazz King."* Seal Beach, CA: Sunrise House, 2005.

Winer, Deborah Grace. *On the Sunny Side of the Street: The Life and Lyrics of Dorothy Fields.* New York: Schirmer Books, 1997.

Yanow, Scott. *Bebop—Third Ear: The Essential Listening Companion.* San Francisco: Backbeat Books, 2000.

Yanow, Scott. *Classic Jazz: The Musicians & Recordings That Shaped Jazz, 1895-1933.* San Francisco: Backbeat Books, 2001.

Zinsser, William. *Easy to Remember: The Great American Songwriters and Their Songs.* Jaffrey, NH: David R. Godine, Publisher, 2001.

INDEX

A

Abbott and Costello Show (tv show)	83
Abbott and Seroff	21
Adams, Mr. (in Eddie Condon anecdote)	142, 143
Adams, Stanley	114
Ager, Milton	5, 7, 79
Ahlert, Fred	97, 138, 232
Ain't Misbehavin (show)	29
Akst, Harry	19, 60, 61
Albert, Don	195
Alexander's Ragtime Band (film)	32
Alexandria Hotel (Los Angeles)	249
Alice in Wonderland (film)	83
Alix, May	93
Allen, Gracie	127
Allen, Henry "Red"	26, 40, 68
Allen, Thornton W.	237
Allen, Woody	173
Alter, Louis	62
Ambassador Hotel (Atlantic City)	233, 249
American Idol (tv series)	79
American Quartet	46, 79, 187, 213
Ames Brothers	230
Amos and Andy	129, 223
Anderson, Irene W.	52
Anderson, Ivy	106, 245
Andre Charlot's Revue of 1924 (show)	122
Andrews, Julie	20
Andrews Sisters	26, 84, 214
Andy Griffith Show (tv show)	103
Anthony, Ray	230
Archey, Jimmy	36
Arlen, Harold	14, 15, 27, 31, 90, 253,
Armstrong, Alpha	207
Armstrong, Lil Hardin	48, 85, 144, 152, 153, 213, 214
Armstrong, Louis	xvi, xvii, 4, 5, 10, 16, 18, 19, 21, 24, 27, 28, 29, 32, 36, 37, 38, 40, 43, 45, 46, 47, 48, 49, 57, 60, 62, 68, 70, 72, 79, 80, 81, 84, 85, 86, 89, 90, 92, 93, 94, 95, 104, 112, 114, 118, 119, 130, 134, 140, 144, 152, 153, 161, 162, 163, 172, 173, 176, 178, 183, 184, 190, 192, 193, 197, 200, 207, 210, 213, 215, 216, 224, 225, 229, 232, 240, 241, 242, 245, 246, 247, 253, 256, 257, 259, 262, 263
Armstrong, Lucille	207
Arnaz, Desi	35
Arnheim, Gus	253
Arodin, Sidney	119
ASCAP	xxi, xxii, 56

Asher, Emily	93, 177	Bates, Charles	79
Astaire, Fred	114, 175, 176	Bauduc, Ray	114
Atkins, Boyd	79, 80	Baxter, Jeff "Skunk"	69
Atkins, Chet	252	Beale Street	xv, 26
Atlantic City Jazz Band	116, 161	Beatles, The	5, 171
Auld, Georgie	22	Bechet, Sidney	xvi, 1, 13, 16, 21, 28, 31, 33, 36, 38, 40, 72, 81, 82, 110, 133, 134, 144, 156, 163, 169, 170, 183, 195, 197, 210, 225, 229, 259
Austin High Gang	71, 156		
Austin, Gene	xvii, 5, 54, 72, 91, 99, 125, 145, 146, 151, 244, 245	Beiderbecke, Bix	xvii, 13, 14, 21, 22, 31, 34, 35, 45, 47, 48, 54, 75, 83, 109, 110, 121, 126, 128, 144, 177, 178, 185, 189, 199, 200, 205, 213, 222, 224, 236, 238, 257
Aviator, The (film)	193, 255		

B

Baer, Abel	115		
Bailey, Bill	27	Being Julia (film)	26
Bailey, Buster	40, 47, 138	Bell, Alexander Graham	xix
Bailey, Mildred	75, 84, 120, 178, 242	Benford, Tommy	197
Bailey, Sarah	27	Bennett, Dave	38
Baker, Belle	31	Bennett, Sanford F.	36
Baker, Blind Bobby	155	Bennett, Tony	49, 83, 90, 95, 106, 131
Baker, Chet	131	Benny Goodman Story, The (film)	19, 45
Ball, Kenny	156		
Ball, Lucille	35	Benny, Jack	170
Baloo (the bear)	105	Benson Orchestra	48
Barbarin, Paul	47, 114, 115	Berigan, Bunny	22, 130, 257
Barber, Chris	169	Berkeley, Busby	256
Barbone Street Jazz Band	110	Berlin, Irving	2, 9, 10, 12, 13, 31, 60, 78, 79, 90, 132, 134, 144, 147, 175, 176, 195, 250, 251, 259
Barbour, Joyce	256		
Barnhart, Jeff	32, 118	Bernard, Felix	54
Barrett, Joe	77, 140	Bernie, Ben	35, 131
Barris, Harry	143, 144, 253	Best Things in Life Are Free, The (film)	105
Basin Street	xv, xviii, 24, 25, 69, 129, 130		

Betsy (show)	31	Boutelje, Phil	44
Betty Boop (cartoon character)	19, 88, 190	Bow, Clara	19
		Bowman, Euday L.	228, 229
Big Boy (show)	105	Brackman, Bruce	154, 240
Big Broadcast of 1932 (show)	170	Brackman, Chuck	240
		Braff, Ruby	49, 88, 123
Big Show of 1916 (show)	172	Braham, Philip	121
Bigard, Barney	49, 62, 104, 259	Braud, Wellman	80, 81
Bigelow, Bob	79	Brecker, Samuel	61
Billy May Orchestra	91	Brecker, Steve	61
Biltmore Hotel	37, 38	Breese, Lou	35
Birth of the Blues (film)	28	Brewer, Teresa	7, 48
		Brice, Fanny	78, 178, 179, 251
Black, James	245	Brilhart, Arnold	152
Black, Johnny	53, 54	Brooks, Harry	29
Blackbirds (shows)	58, 86, 90, 134, 139	Brooks, Shelton	55, 202, 203, 222
Blake, Eubie	53, 139, 140, 143	Brooks, Sonny Jim	258
Blotto (film)	51	Brown, Anna Welker	52
Blue Five	38, 134, 217	Brown, Billie	52
Blue Network	128	Brown, Dewey	84
Blue Skies (film)	32, 133, 175	Brown, Glenn	91
Boardwalk Empire (tv series)	56, 68, 95, 109, 258, 259	Brown, Les	83
		Brown, Lew	28, 29, 105, 120, 157, 196, 257
Bob Scobey's Frisco Jazz Band	51	Brown, William B.	52
Boeddinghaus, David	14	Brown Brothers	56
		Brunies, George	68, 95, 220, 240
Bolden, Buddy	40, 144	Brunies, Henny	13
Bonifay, Fernand (Ferdinand)	72, 169	Brunies, Merritt	13
		Bryan, Alfred	168
Boswell, Connee (Connie)	10, 24, 27, 220	Brymn, J. Tim	18
Boswell Sisters	60	Bublé, Michael	75
Botsford, George	78, 79, 186, 187		

Burnett, Carol	79		Carmichael, Hoagy	49, 74, 75, 86, 114, 119, 120, 154, 155, 177, 178, 207
Burnett, Earl	215			
Burnett, Ernie	151, 152		Carol, Sue	215
Burns, George	127		Carousel (show)	222
Burr, Henry	169, 187			
Burrage, Ryan	156		Carpenter, Charles	256
Burris, Jim (James Henry Burris)	22, 23		Carroll, Earl	89, 90
			Caruso, Enrico	261
Busse, Henry	233, 234, 238		Cary, Dick	49
Butter and Egg Man, The (show)	92		Casa Loma Orchestra	154
Butterfield, Billy	86, 238		Casey, Bob	220
Byers, Pee Wee	92		Cassard, Jules	13
			Castle Jazz Band	68
C			Castle, Irene and Vernon	xxii, xxiii, 141, 261
C-melody saxophone	34, 47, 75, 200		Castle, Lee (Aniello Castaldo)	70, 115
Caesar, Irving	49, 104, 105			
Cahn, Sammy	26		Cates, George	239
Cakewalk	15, 16, 38, 133		Cathcart, Dick	126, 183
California Ramblers	39, 48, 71, 150, 196, 205		Catlett, Sid	49
Callahan, Will J.	201		Cato, Minto	139
Calloway, Cab	19, 27, 89, 90, 189, 190		Celebration of American Music (tv broadcast)	130
Campbell, Granny	178			
Campbell, Manzie	20, 21		Challis, Bill	22, 31
Canal Street	xv, 24, 39, 40		Chaplin, Charlie	200
Cannon, Hughie	27, 28		Chaplin, Saul	26
Cantor, Eddie	xvii, 101, 131, 137, 138, 144, 145, 189		Charles, Ray (Ray Charles Offenberg)	207, 208
Capone, Al	4, 5			
Captain January (film)	220		Charles, Ray (Robinson)	7, 39, 75
Carleton, Bob	106, 107			
Carlisle, Kitty	126			

Charleston Chasers	4, 24, 232	Condon, Eddie	xvii, 1, 12, 22, 27, 28, 29, 30, 36, 39, 43, 45, 64, 76, 88, 98, 101, 105, 128, 134, 142, 143, 156, 177, 181, 183, 186, 210, 213, 220, 245
Charlie Brown Christmas, A (tv show)	112		
Check and Double Check (film)	223	Confrey, Zez	167
Chicago Rhythm Kings	99	Conley, Larry	49
		Connecticut Yankee, A (show)	222
Chinatown	45, 46, 61, 121	Connick, Jr., Harry	40, 64
Christian, Charlie	182	Connie's Inn	84, 142, 210
Cinderella (film)	83	Conrad, Con	137, 164, 165, 199
Clark, Buddy	169	Cook, J. Lawrence	96, 97
Clarke, Grant	30, 133, 134	Cookie Monster	131
Clarkson, Geoffrey	83	Coon, Carlton	56
Clarkson, Harry	83	Coon-Sanders Original Nighthawk Orchestra	56, 118
Clayton, Buck	28, 138		
Clinton, Larry	113		
Clooney, Rosemary	77	Cooper, Gary	175
Cobb, George L.	6, 7	Coots, Fred	35
Coburn, Richard	248, 249	Cotton Club (NYC)	14, 27, 68, 90, 99, 134, 263
Cocoanut Grove (Los Angeles)	143, 223	Cotton Club Parade (1934 show)	14
Cohn, Harry	255	Cottonmouth Rhythm Kings	154
Cole, Bob	159		
Cole, Nat "King"	49, 74, 200, 232	Couesnophone	206
Cole-Johnson trio	159, 160	Count Basie	xv, 21, 208, 229
Collins, Arthur	7, 10, 68, 79	Cox, Jimmy	155
Collins, Jose	169	Crain, Jeanne	138
Columbia Records	xx, 33, 81, 96, 97, 205, 243, 261	Creamer, Henry	3, 57, 212, 213, 237, 238
		Criss, Sonny	7
Como, Perry	208	Croce, Jim	79
Conde, Franz	142	Crosby, Bing	10, 24, 60, 65, 122, 126, 143, 151, 170, 176, 216, 220, 223, 236, 246, 253, 257

Crosby, Bob	13, 14, 166		Dempsey, James	1
Crumit, Frank	158		Denniker Paul	208, 209
Crump, Edward Hull	141		DeSylva, Buddy	7, 19, 28, 29, 39, 105, 120, 170, 257, 258
Cullum, Jim	47, 185, 197		Dickenson, Vic	22, 32
Cutshall, Cutty	114		Dickie, Neville	13, 213
			Dietz, Howard	170, 222

D

			Dixie Duo	139
Dabney, Ford	196		Dixie Syncopators	64
Dalhart, Vernon	228		Dixie to Broadway (show)	133, 134
Daniels, Charles H.	193			
Dapogny, James	112, 219		Dixon, Mort	153, 154
Darin, Bobby	7, 20, 79		Dodds, Baby	62, 81
Daugherty, Doc	95		Dodds, Johnny	23, 163, 173
Davern, Kenny	91, 150, 219		Dodge, Roger Pryor	69
Davies, Russell	16		Donahue, Sam	91, 151
Davis, Benny	19, 137, 138		Donaldson, Walter	2, 17, 34, 131, 144, 145, 146, 147
Davis, Charlie	48			
Davis, Isaac	173		Dorsey Brothers Orchestra	152
Davis, Joe	32, 96, 97, 209, 221, 222			
Davis, Meyer	237		Dorsey, Jimmy	4, 12, 22, 35, 47, 86, 99, 105, 114, 115, 119, 150, 189, 215, 216, 243
Davis, Miles	116			
Davison, Wild Bill	1, 2, 16, 22, 26, 28, 29, 30, 31, 36, 76, 101, 110, 134, 161, 197, 220			
			Dorsey, Tommy	35, 46, 119, 172, 215
			Dowell, Edgar	218
Day, Doris	17		Dreamland Café (Chicago)	85
Day, Edith	11			
Decca Records	26, 114, 216		Dreiser, Theodore	148
DeFranco, Buddy	39		Dresser, Paul	103, 147, 148
Delaney, Tom	109		Dreyer, Dave	21
DeLange, Eddie	62		Dubin, Al	89
Delmar, Harry	90		Duchin, Eddie	255
Delmar's Revels (show)	90		Duffee, Josh	14
			Duke Ellington Orchestra	28, 223

INDEX

Dukes of Dixieland	2, 7, 19, 116	Etting Ruth	2, 5, 17, 21, 58, 70, 105, 258
Dumbo (film)	83	Eubie (show)	139
Dunlap, Louis	256	Europe, James Reese	xxiii
DuPont, Floyd	80	Evans, Bill	39
Durante, Jimmy	251	Evans, Doc	38
Dutch Dixie All Stars	64	Every Day's a Holiday (film)	114

E

Earl Carroll's Vanities (shows)	89, 90
Eberly, Bob	105
Ebsen, Buddy	220
Eckstine, Billy	49, 183
Eddie Cantor Story, The (film)	138
Eddy Duchin Story (film)	6
Edegran, Lars	12
Edison, Thomas	xix, xx, 223, 261
Edmunds, Chris	95
Edwards, Cliff	17, 39, 60, 79, 164
Edwards, Tommy	151
Egan, Ray (Raymond)	91, 92, 108, 109
Eldridge, Roy	28
Elizalde, Fred	205, 206
Elkins, Mollie	203
Ellington, Duke	5, 47, 59, 63, 64, 68, 69, 106, 122, 130, 181, 182, 198, 209, 223, 227, 229, 236, 263, 264
Ellis, Seger	246
English, Peggy (Marguerite Grace)	2
Erdman, Ernie	156

F

Fabulous Dorseys, The (film)	17, 215
Facobs, Jacob	26
Faison, Joseph	189
Fame (film)	257
Fardella, Charlie	154, 227
Feinstein, Michael	70
Ferbos, Lionel	12
Ferko String Band	7
Fess Williams and his Royal Flush Orchestra	190
Fields, Dorothy	58, 70, 89, 90, 139
Fink, Henry	50, 51
Fiorito, Ted	90, 91
Firehouse Five	7, 16, 33, 228, 252
Fischer, Tom	77, 240
Fisher, Dan	255
Fisher, Doris	255
Fisher, Fred	42, 53, 54, 168, 255
Fisher, Mark	246
Fisher, Marvin	255
Fitzgerald, Ella	79, 197, 230, 245

278 | INDEX

Fitzgerald, F. Scott 259, 263
Fletcher Henderson Orchestra 47
Foley, Red 7
Follies (shows) see Ziegfeld Follies
For Me and My Gal (film) 201
Ford, Mary 252
Foster, Pops 1, 36, 117, 210
Foster, Stephen 148
Fountain, Pete 116, 117
Four Lads 65
Fowler, Lemuel 96
Fox, Harry xxii
Frankie Trumbauer Orchestra 128
Freberg, Stan 252
Freeman, Bud 1, 48, 71, 156, 179, 219
Friars Society Orchestra, The 224
Friend, Cliff 115
Frost, Harold G. (Jack) 73
Fry, Stephen 158
Fuller, Walter 183
Fulton, Mike 189
Furber, Douglas 121

G

Galloway, Jim 143
Garber, Jan 20
Garland, Judy 49, 151
Garner, Erroll 176

Gaskill, Clarence 88, 89
Gelber, Jesse 258
Gennett Record Company 40, 41, 48, 62, 71, 224
Gensler, Lewis 126
George Olsen Orchestra 189
George White's Scandals (shows) 28, 29, 105, 120, 257
Gerlach, Horace 215
Gershwin, George xxi, 28, 31, 90, 92, 105, 174, 198, 203, 219, 257, 263
Gibbs, A. Harrington 185, 186
Gibson, Banu 180, 186, 209
Giddons, Gary 43
Gilbert, Ray 144, 220
Gillespie, Dizzy 183, 207, 224
Gillespie, Haven 35
Gillham, Art 13
Giordano, Vince 31, 56, 68, 95, 109, 150, 161, 177, 193, 255
Girlfriend, The (show) 31
Glaser, Joe 216
Gleason, Jackie 220
Glenn Hardman and his Hammond Five 70
Glorifying the American Girl (film) 17, 213
Golden, John L. 171
Goldkette, Jean 31
Goldwyn, Samuel 131

Goodman, Benny	14, 19, 24, 26, 35, 44, 45, 58, 62, 64, 70, 76, 77, 81, 88, 90, 92, 101, 113, 116, 118, 119, 140, 149, 150, 156, 161, 172, 174, 179, 182, 197, 210, 211, 221, 225, 230, 232, 243, 244, 252, 263
Goodwin, Joe	246
Goofus	206
Gordon, Bobby	13
Gorman, Ross	30, 219
Gorrell, Stuart	74
Gotham-Attucks Music Company	196
Grab Bag (show)	245
Grainger, Porter	217
Grant, Sterling	95
Grappelli, Stephane	39, 70, 232, 252
Gray, Chancey	38
Gray, Glen	64
Gray, Jane	2
Great American Broadcast, The (film)	7
Great Gatsby, The (film)	72, 259, 263
Green, Arthur	172
Green, Bud	7
Green, Eddie	75, 76
Green, Freddie	70, 138
Greene, Mort	239
Greer, Sony	223
Gregg, Robert	21
Grey, Joe	185, 186
Griffin, Merv	xxii
Grofe, Ferde	28
Grosz, Marty	22, 115
Guaraldi, Vince	112
Guinan, Mary Louise Cecilia "Texas"	92, 131

H

Hackett, Bobby	2, 32, 107, 112, 142, 155
Haggart, Bob	32, 112
Hall, Adelaide	14
Hall, Edmund	227
Hall, Guy	113
Hamilton, Scott	86, 95
Hamm, Fred	38
Hammerstein, Oscar	31, 127, 128, 222
Hammond, John	182
Hamp, Johnny	29
Hampton, Lionel	70, 140
Handman, Lou	30
Handy, W.C.	17, 18, 25, 26, 40, 76, 140, 141, 159, 191, 192, 254, 261
Handy, Will	159
Hanley, James	102, 103, 178, 179
Hanshaw, Annette	29
Harbach, Otto	127, 128
Harburg, Yip	15
Hardman, Glenn	70
Harlan, Byron	7, 68
Harmonicats	169
Harris, Barry	253
Harris, Marion	30
Harris, Phil	105

Harris, Will J. 214
Harrison, Al 221
Harrison, Charles 169
Harrison, George 27
Harry Richman and the Revelers 28
Hart, Lorenz 31, 154, 222, 253, 256, 257
Harvey, Morton 51
Havens, Bob 134
Havez, Jean 186, 187
Hawkins, Coleman 19, 28, 102
Hayes, Clancy 9, 33, 43, 51, 188
Hayes, Thamon 207, 208
Hayworth, Rita 148
Hegamin, Lucille 110
Heitger, Duke 38, 39, 119, 130
Held, John Jr. 197
Henderson, Fletcher 7, 47, 48, 60, 74, 84, 85, 118, 210, 214, 232, 255
Henderson, Ray 28, 29, 71, 105, 120, 257, 258
Hensen, J. M. 203
Hentoff, Nat 24, 71, 112
Herbert, Victor xxi, 209
Here Is My Heart (film) 126
Here's Howe (show) 50
Herman, Woody 62
Hession, Jim 143
Hickman, Art 128, 180, 181
Higgins, Billy 221
Hill, Alexander 96
Hill, Tiny 14

Hines, Earl 14, 32, 33, 49, 64, 92, 123, 152, 153, 183, 213, 232, 256
Hirsch, Louis A. 127, 128
Hirsch, Walter 58, 188, 189
Hirt, Al 38, 58, 112, 225, 245
His Honor the Barber (show) 196
Hodes, Art 23, 36, 43, 197
Hoffman, Robert 7
Hold Everything (show) 258
Holiday, Billie 62, 138, 151
Hook, Tom 16
Hoover, Herbert 8, 120, 126
Hope, Bob 170
Horne, Lena 14, 58
Hot Chocolates (show) 5, 29, 84, 99
Hot Club of New Orleans 26
Hot Fountain Pen 206, 207
Hot Harlem (show) 210
Hotel Sherman 4
Howard, Darnell 20
Hubbell, Raymond 171
Hucko, Peanuts 142, 210
Hunt, Pee Wee 229
Hutton, Betty 115
Hylton, Jack 35, 49, 121
Hyman, Dick 97, 154, 222

I

I Love Lucy (tv show)	158
I Would If I Could (show)	26
I'll See You in My Dreams (film)	91
Indianapolis 500	103
Ink Spots	64
International Review (show)	70
Iredale, Robert	142
Irene (show)	11
Is Everybody Happy (Film)	201
It Girl	19
Little Italy (NYC)	46

J

Jackson, "Papa" Charlie	192, 193
Jackson, Cliff	122
Jackson, Mahalia	116
Jackson, Michael	200
Jackson, Tony	173, 174
Jarrett, Art	145, 256
Jazz King, The (Ted Lewis)	243
Jazz Singer, The (film)	32, 263
Jazzology Records	128
Jeeves and Wooster (tv series)	158
Jenkins, Gordon	76, 77, 174
Jerome, William	45, 46, 172
Jerry Lewis Show, The (tv show)	200
John, Elton	131
Johnson, Bill	62
Johnson, Bunk	1, 2, 40, 65, 107, 255
Johnson, Buster	233, 234
Johnson, Charles L.	59, 60
Johnson, Clarence	96
Johnson, Enoch "Nucky"	258
Johnson, J. C.	125
Johnson, James P.	96, 123, 125, 142, 196, 224, 227, 262
Johnson, James Weldon	159
Johnson, John Rosamond	159
Johnson, Lonnie	130
Johnson, Ronell	240
Johnston, Arthur	8, 133, 134
Johnstone, Tandy	238
Joker Is Wild, The (film)	17
Jolson, Al	7, 18, 19, 21, 32, 35, 39, 105, 228, 247, 248, 263
Jolson Story, The (film)	19
Jones, Connie	227, 242
Jones, Isham	7, 76, 86, 150, 156, 160, 161, 232, 252
Jones, Jo	21, 70, 138
Jones, Leroy	155, 240
Jones, Spike	158

282 | INDEX

Joplin, Scott	66, 135, 136, 239
Jordan, Joe	162
Joy, Jimmy (Maloney)	98
Jumbo Shrimp Jazz Band	189
Jungle Book, The (animated film)	105

K

Kahn, Gus	2, 90, 91, 131, 144, 146, 147, 156, 160, 161, 173, 174
Kahn, Otto	49, 50
Kahn, Roger Wolfe	49, 50
Kalmar, Bert	223
Kaminsky, Max	22
Kansas City Bar (Tijuana)	117, 167
Kaufman, George S.	92, 170
Kaye, Sammy	255
Kelley, Peck	98
Kellso, Jon-Erik	83, 240
Kelly, Pete	126
Kelly, Wynton	116
Kemp, Hal	256
Kennedy, Jimmy	176
Kennedys (President and Mrs.)	255
Kenny Ball and his Jazzmen	142
Kentucky Club	68
Kern, Jerome	xxi, 31, 54
Kibbey, Ilah	53
Kid Millions (film)	133
Kid Ory's Creole Orchestra	163
King and I, The (show)	222
King of Jazz, The (Paul Whiteman)	236
King of Jazz (film)	122, 144
King of Swing (Benny Goodman)	118
King of the Blues Trombone (Jack Teagarden)	90
King of Polka (Frankie Yankovic)	116
King Oliver's Creole Jazz Band	40
King, Arthur	222
King, Porter	118
Kirby, John	229, 230
Kirk, Andy	77, 143
Kleinkauf, Henry	113
Klickmann, Frank Henri	73
Koehler, Ted	14, 15, 27, 90, 253
Koenig, Martha	40
Kohl, Christopher	26
Kompen, Kristoffer	14
Krupa, Gene	156

L

La Rocca, Nick	162, 224
Ladnier, Tommy	240
Lady Gaga	90, 106
Laine, Cleo	106
Lake Forest Academy	13

Lake Ponchartrain	24, 241	Lewis, George	40, 43, 82, 255
Lake, Meschiya	51	Lewis, Sam M.	60, 61, 71, 199, 227, 228, 247
Lamb, Joseph	239	Lewis, Ted	xvii, 13, 33, 35, 56, 60, 96, 97, 101, 115, 120, 156, 186, 205, 225, 232, 243, 244
Lambert, Donald	123		
Lambert, Scrappy	35		
Lang, Eddie	6, 26, 31, 35, 105, 150, 199, 221		
		Liberace	229
Lang, kd (Kathryn Dawn)	95	Limehouse district (London)	121
Laska, Edward	8	Lincoln Gardens (Chicago)	184
Laughlin, Tim	72, 112, 166, 227	Linger Longer Letty (show)	158
Lauper, Cyndi	131		
Laurel and Hardy	186, 51	Link, Harry	99
Laurie, Hugh	158	Little, Jack	101, 102
Lawrence, Jack	113, 114	Little Richard	20
Lawson, Yank	32, 112	Little Show, The (show)	170
Layton, Turner	3, 57, 212, 237, 238		
Lee, Brenda	256	Little Tramp	200
Lee, Peggy	49	Livingston, Fud	220
Leecan, Bobby	155	Load of Coal (show)	84, 99
Leff, Sidney	71	Lockhart, Eugene	252
Legend of Bagger Vance, The (film)	34	Lombardo, Guy	49, 176, 230
		Long, Avon	14
Lennon, John	171	Long, Johnny	102, 103
Leonard, Eddie	100	Long, Long Trailer, The (film)	35
Lerner, Sammy	104, 105		
Leslie, Edgar	30	Longworth, Alice Roosevelt	11
Leslie, Lew	58, 134, 139		
Let's Dance (radio show)	76	Lopez, Ray	124
		Louisiana Five	9, 240
Let's Face It (show)	1	Louisiana Rhythm Kings	219, 220
Levant, Oscar	4		
Levinson, Dan	12, 48, 74, 174	Love Me or Leave Me (film)	2, 17

Lown, Bert	37, 38		Mazzaroppi, Gary	19
Lunceford, Jimmie	21, 143		McCarron, Charles	32, 33, 51, 154
Lyman, Abe	2		McCarthy, Joseph	11
Lyman, Tommy	145, 152		McCartney, Paul	20, 84, 98
			McDermott, Tom	242
			McGarity, Lou	142
MacDonald, Ballard	102, 103, 178, 179		McHugh, Jimmy	58, 70, 88, 89, 90, 139, 244, 245
MacDowell, Edward	139		McKenna, Dave	232
Mack, Cecil	196		McKenzie, Red	156
Mad Men (tv series)	170		McKibbin, Nikki	79
Madame Butterfly (opera)	171		McKinley, Ray	172
Madden, Edward	67		McKinney's Cotton Pickers	74
Magidson, Herb	207		McPartland, Jimmy	71, 92, 156, 238, 245, 252
Mahagony Hall	69, 129		McPhail, Lindsay	188, 189
Maheu, Jack	72, 166		McPherson, R. C. (Cecil Mack)	196
Mahler, Gustav	125		McShann, Jay	176
Mandel, Johnny	155		Mecum, Dudley	13
Manning, Kate	258		Medina, Mamie	218
Manone, Wingy	74, 98, 162, 240		Meinken, Fred	231
Mares, Paul	13, 70		Melrose Brothers	136, 251, 252
Margie (film)	6, 17, 138		Melrose, Lester	251
Marks, Gerald	35, 104, 105		Melrose, Walter	41, 48, 63
Marsalis, Wynton	130, 172		Mercer, Johnny	83, 119, 120, 155, 174, 236
Marsh, Roy K.	91, 92		Merman, Ethel	120
Marvin, Johnny	58		Mertz and Kurtz	158
Mathis, Johnny	49		Mesterhazy, George	140
Matlock, Matty	33, 102, 227		Meyer, George W.	133, 134, 227, 228, 247
Matthews, Artie	239		Meyer, Joseph	49, 149, 150
Mature, Victor	148		Meyers, Billy	35, 156
Matusovsky, Mikhail	141			

MGM Studios	125, 179, 246	Morris chair	13, 150
Middleton, Velma	49	Morse, Theodore	67, 68
Midiri Brothers	183	Morton, Jelly Roll	25, 26, 41, 43, 63, 72, 77, 81, 111, 117, 118, 136, 139, 152, 161, 166, 167, 172, 174, 197, 198, 225, 239, 251, 252, 263
Midiri, Joe	172, 230		
Midiri, Paul	172		
Midnight Frolics (show)	179	Moten, Bennie	154, 207, 208, 229
		Mueller, Gus	233, 234
Midnight Rounders, The (show)	137	Mullally, Megan	257
		Mulligan, Gerry	131
Miley, James "Bubber"	59, 68, 69, 106, 227	Munro, Bill	243
		Munson, Eddie	100, 101
Miller, Glenn	24, 113, 186	Muppet Show, The (tv show)	34, 106
Mills, Florence	134		
Mills, Frederick Allan "Kerry"	15, 16	Murphy, Stanley	154
		Murphy, Turk	2, 36, 51, 77, 133, 166
Mills, Irving	59, 106, 177, 190, 244	Murray, Billy	9, 10, 54, 158, 174
		Murray, Don	243
Mills, Jack	177	Murray, Elizabeth	6, 7
Mills Brothers	35, 54, 60, 119, 156, 178, 215, 255	Muse, Clarence	242
		Music for Millions (film)	17
Milt Shaw and his Detroiters	35	My Gal Sal (film)	148
Mitchell, George	1	Myers, Colin	189

N

Mitchell, Margaret	104	
Modern Times (film)	200	
Mole, Miff	23, 29, 220, 222	Nabors, Jim	103
Moll, Billy	253	Nance, Ray	69
Monro, Robert	28	Natwick, Myron "Grim"	88
Monroe, Marilyn	151, 186		
Moret, Neil (Charles N. Daniels)	193	Neiberg, Al J.	95
		Nelson, Baby Face	19
Morgan, Carey	32, 33	Nelson, Ozzie	211
Morgan, Russ	114	Nelson, Willie	75
Morris, Kenneth	116		

Index

New Jersey Jazz Society — 88

New Orleans (movie) — 62

New Orleans Moonshiners — 95, 160, 240

New Orleans Rhythm Kings (NORK) — 13, 35, 41, 47, 70, 71, 220, 224, 225, 240, 262

Nicholas, Albert — 81

Nichols, Red — 12, 23, 29, 35, 45, 57, 101, 161, 179, 183, 219, 220, 222, 232

Noble, Johnny — 90

Norton, George A. — 151, 152

Nugent, Drew — 12

Nunez, Alcide — 124

O

O'Connor, Donald — 232

O'Neill, Rose — 179

Ockerse, Taco — 176

Okeh Records — 53, 104

Oklahoma (show) — 222

Oliver, Joe "King" — 40, 43, 48, 62, 63, 64, 68, 81, 85, 96, 163, 172, 184, 190, 213, 214, 225, 241, 251, 262

Olson, George — 17

Onward Brass Band — 47

Original Creole Jazz Band — 184

Original Dixieland Jass Band — 12, 124, 162, 262

Original Dixieland Jazz Band (ODJB) — 11, 12, 33, 34, 46, 47, 53, 56, 70, 103, 109, 110, 124, 137, 162, 164, 165, 185, 192, 199, 203, 213, 223, 224, 235, 243, 262

Original Memphis Five — 205

Orleans Six — 130

Ory, Edward "Kid" — 1, 16, 20, 28, 63, 144, 163, 183, 193, 208, 240

Overstreet, W. Benton — 221

Owens, Harry — 122

P

Page, Oran "Hot Lips" — 208

Page, Walter — 138, 208

Palace Theater (NYC) — 17

Palais Royal (NYC) — 92

Paley, Herman — 51

Palmer, Bee — 2

Palmer, Jack — 69, 98

Palomar Ballroom (Los Angeles) — 118

Papa Tom's Lamentation Jazzband — 116

Paramount Records — 192

Parenti, Tony — 36

Parish, Mitchell — 86, 177

Parker, Charlie — 89, 104, 175, 176, 183, 224

Parsons, Geoffrey — 200

Passing Show of 1916, The (show) — 174

Passing Show of 1918, The (show) — 201

Passing Show of 1923, The (show) — 156

Patton, Charlie — 240

Paul, Les	252	(cartoon)	105
Peck's Bad Boys	98	Porro, Mauro	14
Pee Wee Memorial Stomp	88	Porter, Cole	1, 31, 90
		Powell, Jane	114
Peerless Quartet	51	Prairie Home Companion, A (radio show)	226, 227
Peg o' My Heart (Play)	169		
Pennies from Heaven (film)	216	Preer, Andy	99
		Present Arms (show)	256
Pennington, Ann	29	Preservation Hall	43, 245
Perdue All-American Marching Band	103	Presley, Elvis	215
		Prima, Louis	98
Pete Kelly's Big 7	126, 183	Primrose, George H.	160
Pete Kelly's Blues (film)	2, 35, 79, 91, 126, 201	Primrose, Joe	190
		Prince, Charles Adams	10, 23, 80, 81
Peter Pan (film)	83		
Peters, Mike	115	Provincetown Follies (show)	176
Peterson, Oscar	232		
Pettis, Jack	6, 35	Puccini, Giacomo	19, 171
Philadelphia Musical Academy	44	Purvis, Katharine	245

Q

QRS Music Company	9, 41, 96, 97, 153, 165, 202, 205

Piantodosi, Al	50, 51		
Picou, Alphonse	80, 82		
Pingatore, Mike	122		

R

Piron, Armand K.	93, 94	Rabbai, George	106
Pistorius, Steve	9, 148		
Pitts, Tom	91, 92	Ragas, Henry	34, 46, 47, 165
Pizzarelli, Bucky	86	Rainey, Ma	109
Pizzarelli, John	211	Rainger, Ralph	126, 170
Polcer, Ben	130	Rawls, Lou	49
Polcer, Ed	12, 91, 116, 134	Ray Charles, Singers The	208
Pollack, Ben	12, 58, 118, 215		
Pollack, Lew	219, 220	Raye, Don	213, 214
Popeye the Sailor			

288 | INDEX

Razaf, Andy — 4, 29, 32, 74, 84, 99, 118, 125, 139, 208, 209, 210, 211

Red Hot Peppers — 26, 43, 77, 112, 117, 161, 167, 197, 198, 263

Red Nichols and his Five Pennies — 12, 45

Redman, Don — 74, 120

Reinhardt, Django — 19, 27, 32, 36, 43, 70, 109, 122, 186, 252

Reinhart, Randy — 15, 230

Remick Publishing — 193

Rene, Leon — 242

Rene, Otis — 242

Revelers, The — 28, 49, 60

Reynolds, Ellis — 95

Rhapsody in Blue — 26, 28, 125, 219, 257, 263

Rhody, Matt — 26, 154

Rhythm Boys, The — 126, 143, 144, 223, 253, 257

Rhythmania (show) — 27

Rich, Buddy — xxii

Richman, Harry — 28, 175

Rife, Jerry — 163

Ringle, Dave — 231

Rinker, Al — 143, 253

Ritz Hotel (London) — 175

Ritz-Carlton Hotel (Atlantic City) — 234, 258

RKO Pictures — 125

Roach, Max — 112

Robar, Stanford (Leland Stanford Roberts) — 201, 202

Robbins, C. A. — 237

Robbins, Everett — 217

Roberson, Orlando — 95

Roberts, Allan — 255

Roberts, Lee S. (Leland Stanford Roberts) — 201, 202

Roberts, Luckey — 96

Roberts, Raymond — 252

Robichaux, John (1866-1939) — 16

Robichaux, John (1915-2005) — 12

Robin, Leo — 126, 170

Robin, Sid — 152, 229, 230

Robinson Crusoe, Jr. (show) — 247, 248

Robinson, Russell — 137, 164, 165, 199

Robinson, Scott — 134

Robison, Willard — 49

Rodgers, Richard — 22, 31, 154, 222, 253, 256,

Rodli, John — 154

Rogers, James H. — 38

Rollini, Adrian — 12, 36, 152, 197, 205, 206, 207

Rollins, Sonny — 107, 112

Ronstadt, Linda — 257

Roosevelt, Teddy — 11, 79

Roppolo, Leon (Rapp) — 47, 70, 224, 225, 240

Rose, Al — 62

Rose, Billy — 21, 22, 99

Rose, Fred — 58

Rose, Vincent — 18, 19, 122, 248, 249

Rose of Washington Square (film)	179, 201
Ross Gorman and his Virginians	30, 219
Roulette Records	87
Royal Gardens Café (Chicago)	62, 184
Royal Wedding (film)	114
Royen, John	54
Rubens, George	98
Ruby, Harry	223
Ruby, Herman	149
Runnin' Wild (show)	186, 196
Rushing, Jimmy	116, 208
Russell, Bob	64
Russell, Luis	166
Russell, Pee Wee	1, 2, 13, 22, 86, 88, 98, 101, 105, 156, 179, 219, 220
Ryan, Molly	86

S

Sampson, Edgar	211
Sancton, Tommy	14, 82
Sandburg, Carl	190
Sanders, Joe	56
Sandpiper, The (film)	155
Sarrusophone	133, 134
Saunders, Hal	142
Saunders, Tom	154, 166
Savoy Ballroom (NYC)	211, 214
Sayer, Cynthia	150
Scala, Larry	91, 126
Scandals (shows)	see George White's Scandals
Schmidt, Alice	236
Schoebel, Elmer	35, 70, 156
Schoenberger, John	248, 249
Schroeder, Gene	220
Schumm, Andy	14, 60
Schuster, Ira (John Siras)	101, 102
Schwartz, Arthur	170
Schwartz, Jean	45, 46
Scobey, Bob	2, 43, 51, 188
Scott, James	239
Scott, Richard	156
Secunda, Sholom	26
Seeley, Blossom	238
Seitz, Ernest (Raymond Roberts)	252
Selvin Ben	54, 258
Sesame Street (tv show)	131
Seymour, Charles	166
Shanaphy, Edward	152
Shapiro, Nat	24, 71, 112
Shavers, Charlie	229, 230
Shaw, Artie	89
Shaw, Arvell	49
Shaw, Milt	35
Shay, Larry	246
Sheafe, Mark W.	237
Sheed, Wilfred	153
Sheffield, Leslie	182
Sheik, The (film)	195
Shields, Larry	46, 47
Shilkret, Nathaniel	125, 126

Shipton, Alyn	244	Snow, Robert	154
Shore, Dinah (Frances Rose)	60	Snyder, Ted	10, 78, 194, 195, 250, 251
Show Business (film)	7	Solovyov-Sedoi, Vasily	141, 142
Showboat (film)	125	Some Like it Hot (film)	151, 186
Shuffle Along (show)	134, 139	Somebody Loves Me (film)	115
Signorelli, Frank	221	Somethin' Smith and the Redheads	102
Silver, Horace	107, 204	Song Is Born, A (film)	151, 210
Simeon, Omer	197, 198	Sound of Music, The (show)	222
Simmons, Seymour	35	Sousa, John Philip	xxi
Simone, Nina	145	Spaeth, Sigmund	60
Sims, Zoot	123	Spanier, Muggsy	1, 7, 12, 14, 17, 34, 36, 62, 84, 92, 95, 107, 134, 177, 219, 232
Sinatra, Frank	28, 49, 89, 114, 215		
Singer, Barry	208		
Singleton, Zutty	81, 214	Spice of 1922 (show)	238
Sissle, Noble	139	Spike's Seven Pods of Pepper Orchestra	163
Sjostrom, Frans	14		
Skonberg, Bria	19	Spikes Brothers	251, 252
Smalle, Ed	54	Spotted Cat Music Club (New Orleans)	130
Smith, Bessie	xvii, 3, 10, 21, 40, 53, 109, 130, 155, 192, 210, 217, 255, 262, 263	St. Cyr, Johnny	161, 193
		St. Francis Hotel (San Francisco)	180, 181
Smith, Chris	22, 23, 38, 95	Stabile, Dick	115
Smith, Clara	109, 245	Stacy, Jess	45
Smith, Harry B.	194, 195	Stafford, Jo	225, 232
Smith, Joseph	128, 255	Stark, John	136, 239
Smith, Keely	91	Stark, Will	136
Smith, Mamie	53, 185, 192, 219, 255	Starmer, Fredrick	76
Smith, Pine Top	155	Starmer, William	76
Smith, Trixie	109	Starr, Kay	14
Smith, Willie "The Lion"	27, 123, 142, 224		
Snow White (cartoon)	190		

Steel, John	128, 252
Steele, Porter	80
Steely Dan	69
Sterling, Andrew B.	243
Stern, Joseph	159, 166
Stewart, Rod	131
Stormy Weather (film)	5
Storyville	25, 43, 262
Stride piano	5, 54, 122, 123, 142, 143, 156, 167, 187, 222, 224, 262
Strut Miss Lizzie (show)	213, 238
Sudhalter, Richard	196
Sullivan, Joe	110, 222
Sullivan, Maxine	2, 32, 86
Sunday, Billy	42
Sunset Café (Chicago)	104, 152
Sunshine, Monty	169, 170
Susemihl, Norbert	116, 144, 203
Sutton, Ralph	31, 32, 97, 110, 154
Swanstone, Arthur (Swanstrom)	32, 33
Swarthout, Gladys	252
Sweatman, Wilbur	65, 66, 76, 88,
Sweet & Lowdown (film)	252
Sweet Emma	43
Swing Kids (film)	26
Swing That Music (autobiography)	216

T

Tatum, Art	123, 186, 224, 257
Taylor, Eva	21
Taylor, Irene	144
Taylor, Laurette	169
Teachout, Terry	85
Teagarden, Charlie	114
Teagarden, Jack	xvii, 5, 14, 18, 21, 24, 26, 28, 49, 59, 75, 84, 86, 87, 90, 98, 101, 119, 155, 162, 163, 178, 179, 190, 195, 197, 213, 219, 252
Temple, Shirley	220
Tennille, Toni	79
Teschemacher, Frank	71, 99, 156, 232, 243
Teter, Jack	114
Thiele, Bob	220
This Is the Army (show, film)	17, 133
This is the Life (film)	17
Thompson, Enoch "Nucky" (character, Boardwalk Empire, tv series)	258
Thornhill, Claude	114
Three Suns	169
Tierney, Harry	11
Tijuana Brass	128
Tin Pan Alley	xv, xxi, 60, 61, 67, 95, 102, 115, 144, 146, 148, 153, 157, 158, 159, 160, 161, 163, 166, 177, 187, 195, 205, 208, 209, 228, 244
Tin Roof Café (New Orleans)	225

Tindley, Charles Albert	36		Van Alstyne, Egbert	173, 174
Tintypes (show)	201		Van Brunt, Walter	151
Titanic	261		Van Steeden, Peter	83
Toivola, Katja	240		Vanities (show)	90
Tom Saunders and the Tomcats	166		Vaughan, Sarah	183
Tommy Dorsey and his Clambake Seven	46		Venable, Percy	92, 104
			Venus de Milo	126
Town Hall Concerts	48, 88, 128, 134, 207, 245		Venuti, Joe	6, 26, 31, 49, 60, 75, 99, 105, 119, 150, 215
Trappier, Arthur	36		Victor Military Band	10, 172
Trick, Stephanie	77		Victor Phonograph (Record) Company	xx, 5, 17, 81, 108, 124, 125, 143, 145, 198, 205, 208, 223, 233, 234, 235, 242, 243, 249, 261
Troy, Henry	38			
Trumbauer, Frankie	31, 34, 35, 38, 47, 59, 75, 126, 128, 144, 199, 200, 222, 238, 257			
			Village Follies (show)	170
Tuba Skinny	143, 162, 210		Vince Giordano and the Nighthawks	31, 56, 68, 95, 109, 193, 255
Tucker, Sophie	xvii, 4, 54, 55, 76, 203, 204			
Turk, Roy	133, 134, 138, 232		Virginians, The	30, 219
Turner, John	200		Vocalstyle Music Company	41, 167
Twain, Mark	222			
Tyers, William Henry	165, 166		Von Tilzer, Albert (Albert Gumm)	8, 154, 157, 158
			Voynow, Dick	177

U

Ukulele	205, 261
Up and Down Broadway (show)	46

W

Walker, Aida Overton	166, 196
Walker, George	196
Walker, Sally	148
Walkin' My Baby Back Home (film)	232
Wallace, Oliver	82, 83

V

Vache, Allan	91, 130, 197
Valentino, Rudolphe	194, 195
Vallee, Rudy	120, 131, 175, 209, 264

Waller, Fats	4, 5, 29, 32, 39, 42, 50, 51, 60, 74, 84, 95, 96, 97, 98, 99, 112, 118, 123, 125, 133, 139, 142, 143, 192, 209, 210, 221, 222, 224, 229, 264	White, George	28, 105, 257
		White, Lulu	69, 129
		White Christmas (film)	32, 133
Waller, Maurice	4, 112	Whiteman, Paul	xvii, 4, 5, 22, 28, 30, 39, 45, 54, 57, 64, 92, 105, 108, 109, 121, 122, 125, 126, 128, 131, 143, 144, 145, 156, 181, 189, 219, 233, 234, 235, 236, 238, 242, 243, 248, 249, 250, 253, 257, 262, 263, 264
Ward, Aida	27		
Warfield, Charles	20		
Waring, Fred	115		
Warren, Harry	xxi, 90, 153, 154		
Washington, Ned	86, 214		
Waters, Ethel	29, 60, 80, 86, 109, 193, 219, 224, 242	Whiteman, Professor Wilberforce	143
		Whiting, George	145
Waterson, Henry	195	Whiting, Jack	258
Watson, Maybell E.	152	Whiting, Margaret	35, 193
Watters, Lu	1, 9, 16, 77, 225	Whiting, Richard	35, 108, 109, 145, 193
Weatherly, Frederick	182, 183	Whoopee (show, film)	131, 144, 145
Webb, Chick	211, 230	Wilber, Bob	13, 39
Webb, Jack	2, 126	Wiley, Lee	27, 86
Webster, Ben	123, 176	Williams, Bert	55, 203, 221
Webster, Paul Francis	155	Williams, Clarence	20, 21, 38, 69, 87, 93, 94, 96, 134, 184, 209, 210, 217, 241, 242
Weeks, Harold	82, 83	Williams, Cootie	69, 106
Weems, Ted	145, 205, 221, 232, 258	Williams, Dawn Lewis	244
Welk, Lawrence	116, 134		
Wells, Dicky	27, 36, 109	Williams, Harry	180, 181
Wellstood, Dick	143, 176, 222	Williams, Hugh (Wilhelm Grosz)	176
Wendling, Pete	9		
West, Mae	76, 114	Williams, Mary Lou	32
Wettling, George	76, 220	Williams, Spencer	24, 40, 69, 87, 98, 129, 130, 184, 226
Wheeler, Francis	194, 195	Wilson, Edith	29
When Harry Meets Sally (film)	64	Wilson, Teddy	12, 28, 70, 102, 138, 151, 172

Wilson, Woodrow 8
Winchell, Walter 131
Winfree, Dick 44
Winter Garden Theater 137
Wise, Ed 128
Witherspoon, Jimmy 218
Wizard of Oz, The (film) 15
Wodehouse, Artis 41
Wodehouse, P. G. (Sir Pelham Grenville Wodehouse) 158
Wolverines 48, 177, 224
Wood, Haydn 182, 183
Wood, Leo 185, 186, 204, 205
Woode, Henri 183
Woods, Harry 163, 164
World of Pleasure, A (show) 174
Wrubel, Allie 207

Y

Yankovic, Frankie 116
Yanow, Scott 182
Yellen, Jack 5, 6, 7, 79
Yerba Buena Jazz Band 1
Yip Yip Yaphank (show) 132

You Were Meant for Me (film) 6
Young, Joe 60, 61, 71, 86, 97, 101, 102, 199, 227, 228, 247
Young, Lester xv, 70, 123, 138, 199, 200
Young, Victor 86, 214

Z

Ziegfeld, Florenz 31, 78, 131, 144, 145, 179, 213
Ziegfeld Follies (shows) 78, 133, 145, 169, 179, 189, 251, 257
Ziegfeld's Midnight Frolics 179